WHY GOVERNMENT SUCCEEDS
and Why It Fails

Amihai Glazer

Lawrence S. Rothenberg

HARVARD UNIVERSITY PRESS

Cambridge, Massachusetts

London, England · 2001

Library of Congress Cataloging-in-Publication Data

Glazer, Amihai.
Why government succeeds and why it fails / Amihai Glazer, Lawrence S. Rothenberg.
p. cm.
Includes bibliographical references and index.
ISBN 0-674-00466-3 (alk. paper)
1. United States—Economic policy—1993– 2. United States—Social policy—1993–
3. Political planning—United States. 4. Policy sciences. 5. Rational expectations (Economic
theory) I. Rothenberg, Lawrence S. II. Title.
HC106.82 .G55 2001
338.973—dc21
00-050027

To our children, Daniel Rothenberg, Danielle Glazer,
and Sarah Rothenberg

CONTENTS

Acknowledgments   xi

Introduction: Public Policy—Limits and Possibilities   1

How Economics Interacts with Politics   3
Structure of Analysis   4
Conceptual Apparatus: Economic Constraints   5
What Makes Problems Soluble?   18

1   Macroeconomics: Can Government Control
the Economy?   20

Managing the Economy: Partisan Incentives
  and Political Cycles   21
Monetary Policy and Rational Expectations   25
Fiscal Policy—Is It Just Crowding Out?   33
Exhortation: Persuasion and the Art of
  Equilibrium Selection   35
Spending, Taxes, and Expectations:
  Budget Deficits as Policy Instruments   42
Can Government Control the Economy?   47

2   Redistribution: A Success Story?   48

Economic Constraints and Redistribution   50
Uncertainty and Redistribution: Data   52
Government Commitment to Future Redistribution   57
Implications for Redistribution   58
Effectiveness of Redistributive Policy   59

Why Not Taxes?   68
Conclusions: Redistributive Possibilities   71

3   When Can Government Regulate?   72

The Scope of Regulation   73
Regulating Firms: Possibilities and Pitfalls   75
Regulating Consumer Behavior   89
Conditions for Regulatory Success   94

4   Producing Goods and Services: Getting the Right Mix   96

What Is Production?   98
Crowding Out Private Provision   100
Credibility as an Obstacle to Inducing Production   106
Credibility as an Obstacle to Restricting Production   109
Production Is Difficult   116

5   Economic Constraints and Political Institutions   118

Divided Government and the Politics of Gridlock   119
Federalism and the Devolution of Authority   125
Political and Policy Reform   131
What Do Politicians Know?   136
Institutional Design and Policy Effectiveness   137

6   Final Thoughts   139

What Can Government Do? Five Lessons   141
Conclusions: The Burden of Government   145

Notes   149

References   175

Index   197

FIGURES AND TABLES

Figures

Figure 1.1   Time between price changes   28
Figure 1.2   Multiple investment equilibria: an illustration   40
Figure 1.3   Comparison of deficits and growth in the United States and Japan   43
Figure 2.1   U.S. poverty rates   53

Tables

Table I.1   International comparisons of cigarette consumption   9
Table I.2   Smoking prevalence among U.S. adults, 1965–1994   10
Table 1.1   U.S. economic conditions   23–24
Table 1.2   Wage contracts and national election timing, 1960–1992   31
Table 2.1   Effect of tax and transfer programs on poverty in selected countries   49
Table 2.2   Social Security benefit increases   55
Table 2.3   Labor supply reduction from social insurance and public assistance   61
Table 2.4   Estimated benefits and costs of Social Security by age and earnings, 1985   63
Table 2.5   Male generational accounts by age, 1991   64
Table 2.6   Effective rates of federal taxes   69
Table 2.7   Share of before-tax and after-tax income in the United States   70
Table 3.1   U.S. regulatory agencies   74

Table 4.1   A private contribution game   104
Table 4.2   Per capita health spending and total health expenditures as a percentage of gross domestic product   113
Table 5.1   Important legislation under divided and unified governments, 1947–1990   121
Table 5.2   Spending on environmental and natural resources in U.S. states   127
Table 5.3   Sunset review in U.S. states   132–133

ACKNOWLEDGMENTS

Like any project of this size, many have contributed and we cannot hope to thank them all. However, we would like to single out a few institutions and people who helped this project reach fruition.

First, the two of us met, and the idea for this work was generated, while we were in residence at the Graduate School of Industrial Administration at Carnegie Mellon University, where Glazer served as a visiting professor and Rothenberg was the Bradley Fellow in Political Economy. The program in Political Economy at CMU is greatly missed, as it was both a hospitable and exciting place. We are especially grateful for stimulating discussions with colleagues there, including Dennis Epple, Peter Faynzilberg, Bennett McCallum, Nolan McCarty, Alan Meltzer, Keith Poole, and Richard Romano.

Additionally, we greatly benefited from the initiative, suggestions, encouragement, prodding, enthusiasm, and patience of our editor at Harvard University Press, Michael Aronson. Comments by the anonymous referees solicited by the Press and by Tyler Cowen were also most helpful in the manuscript's final revision.

We would also like to thank the Focused Research Program in Public Choice at the University of California, Irvine, which provided important financial support that made bicoastal collaboration, even in these days of high technology, a good deal easier.

We are grateful to the exceptionally stimulating students in the Program in Public Policy at Hebrew University, where portions of the material from this book were taught, and to the graduate students at the University of Rochester, who read the text at various stages of its evolution.

Finally, we would like to thank our families who put up with us and our project. In particular, we would like to thank our growing children, Daniel Rothenberg, Danielle Glazer, and Sarah Rothenberg, for whom this book has been part of the background noise accompanying most or all of their lives. For the love that they provide, the joy that they bring, and the hope that they give, we happily dedicate this book to them.

WHY GOVERNMENT SUCCEEDS
AND WHY IT FAILS

Introduction:
Public Policy—Limits and Possibilities

A puzzle that has stymied scholars and popular commentators alike has been why government accomplishes some ambitious goals but fails so miserably in meeting others.[1] If government can send a man to the moon, why can it not eliminate poverty? If government can field its soldiers in Kuwait with deadly precision, why can it not control medical costs?

Most explanations for such differences focus on the explicitly political. Typically, inventive analysts who examine a policy's failure or success advance intuitive explanations for the results observed. Since these accountings can be idiosyncratic, others have developed more general principles regarding policy success and failure. Such researchers highlight two related themes:

1. *A policy succeeds only if government officials really want a program to attain its stated goals.* Policy fails when the goals of politicians differ from those formally stated. The intent behind pork barrel projects, for example, may be to spend money in a legislative district, rather than to control floods (e.g., Ferejohn 1974) or to protect the environment (e.g., Ridenour 1994).
2. *Interest groups mold policy in ways that defeat the purpose of the program originally proposed.* Although economic regulation is the classic example cited (Huntington 1953), the deflection of goals by organized interests has been claimed to undermine everything from social initiatives (Lowi 1979) to economic growth (Olson 1982).

Implicit in these analyses is the belief that government could adopt and enforce policies of great benefit to the country if politicians had the right incentives and if special interests were weaker. Government could increase

1

economic growth, eliminate poverty, reduce crime, increase equity, produce public goods,[2] and clean the environment once such obstructions were removed. Many therefore support procedural reforms—limit terms for elected officials, curb campaign contributions, forbid honoraria for government employees, restrict the revolving door by which former officials become lobbyists for firms they regulated—and favor structural changes—unified government (putting legislative and executive control in the same political party), devolution of power to local authorities, strong political parties—as cures for policy ills.[3]

These explanations for policy outcomes, and the proposed solutions, are intuitively appealing and say much about the world. And, although we acknowledge the importance of politicians' incentives and the pressures of organized interests, we think that an exclusive focus on such characteristics gives an incomplete explanation or understanding of policy outcomes. Policy problems may be difficult to solve even for a government with the best intentions, because economic conditions and behavior create constraints, which in some areas make policy ineffective. Studying only the interaction between politicians and constituencies is like investigating the efficacy of medical treatment by looking only at the motives of physicians and ignoring the biology of different diseases. Concentration on politics to the exclusion of economics offers an incomplete examination of many important phenomena: some objectives may be more achievable than others.[4]

We thus contend that, sensible as political explanations are, the response of rational economic actors to a policy—and the context in which such initiatives occur—is crucial for understanding policy outcomes. Despite their usefulness, conventional political explanations neglect the potentially crucial interaction between politics and economics.

Notwithstanding the large research in public choice and in political economy, the vast literature on public policy does not comprehensively investigate how economic constraints structure policy outcomes. As mentioned, some fine research, particularly in macroeconomics, discusses several economic issues (for surveys, see Persson 1988, Persson and Tabellini 1990, and Cukierman 1992; for a more explicitly political perspective, see Alesina and Rosenthal 1995, Alesina 1995, and Keech 1995). Much of this research is excessively technical for many persons interested in policy; it omits much that interests a scholar generally interested in policy; its treatment of politics is strange to students of politics or policy (for example, by assuming that government maximizes a social welfare function); and, of course, it fails to demonstrate how findings generalize to other policy areas. Other recent work, notably that by Dixit (1996), discusses elegantly and at some length the difficulty that government has in committing to future policies and the consequences of that difficulty. But, in not applying the concepts to diverse policies and in not asking what types of problems government can solve, Dixit's focus differs from ours. In short, though important works apply economic concepts to both politics and public policy, the gulf between analyses of public policy and analyses of rational responses to changing conditions has probably grown in recent years as new insights from economics and game theory have increased faster than their applications. As a result, many important advances have been missed by students of policy.

How Economics Interacts with Politics

The claim that economics interacts with politics may seem obvious and even mundane. What makes it an important and interesting assertion is that the effects derived from an analysis of their interaction can be subtler than may be initially believed and, indeed, often counterintuitive.

Accordingly, we aim here to fill a gap in the analysis of public policy by bringing economic behavior to the forefront. The following study addresses our basic concern—what government can do—by stepping back from political machinations and assuming an idealized political state where forward-looking politicians in a democracy attempt to realize, rather than to subvert, policy objectives. Though, as will become clear, we refer to core features of democracies (most notably, how political turnover affects policy success and how endogenous support for a policy can make it more effective), we integrate them with considerations of economic behavior. Similarly, we neglect institutional and constitutional differences; though, for example, we often discuss the United States, our study aims to be generic and rarely relies on special features of the American system, such as the separation of powers and federalism. Only at the end of the book do we investigate how such variations can condition the policy processes and the outcomes observed.

To meet our ambitious goals, we use several approaches. The book contains both theoretical materials (with an emphasis on making them accessible) and detailed empirical data to draw inferences about what government can accomplish. In the same spirit, we deliberately juxtapose broad sweeps of issues with specific, in-depth, examples to develop insights about what is within government's grasp.

Thus, on the one hand, we offer some general global statements about public policy that answer questions of widespread concern. Which societal problems are potentially amenable to government intervention? Are certain types of policy more likely to fail because of economic constraints? On the other hand, we ground our research in the real world with empirical examples that illustrate the themes of our analysis and test our hypotheses (or, at least, illustrate why we think they are correct).

We believe that balancing broad generalizations with detailed examinations helps us make an important contribution to the public policy literature. We focus more sharply on policy and employ less technical detail than do books applying game theory to politics (e.g., Shubik 1982, Ordeshook 1986, Mueller 1989). But we also adopt a more positive, micro-level, approach to understanding government activity than is found in research concentrating on designing policies to solve market failures (e.g., Stokey and Zeckhauser 1978, Weimer and Vining 1999).

Political scientists and policy analysts (to whom we do not propose to teach politics) should find our book helpful for its explication and application of relevant economic ideas and theories; economists (to whom we do not propose to teach economics) should find it useful for learning about how their theoretical models relate to the political world. Rather than expanding on the latest economic theory, we strive to explain, in a way previously unavailable, generic processes that underlie government behavior.

More broadly, we hope that our approach changes the way readers view policy issues. For some, their conception of policy analysis may change a bit. Others may find that their normative assessments of governmental performance should consider which policy goals are attainable and which are not. And still others may discover linkages between policy areas that they had previously missed.

Structure of Analysis

The four chapters that follow investigate the core issue of what government can do according to policy functions. We then turn our attention more squarely back to politics by developing additional implications for how institutional political arrangements may influence policy.

Specifically, we investigate four policy areas:

1. *macroeconomics*, policies to promote employment and growth;
2. *redistribution*, policies to transfer income and wealth between persons;
3. *production*, policies by government to manufacture goods or to supply services or to buy them; and
4. *regulation*, policies to direct the specific behavior of firms or individuals.

These four activities do not constitute everything that government does (in particular, we largely ignore foreign policy and national defense). But this enumeration does cover most domestic governmental activities and is more comprehensive than standard definitions of policy (e.g., Lowi 1964, 1972).[5]

After largely putting institutional nuances aside, the final substantive chapter brings such characteristics back to the forefront. Thus, we investigate the policy effects that alternative institutional arrangements may have on government outputs, particularly given the insights garnered from investigating what an angelic government can do subject to economic constraints. Specifically, we "bring politics back in" by turning our focus to current debates about desirable institutional arrangements: divided government, devolution of power in federal systems, and limits on legislators' terms. In doing so, we show how it is possible to blend our approach of what public policy can accomplish with variance in institutional design.

Conceptual Apparatus: Economic Constraints

We orient our substantive discussion with the aid of four organizing concepts or economic constraints. After considering a broad range of academic research and real world policies, we believe that several interrelated factors that are rarely mentioned in political analyses of public policy provide important conceptual keys for unlocking what government can do. Although some are more important than others for understanding some policy areas (and some are perhaps more important in an absolute sense), we are impressed that these constraints are generally germane for understanding policy. These concepts are

1. *Credibility.* Credibility requires officials to persuade others that government will follow through on the actions promised. Credibility will be especially important when the success of a policy requires government to induce firms and individuals to make costly, irreversible investments. But for an elected government subject to the vicissitudes of elections and to sea changes in public opinion, and lacking many commitment methods available to firms or consumers, credibility is often problematic.

2. *Rational expectations.* Rational expectations refer to the collection of, and the sophisticated response to, information by decisionmakers. Not all economic actors will have rational expectations (generally, we expect larger economic actors such as firms to have better foresight than smaller economic agents such as consumers). But many do, so policymakers should not assume that economic actors will react only in ways that suit a given policy. In general, policies readily anticipated and easily manipulated by economic agents are most prone to fail.

3. *Crowding out / crowding in.* Crowding out or, alternatively, crowding in, appears when the consumption or production of a good varies with the amount other firms or persons consume and produce. With crowding out, activity is reduced (for example, as we will discuss in our analysis of production, philanthropic donations to museums and orchestras may decline after government increases its grants). With crowding in, activity is increased (for instance, with fad behavior, where the participation by some in an activity makes it attractive to others). Depending on whether the activity in question eases or obstructs the achievement of government goals, crowding out or crowding in may have different effects on what government can accomplish.

4. *Multiple equilibria.* Multiple equilibria refer to the theoretical and empirical possibility that different outcomes are produced by the same circumstances. For us, the important point is that on some issues government may determine which equilibrium is brought about. Thus, some government policy can be viewed as an attempt to nudge behavior toward a particular equilibrium. Though the ex-

istence of multiple equilibria does not guarantee the success of policy, it can provide opportunities for success, since government actions can induce a switch from a bad to a good equilibrium.
Multiple equilibria may also be hazardous, as the economy may settle into an undesirable equilibrium.

It might be asked whether all four of these concepts are central and, if so, why these four concepts and not others? In large part, we focus on these concepts because we observe that government faces more severe credibility problems than other organizations. Though subtleties are involved, other organizations have means of commitment that can effectively bind their behavior but are not available to government: most obviously, firms can enter into contracts, enforceable by the courts, that can constrain their future actions. More generally, government is uniquely situated both to establish and to abolish property rights in a manner that qualitatively distinguishes it from private decisionmakers and that makes credibility far more of an issue. To understand when governmental policy is credible, we must therefore look not at the pronouncements of politicians but examine under what conditions government can be expected to indeed follow a policy that it claims it will. Though we will see that rational expectations, crowding, and multiple equilibria may have additional impacts on public policy independent of credibility concerns (and we do not wish to underestimate such impacts), these three concepts also stand out because they significantly explain the conditions that make policy more or less credible.

To elaborate this last point, often the beliefs of firms and consumers about what government will do, and the reactions of economic actors to the policies, are based on a rational analysis of what incentives or pressures government will face or what changes will occur (for example, through elections). Therefore, under many circumstances, to ascertain the credibility of a policy it is necessary to consider rational expectations of what policy will be in the future. And to determine the effects of a credible policy it is also necessary to consider the behavior of economic actors in response to the policy, which can depend in part on what people expect (including what they should rationally expect) the effects to be. Similarly, issues of crowding can be prominent, as when a change in the behavior of some people induces others to react in the same way (perhaps changing political pressures and expectations about policy along the way), thereby weakening or strengthening credibility. Under some, but not all, conditions these altered pressures and updated expectations can reinforce the private behavior that government desires. The existence of multiple equilibria is one manifestation of how any one actor's behavior can affect the behavior of others, with the special characteristic, however, that it allows a temporary policy to have permanent effects. In other words, when multiple equilibria are possible, which one is eventually realized may be a key component of whether policy credibility, and hence policy goals, can be realized.

Viewed differently, our four concepts allow us to predict when a policy will be self-defeating and when it will be self-sustaining. When the desired behavior by individuals or firms generates crowding in of that behavior, when people anticipate such crowding in, and when they believe that government is committed to pursuing the policy, they become yet more willing to engage in that behavior, thus making the policy self-sustaining. In an extreme case, the crowding in may be sufficiently powerful that the economy will move from one equilibrium to another, with individuals and firms continuing to behave in the manner that government desired even if government no longer conducts an active policy in the designated area. When some or all of these conditions are absent, a policy can be self-defeating, making success unlikely.

We conclude this chapter with examples that demonstrate how applying the concepts of credibility, rational expectations, crowding out, and multiple equilibria can give a plausible, if not a definitive, understanding of seemingly anomalous results. Specifically, we consider two types of behaviors that share many similarities, but where the outcomes diverge: the emission of noxious fumes by cigarette smoking and the emission of noxious fumes by cars with defective or improperly tuned emissions equipment. A brief look at the evidence suggests that, despite the obvious similarity that in both acts consumers generate noxious gases, state governments in the United States (on which we focus here) have reduced smoking while they have failed at inducing people to maintain their emissions equipment. These two cases have other similarities that make them good subjects for comparative study: they concern consumer behavior, they are subject to few regional or partisan conflicts, they generate externalities, they deal with the broad issue of public health, and they are heavily influenced by state regulation. What can explain this discrepancy between government success and failure?

A Success: The Decline of Smoking

Consider first cigarette consumption. Table I.1, which presents cross-national data, indicates that the 28 percent decline in per capita consumption in the United States' is impressive; of the countries listed, only the United Kingdom had a greater decrease. In contrast, several countries had increased per capita consumption, including Japan, France, and China (at an amazing 160 percent). Following this pattern, Table I.2, which lists U.S. cigarette consumption over three decades, shows that the proportion of adults smoking cigarettes in the United States fell from 42 percent in 1965 to 25 percent in 1994. Similarly, the proportion of former smokers in the population increased from 18 percent in 1970 to 24 percent in 1985 (Viscusi 1994). In short, the United States seems to be doing something right.

Yet, given the distribution of pressure groups and political preferences, standard political stories incompletely explain this success. U.S. cigarette producers are concentrated among a few large corporations, which are well

Table I.1 International comparisons of cigarette consumption (adult per capita consumption and prevalence by males by country)

Country	Annual cigarette consumption per adult			Prevalence* (percentage smoking)
	1970–72	1980–82	1990–92	
Australia	3,410	3,440	2,710	29.0
Belgium	3,090	2,880	2,310	31.0
China	730	1,290	1,900	61.0
Denmark	2,050	2,020	1,919	37.0
France	1,860	2,080	2,120	40.0
Germany	2,430	2,420	2,360	36.8
Ireland	3,050	3,030	2,420	29.0
Italy	1,800	2,310	1,920	38.0
Japan	2,950	3,430	3,240	59.0
Korea	2,370	2,750	3,010	68.2
United States	3,700	3,560	2,670	27.1
United Kingdom	3,250	2,740	2,210	28.0

Source: World Health Organization, Tobacco or Health Programme, *Tobacco or Health: A Global Status Report: Country Profiles by Region, 1997.* http://www.cdc.gov/tobacco/who/whofirst.htm
*All data are from 1993 or 1994 except China (1984), Germany (1992), and Korea (1989).

Table I.2 Smoking prevalence among U.S. adults, 1965–1994 (percentage of
regular smokers, 18 years of age and older)

Year	Prevalence
1965	42.4
1966	42.6
1970	37.4
1974	37.1
1978	34.1
1979	33.5
1980	33.2
1983	32.1
1985	30.1
1987	28.8
1988	28.1
1990	25.5
1991	25.7
1992	26.5
1993	25.0
1994	25.5

Source: Office on Smoking and Health, National Center for Chronic Disease Prevention
and Health Promotion Centers for Disease Control and Prevention, July 1996.
http://www.cdc.gov/tobacco/prevali.htm

Note: Estimates since 1992 incorporate "some-day" smokers.

organized politically, whereas opponents of smoking are widely dispersed
and, although they have their advocates such as the "Big Three" health associations (the American Heart, Lung, and Cancer Associations), their political operations would seem to be no match for the tobacco companies.
Furthermore, politicians are not exceptionally united around the goal of
reducing cigarette consumption. Governmental ambivalence toward tobacco producers has often been demonstrated by the coexistence of agricultural assistance for tobacco farmers with public programs to reduce
smoking.[6]

Of course, smoking might have declined even had government done
nothing. Nonetheless, it is not readily evident which social forces would
have driven such a decline.

Most notably, income effects alone do not explain change in the United
States or in other developed countries. For example, the cross-national evi-

dence in Table I.1 suggests that economic growth does not determine smoking rates.[7] Some rich countries, such as Japan and France, have had increased smoking while others had declines. Similarly, differences in economic development would not explain why the rate of smoking among men in Japan is now double that of the United States. Indeed, the huge increase in cigarette consumption in China seems to be sweeping much of Asia: the *New York Times* reports that while "American cigarette sales are expected to decline by about 15 percent by the end of the decade . . . [i]n Asia, smoking is not only tolerated, but is fashionable" (Shenon 1994, sec. 4, p. 1). So accepted is smoking in China that the standard greeting between men goes like this: "Smoke?" while offering a pack in outstretched hand. The only polite response is to take one, light up, draw, and only then to start the conversation (see Rosenthal with Altman 1998).

These differences across developed nations also suggest that increased knowledge about the hazards of smoking—the harm to smokers themselves and to persons around them through secondhand smoke—cannot be the main explanation for declines in cigarette consumption. The increased smoking in so many countries, several of them with highly educated populations, is inconsistent with a knowledge-based explanation.

Rather, it appears that, although political conditions make government initiatives seem ripe for failure, consumption has declined at least partly because of governmental efforts. For example, in California alone (which has some of the nation's most stringent antismoking policies), increased taxes and a government-initiated antismoking media campaign are estimated to have reduced cigarette consumption by 1.56 billion packs of cigarettes over four years, or by about seventeen packs per person annually. Statistical analysis finds that smoking declined in California at three times the national rate after the state's 1988 passage of Proposition 99, which increased the tax on cigarettes from 10 to 35 cents per pack and allocated 20 percent of revenues raised for educational programs to reduce tobacco use (Sung et al. 1994, Hu et al. 1995a, b).

A Failure: Automobile Emissions

Government policy has reduced smoking, but policies designed to reduce emissions of vehicles once they are in the hands of drivers have failed. Cars are major polluters—they account for 62 percent of total U.S. carbon monoxide emissions, 32 percent of total emissions of nitrous oxides, and

26 percent of total volatile organic compounds (Davis 1995); the annual damage from automobile emissions in the United States is about $50 billion.[8] It also appears that a minority of cars generate most of the air pollution.[9]

In the United States, many state governments, in response to federal mandates, require automobile owners to have their vehicles' antipollution devices checked. Thirty-eight states require such tests (known as "smog checks"), affecting some 33 million vehicles.

Regular smog checks may seem a simple and easy solution to an otherwise troubling problem.[10] Yet reality has proven far more problematic than such a straightforward policy prescription might imply. Even optimistic studies show that emissions reductions in the United States were, at most, half of those expected. More pessimistic analyses find *no* effect and point to rampant problems: garages often fail to repair pollution abatement equipment and yet pass defective automobiles on the tests, repaired cars break long before their next inspection, and owners tamper with their repaired cars after successful inspection. The end result is a failed program. Thus, a study of air quality in Minnesota finds that, at most, 1.3 percent of the improved air quality in that state can be credited to the inspection system (Scherrer and Kittelson 1994); depending on the vagaries of interpretation, these data are even consistent with the hypothesis that smog checks increase emissions. An Arizona study found no significant differences in emissions between cars that were and were not subjected to smog checks (Zhang et al. 1994). Similarly, studies in California find that cars are no cleaner after a smog check than they are before inspection (see references in Glazer, Klein, and Lave 1995).

For our purposes, the issue of automobile emission reductions offers a useful comparison because, in many ways, it resembles efforts to reduce cigarette smoking. Support for limiting automobile emissions appears about as strong as for reducing smoking. Once again, the major interests are better organized on the producer side—in this case, the automobile producers. If anything, producer support for smog checks is stronger than it is for reducing smoking, since smog checks diminish the need for manufacturers to invest in lessening new-car emissions. The existence of public interest environmental organizations that campaign for reduced automobile emissions strengthens the proposition that the two cases examined have similar characteristics. Also, comparable to the situation with cigarettes, politicians are frequently divided about reducing car emissions. Political leaders appreciate the economic importance of the automobile industry, the value constituents place on high-performance cars, and the desire of citizens to reduce pollution.

Admittedly, the two goods examined show several economic differences. It is not clear, however, that these discrepancies make the likelihood of reducing smoking greater than of reducing emissions:

- *The externalities the good creates.*[11] Although others may also suffer, the people most harmed by cigarette consumption are the smokers themselves.[12] In contrast, a driver does not suffer from his own car's emissions (indeed, a car's occupants typically leave the exhaust behind them and suffer from the pollution created by vehicles in front). Reducing consumption of externality-producing goods is generally more difficult because the consumer does not pay the costs created by the externality.
- *The technical difficulties of solving the problem.* Related to the first point, it might initially appear that reducing emissions through automobile maintenance is technically more difficult than is quitting smoking. Certainly, at one level, this is true. Garage mechanics may fail in repairing equipment, and broken emissions systems may be undetected for some time. Cigarette smokers need merely stop lighting a match.

Given, however, that smokers may be psychologically and physiologically addicted to nicotine, it is questionable that it is easier to reduce smoking than to reduce smog.[13] Addiction may make smokers insensitive to increased costs of smoking and, consequently, make policy less effective.

Explaining the Discrepant Outcomes

Thus, making a strong case that the clout of smokers or the producers of cigarettes is much weaker than that of automobile drivers is difficult. Relative political strength does not explain why smokers and cigarette producers are penalized and drivers are not. Nor is it obvious that the characteristics of smoking compared with emissions make one set of related problems easier to solve than another. Rather, a qualitatively different explanation for policy success or failure is required.

We claim that the interaction of economics with politics highlights some important differences between smoking reduction and emissions controls and could explain the contrasting outcomes of the government programs. Specifically, consider how economic constraints such as credibility, expectations, crowding out, and multiple equilibria can give insights absent in other viewpoints.

Perhaps most notably, cigarette smoking appears subject to crowding out and crowding in.[14] An important characteristic of smoking is that persons are likely to find the activity more enjoyable and less difficult if others around them also smoke. Smokers will be socially accepted, hear fewer complaints by fellow consumers, find it easier to borrow a lighter or a cigarette, and face fewer restrictions if restaurants, airlines, and other businesses consider it profitable to accommodate rather than to restrict smoking.

The Surgeon General of the United States (Centers for Disease Control and Prevention 1994), in discussing tobacco advertising, has recognized these pressures:

> Current research suggests that pervasive tobacco promotion has two major effects: it creates the perception that more people smoke than actually do, and it provides a conduit between actual self-image and ideal self-image—in other words, smoking is made to look cool. Whether causal or not, these effects foster the uptake of smoking, initiating for many a dismal and relentless chain of events . . .
>
> Among environmental factors, peer influence seems to be particularly potent in the early stages of tobacco use; the first tries of cigarettes and smokeless tobacco occur most often with peers, and the peer group may subsequently provide expectations, reinforcement, and cues for experimentation. Parental tobacco use does not appear to be as compelling a risk factor as peer use.
>
> How adolescents perceive their social environment may be a stronger influence on behavior than the actual environment. For example, adolescents consistently overestimate the number of young people and adults who smoke. Persons with the highest overestimates are more likely to become smokers than are persons with more accurate perceptions. Similarly, persons who view cigarettes as easily accessible and generally available are more likely to begin smoking than are persons who perceive more difficulty in obtaining cigarettes. (pp. vii, 5–6)

The same idea regarding crowding can be applied to understand policies that reduce smoking. If government reduces smoking by some persons, it will induce reduced smoking by others. Policy will benefit from a multiplier effect. For instance, restrictions on smoking may change the peer pressures that young people face that may lead them to take up the habit (Sunstein 1990). Put another way, we expect to see either many or few persons smoking. Similarly, we expect an uneven distribution of smokers, with heavy smoking in some groups that interact socially and little smoking in other comparable groups.[15]

Comparatively, although automobile emissions are public bads, crowding in is limited when it comes to maintaining emissions equipment. It may be no easier or no cheaper to fix emissions equipment when others maintain their own devices (for example, the availability of qualified mechanics may increase, but the demand for their services may outstrip the increased supply). Nor should one expect that the satisfaction, or the reduction in social pressures, that citizens feel from fixing their emissions equipment will be greater when they know that others are doing so. Social pressures are also small because, except in extreme cases when it is clear that a car is producing foul gases, failed car emissions systems can be detected only with the aid of expensive equipment. Therefore, neighbors, friends, or coworkers will exert little social pressure to fix pollution devices even if others are complying.

The relevance of crowding in for explaining the differences between smoking and smog checks may be reinforced when the existence of multiple equilibria allows government to determine which equilibrium is established. Since changing one person's smoking behavior can change the actions of many, it is easy to imagine smoking as characterized by multiple equilibria, where many people smoke or just a few do (or where persons in isolated subgroups either smoke in large or in small numbers). Furthermore, because social acceptance and convenience—or the lack thereof—are likely to be part and parcel of these multiple equilibria, the equilibrium established is likely to be stable. In contrast to controls on smoking, mandates for automobile emission repair and maintenance do not generate crowding in: governmental effects associated with smog checks will be limited to those persons directly induced to reduce emissions. As a result, the existence of multiple equilibria is less likely.

Thus, antismoking policy may be effective whereas smog checks are not because only for smoking can policymakers influence which equilibrium holds. Specifically, if one possible equilibrium in the absence of government intervention is for most people to smoke (thereby making it attractive for each consumer to smoke), and another is for most people not to smoke (leading potential smokers to realize that the habit will be inconvenient), government may help determine which one holds. For example, government warnings about the dangers of smoking may induce enough people to quit smoking so that crowding in takes place and the low-smoking equilibrium comes about. Furthermore, government may adopt policies, such as high or low cigarette taxes, that make political support for one equilibrium or another unravel; for instance, high taxes may make some persons quit smoking, lowering the rate of smoking in the population and, hence, increasing political support for raising tobacco taxes further. This circular process will continue until the low-smoking equilibrium is attained.

The existence of multiple equilibria suggests that policy can not only be effective but also that short-lived public policies may have effects for a long time afterwards, allowing government policy to be potent. For example, by moving behavior from one equilibrium to another, reductions of smoking caused by temporary tax increases or by temporary antismoking campaigns may be long-term.[16] Alternatively, when the equilibrium for a given policy is unique, as with vehicle emissions, temporary policies will have only temporary effects. The distinction is analogous to one found in medicine. Treatments are most effective when they consist of intense inhibition therapy, which kills all the viruses or bacteria causing a disease. Therapy is less effective when continued maintenance, requiring patients to take drugs for years, is necessary. A shift from one equilibrium to another resembles inhibition therapy; maintenance therapy resembles a policy that must be implemented for years.

Related to the use of crowding out and of multiple equilibria, the different achievements on smoking and on emissions may also depend on expectations. For instance, if consumers and firms expect government regulation of smoking to be effective and regulation of automobile emissions to be ineffective, then they may rationally believe that the regulatory programs will respectively be supported or allowed to flounder. In reaction, cigarette smokers will be more inclined than drivers to incur costs that have long-term payoffs. For example, smokers may be willing to enter smoking cessation programs and, generally, to accept the high cost of kicking an addictive habit.[17] Drivers, by contrast, will avoid spending much on emissions repairs if they believe future regulations will be weak.

Clearly associated with rational expectations are issues of government credibility. Our earlier discussion might seem to suggest that credibility cannot explain why smoking policy succeeded and emissions policy failed since the two cases appear, a priori, similar. When put in context with the other features already discussed, however, the potential impact of credibility becomes clear. Once policies succeeded and failed, as new equilibria were established and expectations were updated, consumers likely began to see government's policies as credible for smoking but not for emissions.

Also, to follow up this and an earlier point, investment, particularly by current smokers for whom quitting is costly psychologically and sometimes financially, will most likely be made when benefits are expected to continue far into the future. Consumers who believe that government will reverse itself and again promote smoking will not invest. Analogously, firms will internalize beliefs about credibility in their investment decisions in ways that make smoking less desirable (on the efficacy of such efforts, see Borland et al. 1990, Brenner and Mielck 1992). For instance, airlines that anticipate bans on smoking may not install ashtrays in their planes and may select less expensive air circulation systems that replace the air in a plane less frequently. Such strategic complementarities magnify the direct effects of public policies.

Conversely, as mentioned, citizens may invest little in durable repair of emissions equipment if they believe that the government's emissions policy will be short-lived. Of potentially even greater importance, garages that might service automobile emissions equipment, but believe that government is imperfectly committed to smog checks (so that it may relax a policy or change it), may not invest in the training and equipment necessary to make the policy succeed. Indeed, a frequent complaint of garage owners is that investment in certain types of antipollution equipment is unprofitable because government so often changes the type of expensive equipment required to meet current requirements. In response, many garages decline to offer the required tests and repairs (Gates 1991).

At another level, however, credibility may be more subtle, also working through political processes. As the previous discussion suggested, smoking policy may have greater credibility than emissions policy because initial success in reducing smoking will increase political support for antismoking policy and make it difficult for government to backtrack. Ex-smokers and firms that invest on the assumption that smoking will be discouraged will be outraged if policy is reversed, thereby making the government's antismoking policy credible. Although consumers of low-emissions cars or producers of them would increasingly support antiemissions programs, car owners forced to repair their exhaust systems will not be especially committed to the policy.

Thus, along with crowding out, multiple equilibria, and rational expectations, credibility may be important in determining policy success or failure. A credible policy may succeed by changing behavior and political attitudes.

In summary, the different outcomes from government policies on smoking and on emissions maintenance may be explained by economic constraints. At least implicitly, policymakers may have taken advantage of crowding in by moving behavior from an equilibrium with much smoking to one with less smoking. It is reasonable to assume that this change was aided, particularly once some success was realized, by the expectations of citizens and firms and by the credibility that government gained for continued antismoking policies. It appears that, faced with these beliefs and the credibility of antismoking policy, more smokers found ways to quit, potential smokers more frequently abstained in the first place, and the sellers of complementary services acted as if they expected a decline in the number of smokers.

By contrast, policy toward emissions floundered without crowding in. Drivers were given little reason to change their expectations about the pressures they would face to maintain their equipment, little basis for believing that government was committed to its policy for the long haul, and few incentives to invest in maintaining their emissions systems over a sustained period.

What Makes Problems Soluble?

As already implied, we start from a simple, but we believe an underdeveloped, perspective: some problems are inherently more soluble than others. Scholars and practitioners interested in public policy may want to think more carefully about what problems are amenable to government intervention and through what means—how economics and politics fit together—than is the convention. The rest of this book more thoroughly develops this view and its implications by shedding light on the possibilities for "good" policy given economic constraints. That is, it explores which problems government can solve given the behavior of individuals and firms and how such behavior feeds back into the political world.

We begin our examination of different policy areas with macroeconomic policy. Such policy is substantively important. Moreover, for our purposes, starting with a study of how government deals with economic growth or with unemployment has additional attractions. All four of the principal concepts we outlined are important for understanding macroeconomics, and it is the area where practitioners and researchers have paid the most attention to them, particularly to credibility and rational expectations. With this foundation, we will proceed to compare and contrast the possibilities of government success with redistribution, regulation, and production, to suggest what importance some basic feature of democratic government might have, and to draw some inferences about the possibilities for government success and failure.

1

Macroeconomics:
Can Government Control the Economy?

Economic prosperity is crucial for a politician's success. Indeed, it can determine whether a president wins an election (e.g., Fiorina 1981). Yet it is unclear whether, or to what extent, government can influence the performance of the aggregate economy. One reason the effects are unclear is that economies fluctuate regardless of which policies are pursued, making partitioning of government's impact relative to that of other economic forces difficult.[1] And, as we will discuss in more depth shortly, government policy cannot merely be assumed to be effective, as it must overcome roadblocks before even the most sophisticated attempts to control the economy can succeed. Further obscuring the effects of policy, politicians may claim credit for good economic conditions that they did not bring about and blame economic downturns on forces outside their control—even when such events result from political ineptitude or a pursuit of short-term goals (for example, reelection) that lead presidents to sacrifice long-term prosperity (see Tufte 1978).

Moreover, managing the economy requires levels of political coordination and dexterity that seem unattainable by any democracy, regardless of which institutional arrangements are adopted. Thus, students of politics have examined, for example, whether politicians can adeptly control and coordinate agencies that oversee the economy, with particular attention paid to presidential and congressional influence over the Federal Reserve Board (FRB) in the United States (Grier 1989, 1991, 1996; Chappell, Havrilesky, and McGregor 1993; Krause 1994).

Consistent with the spirit of our endeavor, we concentrate on asking whether government can manage the economy rather than on whether politicians pursue the wrong goals. Consequently, we aim to develop inferences about the feasibility of managing the economy, assuming that political actors are both competent and cooperative.

To address these concerns, we highlight the principal tools government may use to manage the economy:

- *monetary policy*, directed at manipulating interest rates or the money supply;
- *fiscal policy*, directed at setting levels of government spending and taxes;
- *exhortation*, directed at persuading economic actors to change their behavior; and
- *budgetary policy*, directed at raising and lowering levels of government indebtedness by changing the mix of taxes and borrowing used to finance government spending.

For expository reasons, we will largely focus on the United States. But consistent with our goal of discerning what can be accomplished generically, our analysis typically extends to other democracies, including to parliamentary regimes.

We will find that the features we emphasize—credibility, expectations, crowding out, and multiple equilibria—constrain the effectiveness of macroeconomic policy, although different constraints are more important for some policies than for others. In particular, rational expectations are important for monetary policy; crowding out is important for fiscal policy; multiple equilibria and credibility are fundamental for manipulation by exhortation; and rational expectations and crowding out are important for budgetary policy.

When all these economic constraints are taken into account, it appears that government can guide, but cannot control, aggregate economic performance. Although the political considerations that we downplay also affect the economy, our analysis of what government can accomplish is roughly consistent with the observed level of political influence on economic performance.

Managing the Economy: Partisan Incentives and Political Cycles

To expand on our last comments, it helps to discuss the extent to which politicians manage the economy before we examine which tools they may use. To this end, we will sketch the degree to which economic conditions are a product of governmental intervention.

If all incumbents adopted the same policies, establishing that politicians can affect the economy would be difficult. Two political features, however, appear to lead politicians to vary systematically in their approach to the economy.

The first is partisanship. Political parties have different reputations and constituencies, which make them prefer different economic outcomes (Hibbs 1977). In the United States, for example, Democrats are usually viewed as the party of workers and of the poor, preferring low unemployment even at the expense of higher inflation, whereas Republicans are generally considered the supporters of business who favor low inflation even at the cost of higher unemployment.[2]

The second feature is that politicians who believe voters weigh economic conditions just before an election more heavily than conditions early in an incumbent's term will prefer bad economic news in the beginning rather than at the end of their terms. As Fair (1988) summarizes the evidence, voters favor parties that rule during good economic times in the immediate past:

> Voters look back between about six and nine months regarding real [per capita] growth rate and about two years regarding the inflation rate. This rather short horizon leaves room for an administration to increase the chances of its party getting reelected. Whether administrations in fact behave this way, thus creating "political business cycles," is, of course, a different question . . . The only point here is that voters seem to behave in a way that provides an incentive for such manipulation.[3] (p. 177)

Thus, as the election year data in Table 1.1 illustrate, over 1952–1997 annual economic growth (as measured by the change in gross domestic product, or GDP)[4] averaged 4.48 percent in years when the incumbent party retained the U.S. presidency (in 1956, 1964, 1972, 1984, 1988, and 1996), compared with 3.1 percent when the incumbent party lost (in 1952, 1960, 1968, 1976, 1980, and 1992). Inflation was also lower when the incumbent party won (3.17 percent compared with 4.53 percent), although differences in unemployment were small (5.55 compared with 5.73 percent).

Table 1.1 can also be used to investigate whether American presidents manipulate the economy, by examining whether inflation or unemployment varies under different political parties. The results show that infla-

Table 1.1 U.S. economic conditions, by presidential administration, party, and year

| Administration (party) | Year | Economic conditions (percentage) | | |
		Real GDP growth	Inflation	Unemployment
Truman	1949	−0.8	−2.1	5.9
(Democrat)	1950	8.9	5.9	5.3
	1951	7.6	6.0	3.3
	1952	3.7	0.8	3.0
Eisenhower	1953	4.6	0.7	2.9
(Republican)	1954	−0.7	−0.7	5.5
	1955	7.1	0.4	4.4
	1956	2.0	3.0	4.1
	1957	1.9	2.9	4.3
	1958	−1.0	1.8	6.8
	1959	7.4	1.7	5.5
	1960	2.4	1.4	5.5
Kennedy/Johnson	1961	2.3	0.7	6.7
(Democrat)	1962	6.1	1.3	5.5
	1963	4.3	1.6	5.7
	1964	5.8	1.0	5.2
	1965	6.4	1.9	4.5
	1966	6.5	3.5	3.8
	1967	2.5	3.0	3.8
	1968	4.7	4.7	3.6
Nixon/Ford	1969	3.0	6.2	3.5
(Republican)	1970	0.1	5.6	4.9
	1971	3.3	3.3	5.9
	1972	5.5	3.4	5.6
	1973	5.8	8.7	4.9
	1974	−0.6	12.3	5.6
	1975	−0.4	6.9	8.5
	1976	5.4	4.9	7.7
Carter	1977	4.7	6.7	7.1
(Democrat)	1978	5.4	9.0	6.1
	1979	2.8	13.3	5.8
	1980	−0.3	12.5	7.1

Table 1.1 (continued)

| Administration (party) | Year | Economic conditions (percentage) | | |
		Real GDP growth	Inflation	Unemployment
Reagan	1981	2.3	8.9	7.6
(Republican)	1982	−2.1	3.8	9.7
	1983	4.0	3.8	9.6
	1984	7.0	3.9	7.5
	1985	3.6	3.8	7.2
	1986	3.1	1.1	7.0
	1987	2.9	4.4	6.2
	1988	3.8	4.4	5.5
Bush	1989	3.4	4.6	5.3
(Republican)	1990	1.2	6.1	5.6
	1991	−0.9	3.1	6.8
	1992	2.7	2.9	7.5
Clinton	1993	2.3	2.7	6.9
(Democrat)	1994	3.5	2.5	6.1
	1995	2.0	2.5	5.6
	1996	2.8	3.3	5.4
	1997	3.8	1.7	4.9
Average	All years	3.3	4.0	5.8
	Election years	3.8	3.8	5.6

Sources: GDP data 1949–1996, Survey of Current Business, Table 2A, August 1997; 1997 from *Economic Report of the President,* 1998, Table B-2; inflation (CPI) data from ftp.bls.gov/pub/special.requests/cpi/cpiai.txt, Bureau of Labor Statistics, CPI-U, October 16, 1998. Unemployment rate from Bureau of Labor Statistics, ftp.bls.gov/pub/special.requests/lf/aat1.txt.

tion is 0.12 percentage points lower and unemployment is 0.81 percentage points lower when a Democratic rather than a Republican president is in office, with the slightly lower inflation under Democrats largely attributable to the Clinton years. Our simple analysis is broadly consistent with the more detailed and sophisticated empirical estimates reported by Alesina, Roubini, and Cohen (1997). Although the partisan differences are small, Democrats, compared to Republicans, do care more about unemployment than about inflation.

The evidence for manipulation of the economy around the time of a presidential election is weak. Although, as seen in Table 1.1, inflation and unemployment are slightly lower in presidential election years than in other years, and economic growth is greater, deeper examination (which, for example, considers changes from previous years) finds no difference in economic performance in election years (for a summary of the evidence, see Alesina 1995).

The data thus indicate that political control of the economy is limited. Different political parties may guide the economy in different directions and somewhat stimulate the economy every fourth year. But neither partisan control nor political cycles seem to produce dramatic changes. Of course, even if one accepts these inferences, developing an intuition about what underlying processes are operating requires further investigation into whether economic feasibility, political will, or ineptitude is the driving force at work.

Monetary Policy and Rational Expectations

Clinton's face turned red with anger and disbelief. "You mean to tell me that the success of the program and my reelection hinges on the Federal Reserve and . . . bond traders?" . . . Nods from his end of the table. Not a dissent. Clinton . . . perceived at this moment how much of his fate was passing into the hands of the unelected [Chairman of the Federal Reserve Board] Alan Greenspan and the bond market. (Woodward 1994, p. 84.)

The above quotation from a popular description of the early years of the Clinton administration highlights a frustration facing national leaders. Specifically, their ability to employ monetary policy to stimulate the nation's economy during an election year or during their term in office largely depends on policies adopted by other political decisionmakers—in the United States, the Federal Reserve Board—toward money supply and interest rates and on responses taken by private decisionmakers, such as those driving the bond market. As already mentioned, much of our analysis implicitly views government as one unit, with no conflicts of the type claimed to exist between the FRB and the American president (or legislature). Rather, we shall consider how bond traders, firms, workers, and consumers react to government policy.

Still, it is important to explain how the money supply can be such a powerful tool. This issue can be examined at two levels. One highlights the sheer mechanics of money supply expansions and contractions in the absence of the sophisticated behavior discussed in our book, which we label the traditional view; the other integrates rational expectations. Since understanding the traditional response is a prerequisite for appreciating the contemporary one, we examine these perspectives sequentially.

The Traditional View of Monetary Policy

The traditional view of monetary policy concentrates on the multiplier effects of increases in the money supply. Money—which may be defined as the sum of currency and of deposits in checking accounts—is seen as lubricating the operation and expansion of the economy.[5] In the United States the Federal Reserve Bank, not the Congress or the president, controls monetary policy. The control is indirect, relying largely on buying and selling treasury bills from private investors.

To illustrate, suppose that the FRB puts additional money into circulation by buying a consumer's $10,000 U.S. Treasury bill for its current market price of $9,500.[6] The consumer exchanging noncash assets for money may want to spend his additional cash. Or he may buy a different financial asset, with the person selling him the asset in turn buying goods. Or the increased purchases of assets by this consumer and others like him may increase asset prices, make people and firms feel wealthier, and thus induce them to spend more on goods, equipment, machines, and so on. And as this cash circulates through the economy, its new holders may also buy goods, further increasing consumption.[7]

Additionally, because the FRB's purchases of Treasury bills increase their market price, the rate of return on these bills will necessarily drop. For example, an increase in the market price of six-month bills with a $10,000 redemption value from $9,500 to $9,600 reduces their annual interest rate from 10.3 percent to 8.2 percent. Such lower interest rates should further stimulate the economy.

Federal Reserve purchases of bills from commercial banks may also stimulate the economy by increasing bank loans. Since commercial banks use cash or deposits at Federal Reserve Banks (which are cash equivalents) as reserves, an increase in FRB purchases will increase bank reserves. Banks may now be more willing to make commercial loans, thereby leading to a decline in market interest rates.

Lastly, if capital moves easily across borders and if exchange rates are flexible, then an increase in the money supply may indirectly cause an increase in exports and a decline in imports. By lowering real interest rates,[8] an increased money supply reduces the expected return of investing in American financial assets and induces portfolio managers to shift assets abroad.[9] The resulting decline in demand for the dollar makes it cheaper relative to other currencies, thereby reducing imports and increasing exports, which further stimulates the domestic economy.[10]

In short, the traditional view considers monetary policy a powerful, probably the most powerful, instrument for managing the economy. When the economy needs stimulus, government can increase the money supply. The additional cash churns through the economy in several ways: consumers with more cash spend more, lenders with more loanable funds lower their interest rates and lend more, and investors faced with lower domestic returns look abroad and indirectly lead to higher exports.

The Rational Expectations Perspective

The conventional version of how monetary policy functions gives much room for effective monetary policy. Such a view, however, assumes that economic decisionmakers have imperfect foresight.[11]

Alternatively, if these actors have rational expectations, the stimulus from increases in the money supply may be short-circuited. Farsighted decisionmakers may merely raise prices and wages commensurate with the increased demand for goods produced by a higher money supply. The result will be inflation, not higher employment or growth.

Given rational expectations, whether expansionary monetary policy stimulates the economy or instead increases inflation depends on how prices and wages respond to changing conditions. If prices and wages adjust quickly, then inflation will result; if the adjustment is slow, then some economic stimulation can occur. Put another way, *price rigidities and wage rigidities* are essential for making monetary policy effective when economic agents have rational expectations.

Are prices and wages sticky? The answer is mixed. Wages and prices do adjust, but they often take time. Consequently, over the short-term government can stimulate the economy by increasing the money supply, but rational expectations make permanent increases in economic activity unlikely. Specifically, if the change in demand is small and if the economy is not initially overheated, then increases in the money supply may provide a short-term economic stimulus (for example, one year). However, because many of the industries most sensitive to macroeconomic changes anticipate shifts and adjust accordingly, the economic boost may be small. So if the change in demand is large, if the economy is working at capacity, and if the period under consideration is sufficiently long, then firms increase prices and wages; only inflation is produced.

Several empirical regularities lead to the conclusion that short-term stimulation through monetary policy is possible under the right conditions, but that the effects are unlikely to persist for long. One is that prices are, indeed, sticky over the short term, suggesting that monetary policy can at least temporarily stimulate the economy. Although, in extreme cases, firms absorb declines in the real price of their goods for a long period before increasing their nominal prices—for example, Cechetti (1986) finds that publishers of U.S. magazines allow inflation to erode the real value of their products by 25 percent before increasing prices, which, in an economy of modest inflation, can take years—the more typical period between price increases is annual.[12] Figure 1.1, which lists the average length of time

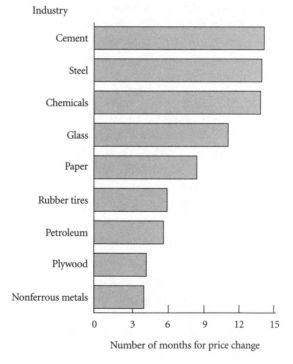

Figure 1.1 Time between price changes (average for various industries). *Source:* Carlton (1986).

between price increases for several American industries, illustrates the extent of such price stickiness.[13] Though practice varies across industries, none adjusts prices as frequently as quarterly and none waits much more than a year. The delay in price adjustments allows monetary policy to stimulate or dampen the economy over the short run.

Other evidence for the proposition that monetary policy is undermined would be data indicating that changes in policy are anticipated. As mentioned, monetary policy will be ineffectual if policy changes are anticipated by firms and consumers. In such circumstances, firms and employees with perfect foresight would increase prices and wages, neutralizing the attempt to increase employment and production by increasing the money supply. Even if firms keep prices constant over the course of a year, they would undercut the stimulative effect of increases in the money supply by perfectly anticipating all the increases that would occur, and setting prices that reflect expected future inflation.

Whether, however, such nimble reactions actually occur has been inadequately investigated. The obvious means of studying such phenomena is to examine behavior around the time of elections. For instance, if different political parties have different preferences over monetary policy and if firms and workers have rational expectations, then prices charged by firms, and wage contracts signed with workers, should depend on who wins the election. In the United States price and wage increases would be greater when the Democrats rather than the Republicans are the clear winners, and firms should wait until just after an election to set prices or wages.[14]

As data on union contracts are more readily available than data on product prices, we concentrate on them.[15] Nevertheless, we would expect findings for price changes to be comparable.

For our investigation we compiled data on all major contract agreements in the United States for the years 1960–1992. Specifically, we examined the 6,105 contracts involving more than 3,000 workers for which the month and the year are reported by the Department of Labor. Since presidential elections occur in early November, we classify the date of the agreement into either one of the two pre-November quarters—May, June, and July or August, September, and October—or one of the two post-October quarters—November, December, and January or February, March, and April.[16] We also create variables that measure whether the contract (1) has a length of no more than two years; (2) is signed in an election year (congressional or presidential); and (3) is signed in a presidential election year.[17]

We employ these data to test three hypotheses about whether monetary policies anticipated from electoral outcomes are incorporated into economic choices:

1. Assuming monetary policy is mitigated by offsetting behavior, more contracts should be signed after October in election years than in nonelection years.
2. Because presidential elections are more important than congressional elections for macroeconomic changes, effects should be greatest in presidential election years.
3. If industries most vulnerable to macroeconomic changes sign shorter-term contracts, the dates at which short-term contracts are signed should be most sensitive to electoral outcomes.

The data in Table 1.2 indicate that monetary policy's effects are likely reduced, but not eliminated, by reactions to election outcomes.[18] Contracts in presidential election years are more often negotiated in the two quarters after October compared with the pattern in nonelection years. But even many of those firms most likely influenced by macroeconomic conditions ignore electoral impacts.[19]

In particular, the data on short-term contracts comparing the proportion of contracts signed in the six months before a presidential election to the proportion of contracts signed in the six months after an election demonstrate an anticipatory effect. One-half of all contracts are signed in the two post-October quarters when a president is elected, but only 39 percent are signed in these two quarters in other years; this correspondence is particularly strong in the immediate post-October quarter (26 compared to 18 percent). Nevertheless, even in presidential election years, roughly half of all agreements are signed before the election. Additionally, when both midterm and presidential elections are compared to years with no election, the difference between the proportion of contracts signed in the last two quarters is slight (43 to 41 percent).[20] Thus, our findings indicate that those industries most influenced by changes in demand induced by monetary policy will be more likely to enter into short-term contracts that can be settled when a presidential election outcome is known.

The results for longer-term contracts are consistent with the belief that changes in aggregate demand of the size produced by varying money sup-

Table 1.2 Wage contracts and national election timing, 1960–1992 (percentage of all contracts approved)

Contract duration	May–July	August–October	November–January	February–April
		Quarter		
All lengths				
All years (election and nonelection)	36	24	19	21
Two years or less				
No election	36	23	18	23
Election	37	20	23	20
No presidential election	38	23	18	21
Presidential election	32	19	26	24
More than two years				
No election	34	26	20	21
Election	37	25	18	20
No presidential election	35	26	19	20
Presidential election	36	24	19	21

Source: U.S. Department of Labor, *Current Wage Developments,* for years 1960–1993.
Number of cases = 6,105

ply are unimportant for the industries that sign long-term contracts. Regardless of how the information is examined—by election years, by presidential election years, by comparing the third quarter to all others, by comparing the last half of the year to the first half—no relationship emerges.[21]

Some further evidence that monetary policy can be effective given rational expectations, at least in influencing interest rates, is found by examining how the creation of the Federal Reserve Bank influenced financial behavior. In the years before its establishment in 1914 (specifically from 1890 to 1910), short-term interest rates were highly seasonal, with rate increases usually followed by declines to the average value. In contrast, in the years 1920–1933 short-term interest rates showed little seasonality, and the interest rate in any one period was likely to persist in the future (see Mankiw, Miron, and Weil, 1987). Not only did the pattern of short-term interest rates change, but the behavior of long-term rates came to track changes in short-term rates more closely, suggesting that investors in long-term assets changed their expectations of the behavior of the economy following the establishment of the Federal Reserve.

The performance of the economy can depend heavily on the reputation of the central bank. Suppose that the public expects the central bank to increase the money supply. Then in anticipation firms may increase wages and prices, thereby reducing demand for goods and for labor. The central bank would then want to stimulate the economy to avoid an incipient recession, and would therefore increase the money supply. The anticipated, and realized, increased money supply would then leave the economy with the same output and employment, but with higher prices. If, instead, firms and workers did not expect the central bank to increase the money supply, they would not increase prices and wages, and the economy would enjoy the same level of output with lower prices.

Central bankers agree that credibility is central to maintaining low inflation. A survey of eighty-four heads of central banks asking them to rank the importance of credibility on a five-point scale (with 4 meaning "quite important" and 5 "of the utmost importance") produced a mean response of 4.83, with no respondent choosing a number below 4. The need "to keep inflation low" was viewed as credibility's most important feature. Indeed, over 90 percent of respondents said that credibility and dedication to price stability were either "quite closely related" or "virtually the same" (Blinder 1999). Credibility may be established by binding the central bank in different ways (such as the imposition of constitutional constraints) and isolating the central bank from political pressures to inflate (indeed, some studies find that inflation is lower in countries with independent central banks)[22] or imposing penalties for failing to fight inflation (for example, New Zealand stipulated that the central bank governor can be removed if the 0–2 percent inflation target band is not met; see McCallum 1999). Central bankers themselves, however, find such means unimportant, claiming instead that credibility is established by establishing a record of low inflation (Blinder 1999). If so, then under some circumstances credibility increases when a person in authority—for example, a central bank head with a strong reputation for opposing inflation (Rogoff 1985)—has discretion.[23]

In summary, government can influence economic conditions in the short term through changing the money supply, although the long-term effect of such influences will be small. Rational expectations and adaptations by firms, workers, and consumers weaken, but do not eliminate, the stimulative effects of manipulating money supplies and interest rates. Monetary policy cannot assure *long-term* prosperity.

Fiscal Policy—Is It Just Crowding Out?

Another frequently voiced claim is that politicians can stimulate the economy by increasing government spending. Typically, it is suggested that incumbents can prime the economy in anticipation of an upcoming election with an appropriately timed infusion of spending.

Whether fiscal policy can, however, effectively stimulate the economy is questionable. Even if changes in spending affect the economy, fiscal policy is a crude tool for economic stimulation, both because the time when the desired stimulus is felt may be hard to control and because much cooperation and skill are needed from the politicians and the bureaucrats charged with formulating and implementing a stimulus package. The economic stimulus that election-minded politicians desire may come too early before an election to influence voting, or it may be realized only after the election is decided.

But even when such obstacles are nimbly overcome (as is consistent with our general analytic approach), the question remains: does government spending increase total spending or does it merely cause switches between different types of spending? The answer to this query appears to be that, without government tailoring spending in specific ways, little stimulus is felt as crowding out by rational economic agents mitigates the stimulus of fiscal programs. If government largely purchases goods desired by the citizenry or makes investments with immediate payoffs, public spending may merely supplant private spending. Given these restrictions created by crowding out, the aggregate effect of fiscal policy on the macroeconomy is modest.

To understand the source of such constraints, consider the typical characterization of aggregate demand as the sum of several spending choices:

Output = expenditures on consumption goods (domestic and imported)
+ Investment + Government purchases of goods and services
+ Exports − Imports.   (1.1)

When (1.1), which is often written as $Y = C + I + G + X − M$, is viewed as describing *desired expenditures* (rather than as an accounting convention), it helps explain how government spending can crowd out private spending. The sum $C + I + G + X - M$ summarizes what government, firms, consumers, and foreigners wish to buy.[24] The economy is in equilibrium when desired spending equals aggregate output. Neither excess supply nor excess demand for goods and services exists, and firms face no pressure to change their output levels.

This view generates an ironic implication, already mentioned, regarding which purchases will most stimulate the economy. As government spending on projects with large current benefits but small future rewards is likely to crowd out current consumer spending, stimulus is greatest when spending is on *worthless* goods or on investments with payoffs far in the future. Projects with immediate returns make consumers better off in the current period relative to future periods; consumers may offset their increased current consumption arising from stimulative expenditures by saving more.

In contrast, wasteful spending reduces the welfare of consumers in the current period, inducing these consumers / taxpayers to spend now rather than to save for a future when less waste is expected. The lower savings make crowding out small; the sum of consumption and government spending $(C + G)$ in the current period will increase.[25] Analogously, public spending on projects producing only future benefits (for example, investment in infrastructure or in pure research) impels consumers to substitute current spending for later spending, as consumers will enjoy the benefits of present government expenditures by getting more services in the future.

Furthermore, the crowding out of fiscal stimuli may be amplified in economies with much foreign trade, since increased domestic sales are offset by reduced exports.[26] For instance, heightened demand in the United States created by a stimulus raises interest rates, which induces portfolio managers searching for higher rates of return to shift their investments to America. Increased demand raises the dollar's value relative to other currencies, making imports cheaper and exports more expensive. Eventually, exports will decline and imports will rise until aggregate demand and interest rates return to their initial levels.

Thus, besides the sheer technical difficulty of proper timing, the effectiveness of fiscal policy is limited by crowding out and is distinguished by ironies. Fiscal stimuli will work best when spent on projects that give consumers small immediate returns or none whatsoever. In contrast to monetary policy, crowding out reduces the effectiveness of fiscal policy in an open economy.

Not surprisingly, fiscal stimulus packages that avoid crowding out are frequently derided as paying for pork barrel or wasteful goods. *Time* magazine dubbed the impasse that led to a successful filibuster of Bill Clinton's 1993 economic stimulus proposal as "porklock" (Duffy 1993); proposals to spend $2.5 billion on "ready-to-go" projects such as an "alpine slide" in Puerto Rico were widely derided, although our analysis suggests that such projects may be appropriate for a fiscal stimulus. Similarly, the $100 billion economic stimulus plan that Japanese Prime Minister Miyazawa outlined that same year, which included such luxurious infrastructure investments as $10 billion for electronics equipment ranging from supercomputers for universities and research institutes to desktop computers for high schools (Patton 1993), was stalled and eventually abandoned. In practice, justifying projects without immediate payoffs, particularly when speedy implementation is essential, limits the effectiveness of fiscal policy, even when the "right" projects are selected. Added to the problems posed by crowding out and the difficulty of getting the timing correct even for the most able economic planners (for example, Clinton's proposal was discredited by an embarrassing growth in employment), these obstacles limit the effectiveness of fiscal policy.[27]

Exhortation: Persuasion and the Art of Equilibrium Selection

We have so far focused on government's formal powers to issue or to spend money. Complementing such tools are informal instruments that government can use to improve economic performance—what we label exhortation. We view the effects of exhortation broadly, to encompass both unsubstantiated rhetoric ("cheap talk")[28] and persuasive efforts that depend on costly actions to be credible.[29] By our definition, exhortation is distinguished by making policy more effective than the policy's mere content would lead one to expect.

Obviously, exhortation is more nebulous and less concrete than monetary or fiscal instruments; it touches on the vicissitudes of politics rather than on the sterile world of the policy expert. Yet exhortation may affect what government can accomplish. Furthermore, the generic economic constraints discussed throughout our larger analysis are important for understanding the processes at work. Most notably, taking advantage of opportunities for establishing credibility, encouraging crowding in, and shaping expectations through exhortation may guide the selection of equilibria.

Although we do not want to exaggerate the importance of exhortation, it can improve the inflation / unemployment trade-off, lower interest rates, and induce investment.

Inflation and Growth

Politicians want low inflation and high growth, but there is a significant tension between the two. As the trade-off between inflation and economic growth (and, with growth, high employment) can vary with expectations, whether or not they are rational, exhortation may influence which inflation / growth equilibrium is attained.[30] Historically, the percentage of a year's gross national product (GNP) necessary to reduce inflation by one percentage point, the *sacrifice ratio,* has been roughly five to one (a one percent decline in inflation costs five percent of one year's GNP). But the sacrifice ratio can vary substantially. In the early 1980s the U.S. sacrifice ratio was about 2.4, as an inflation decline of 6.7 percent was associated with "only" a 16 percent drop in GNP over its trend value. As annual U.S. GNP was then about $6 trillion, this reduction in the sacrifice ratio resulted in a savings of roughly $1 trillion, or $4,000 per capita, relative to the historical ratio.

Why the sacrifice ratio varies is explicable at two levels. At a mechanical level, we can point to expectations about future inflation. Since, as already established, prices may be rigid in the short run, the sacrifice ratio will be especially low or high if firms (and consumers) generally underestimate or overestimate inflation.

The other level focuses on the underlying process generating the sacrifice ratio, suggesting that expectations can be self-fulfilling: different equilibria may be associated with different sacrifice ratios. Anticipation of high inflation may lead to large immediate price increases, whereas expectations of low inflation can produce small price increases.

It is the possibility that self-fulfilling beliefs lead to different equilibria that makes exhortation potentially important. Successful governmental leaders may convince businessmen that inflation will be low and thus induce firms to restrict price increases. Consequently, the relationship between inflation and employment can depend on politicians' (and the central bank's) abilities to guide which equilibrium out of the possible equilibria is realized.

Sometimes such actions will be blatant. One well-known and successful instance in the United States occurred in 1962 when the Kennedy administration demanded that steel producers rescind price increases and threatened to have the Justice Department sue for antitrust violations if they did not comply (Malabre 1994). Similarly, in the face of potential political repercussions, large oil companies such as Standard Oil in the 1920s (Olmstead and Rhode 1985) and Mobil and Exxon in the 1970s set their prices below what the market would have otherwise dictated (Erfle, Pound, and Kalt 1981, Erfle and McMillan 1990).

More frequently, exhortation is subtler. For example, the Reagan administration and FRB Chairman Paul Volcker were both committed to reducing high inflation rates in the 1980s. In thinking about how to reduce inflation with the least pain, David Stockman (future director of the Office of Management and Budget) and Jack Kemp (a leading Republican congressman) wrote a memo to President-elect Reagan in 1980 that emphasized the need to lower expectations by making "decisive, credible" cuts in outlays (quoted in White and Wildavsky 1989, p. 132). After leaving government, Stockman (1987) would recount:

> I had acquired some amateur's knowledge of rational expectations theory and the mechanics of financial markets. This permitted me to sidestep the precipice of recession with a *fiscal expectations* theory of rapid and dramatic financial market recuperation resulting from the new administration's policies. The markets would soon see that we were not fiscal con men or practitioners of "voodoo economics," waiting for economic magic to balance the budget, as the opposition had charged. The real Reagan supply-side program would embody a solid and sweeping anti-free lunch plan, based on unprecedented retrenchment of federal entitlement, subsidy, and cheap credit programs. (p. 78)

The Reagan administration, with Volcker's aid, convinced the public that it was serious about reducing inflation. The result was the deepest recession since the Great Depression, coupled with such a sharp fall of inflation that the sacrifice ratio was roughly half that historically observed. The administration may be credited with guiding which self-fulfilling equilibrium was selected.

Thus, although exhortation is difficult to quantify, it does appear to influence the inflation / unemployment trade-off. By guiding the process that determines the sacrifice ratio, exhortation can determine which equilibrium is established and the severity of the trade-off that is realized.

Jawboning Interest Rates

Similar exhortation, often called jawboning in this context, can affect interest rates. When threats are credible—for example when government's attention is firmly on interest rates—jawboning can reduce rates beyond the effects generated by monetary policy.

For instance, it appears that government may influence the prime interest rate that banks charge. Consider events in the second half of 1979 when the United States was first preoccupied with a deteriorating economy and then galvanized by a crisis in Iran marked by the taking of American prisoners (see Glazer and McMillan 1992). If exhortation is important and works when threats are credible, it should have been more effective before the international crisis, when attention was squarely on high interest rates generally and on the prime rate specifically, than during the crisis itself when bank behavior was little noticed.

The evidence supports this proposition. The outcry was great when interest rates rose sharply before the hostage seizure. Whereas the prime interest rate was stable at 11.5 percent in the first seven months of 1979, it increased to 13.2 percent by October 12; by October 29 Citibank, the largest New York City bank, had raised its prime rate to 15.25 percent. Although this increase was justified by corresponding rises in commercial interest rates (for example, the gap between Citibank's prime rate and commercial paper was only 1.15 percentage points), public officials were agitated. With the political eyes of the nation on the economy, FRB Chairman Volcker warned banks not to increase their rates and Congressman Henry Reuss, chairman of the House Banking Committee, sent a telegram to Citibank requesting a reduction in its prime rate. Although Reuss's specific request was not honored, only one bank, First National of Pennsylvania, followed Citibank to 15.25 percent in the face of this pressure.[31]

At this point, Iranians seized American hostages and political attention switched to foreign affairs. If exhortation is ineffective when little used or little noticed, the gap between prime rates and commercial rates should have widened once the president was trapped in the White House Rose Garden awaiting the hostages' release.

This expectation is borne out. Citibank raised its prime rate to 15.75 percent the week of the hostage seizure, readjusting its lending rate to the level called for by the formula that it normally used to adjust the prime in line with other market rates (its earlier 15.25 percent rate had fallen below that implied by this formula). Although Congressman Reuss complained about Citibank's action, nobody else in Congress appeared to notice, and the administration remained silent.

The absence of political response to bank actions became more dramatic as the crisis in Iran intensified. While interest rates on commercial paper declined, the prime rate was stable. When the gap between commercial paper and the prime increased to 2.25 points by mid-February, no one in Congress or in the administration complained. The finishing touch occurred in the weeks immediately after a failed attempt to rescue the hostages on April 25, 1980, raised a firestorm of controversy among the American public. In the aftermath of this disaster, banks raised the prime rate to levels that far exceeded other interest rates. The difference between the prime rate and the rate on commercial paper increased from 4.25 percentage points to 6 points in a week and to 7.5 points in two weeks. Only on May 23 did the White House publicly complain about the prime rate, provoking a fall in the prime interest rate and a decline in the prime / commercial gap to 4.2 points by the end of June.

Consequently, although its power is restricted, jawboning may lower interest rates. Furthermore, the effectiveness of jawboning is likely to be conditioned heavily by whether the potential sanctions faced by banks are viewed as credible.

Investment and Partisan Cycles

Related to our earlier discussion of exhortation and the selection of equilibria, a government may be associated with high-investment equilibria if firms expect higher investment by others under that government. Such expectations can create a partisan business cycle with different parties associated with different levels of economic activity.[32]

Specifically, even if all politicians favor high investment, exhortation may produce partisan cycles. Suppose, for instance, that the identity of current and future administrations are known with certitude, for example, that Democrats will govern in period one and that Republicans will succeed them in period two. Suppose, further, that one party's assurances about the profitability of investment are more believable than the other's, and that each party claims that it will promote investment (even by adopting the same policy). Nonetheless, each firm profits by shifting investments to the period when it expects the party associated with high investment to hold office. The belief that investment will be higher under one party is self-fulfilling, creating a partisan cycle and reinforcing the belief that the economy does better under one of the parties.[33] In short, the abilities of political parties to generate investment may vary systematically and may help explain why some have historically produced higher growth rates.

This is especially likely if strategic complementarities induce some firms to invest when others do. Consider two equilibria: an equilibrium (e_L) characterized by low investment, and an equilibrium (e_H) characterized by high investment, as shown in Figure 1.2. The horizontal axis shows the average investment (e) by firms in the economy, and the vertical axis shows one firm's desired investment (e_i). As shown by the curve in Figure 1.2, a firm may want to invest more when others firms also invest: if firm i can observe investment and finds that investing when others do is profitable, then e_i will increase with e. An equilibrium also requires that average investment equals each firm's investment, which is depicted by points along a line with a slope of 45 degrees. The equilibria are thus depicted by points

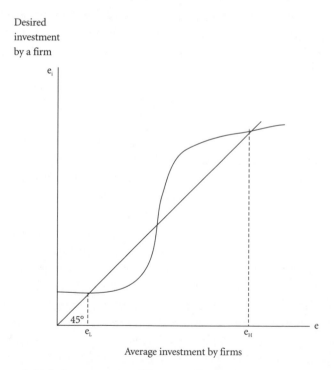

Figure 1.2 Multiple investment equilibria: an illustration.

where the straight line intersects the curve. Partisan business cycles may, therefore, appear when one party is associated with expectations of higher investment, leading still other firms to follow suit and a high investment equilibrium to be realized.

For an example of how complementary investments can arise, think of some firms making hard disk drives and of other firms producing personal computers (PCs). A manufacturer of hard drives may invest in producing them only if he expects PC manufacturers to buy hard disks. The more investment in factories the hard disk manufacturer sees by PC manufacturers, the more the hard disk manufacturer will invest in his own factory. On the other side, PC manufacturers will fear investing in more capacity if they anticipate shortages of hard disks. Thus, investment by PC firms will be higher when they anticipate high investment by hard disk manufacturers.[34]

The example we just gave arises when specialized inputs will be available only when demand is high. But other complementarities can also make the profits from investment increase with the amount invested by other firms (Hall 1991):

- *Business costs decline in places where, or during times when, sales are high.* For example, many retailers find selling cameras profitable in midtown Manhattan because the large clientele more than makes up for the sharp competition.
- *Divisions between periods of intense work and no work, rather than spreading work evenly, may be optimal if employees incur a fixed cost for each day or period they labor* (Rogerson 1988).
- *Incentives to work, and productivity, may increase if workers can more easily find satisfying jobs when employment is high.*[35]
- *Investment may rise if rational managers find it in their self-interest to mimic other managers* (Scharfstein and Stein 1990). If some managers invest more, others may follow suit, not necessarily because profits are higher, but because each manager will not fear to be the sole one who fails.

These features suggest that politicians may guide equilibrium selection by inducing investment from at least some to crowd in others. For instance, if government convinces citizens that prosperity is coming—for example, Matsusaka and Sbordone (1995) find that between 13 percent and 26 percent of the variation in GNP over time can be attributed to changes in consumer confidence—then some firms may be induced to invest, which encourages others to follow suit. Alternatively, government can appeal directly to potential investors and get some to invest in order to encourage others to invest. For example, in his discussion of "indicative" planning in Japan, Ito (1992) summarizes the potential impact of government efforts to stimulate investment:[36]

> Those who find indicative plans effective emphasize the importance of the government's signal and its commitment to growth. It is often the case that investment in structures and equipment in a particular industry will not take place unless sales projections are favorable. Uncertainty might make investors pessimistic and keep the economy in a low-demand equilibrium. If an announcement by the government provides credible information on output projections for various industries and government expenditures, it stimulates investment decisions in the private sector. When the private sector believes the plan and behaves accordingly, the plan becomes self-fulfilling. Indicative planning can select a particular equilibrium among many possible equilibria. (pp. 65, 67)

Seen through the lens of our analysis, appeals such as those reflected in indicative planning create a focal point for settling in an equilibrium with high output.

In short, given the importance of credibility, which politician is doing the exhorting to induce investment may determine exhortation's efficacy, generating partisan cycles. Such partisan cycles as a function of expectations and exhortation may be particularly likely if strategic complementarities make a firm's profits from investment increase when other firms invest. Since there is crowding, politicians need only induce investment by some actors to assure investment by others.

Spending, Taxes, and Expectations: Budget Deficits as Policy Instruments

> As a very important source of strength and security, cherish public credit . . . [avoid] the accumulation of debt, not only by shunning occasions of expense, but by vigorous exertions in time of peace to discharge the debts which unavoidable wars may have occasioned, not ungenerously throwing upon posterity the burden which we ourselves ought to bear. (George Washington, Farewell Address, 1797)

In the tradition of George Washington, it is frequently heard that politicians help or harm the economy by producing balanced or deficit-ridden budgets. Certainly, countries such as the United States have experienced large reversals in the balance between government revenues and expenditures. In the first sixty years of the Republic the federal government ran an annual surplus averaging 6 percent of expenditures, while 20 percent deficits were commonplace in the 1980s.

Can the government help or harm the economy by running balanced or unbalanced budgets?[37] At first glance, it is difficult to argue that deficits matter. For example, despite Japan's economic success in the first forty-five years after World War II, over that period the United States and Japan both ran deficits that averaged between 3 and 4 percent of GNP. For further detail, Figure 1.3 compares deficits and growth in the two countries. The

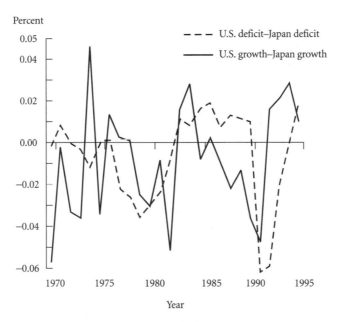

Figure 1.3 Comparison of deficits and growth in the United States and Japan (note: Deficits are measured as a percentage of GNP; growth is the annual percent increases in GNP. *Source:* Deficits 1970–1990, Ito (1992), tables 6–7; 1991–1996, *OECD Economic Outlook,* December 1997, Annex Table 30. Japan GDP calculated from *OECD National Accounts,* vol. 1: *Main Aggregates, 1960–1995,* Line 56. U.S. GDP calculated from *Survey of Current Business,* August 1997, Summary National Income and Product Series.

solid line shows annual economic growth in the United States minus annual economic growth in Japan. The dashed line shows the government deficit in the United States as a fraction of GDP, minus the corresponding value in Japan. A negative number means that the United States deficit was smaller. In some years, such as in most of the 1980s, the United States had lower growth and higher deficits. But in other years, such as in much of the 1970s, Japan enjoyed higher growth than the United States while incurring larger budget deficits. Although such data are only suggestive—for instance, Japan may have grown more without budget deficits—they indicate that deficits can be compatible with economic growth.

Nevertheless, four related troubles have been attributed to deficits: (1) inflating prices by increasing aggregate demand;[38] (2) reducing current saving and investment and therefore lowering economic growth; (3) increasing interest rates; and (4) burdening future generations who must repay the accumulated debt. Some argue (as the Clinton administration did in its early years) that reducing inflation and interest rates while increasing investment and savings is possible only if the deficit is cut.

Others disagree, maintaining that offsetting behavior mitigates or eliminates the perceived damages produced by a budget deficit. That was the view of Franklin Roosevelt (1941), the first American president to advocate deficit spending to jump start the economy, when he stated in a 1939 speech that "Our national debt after all is an internal debt owed not only by the Nation, but to the Nation. If our children have to pay interest on it they will pay that interest to themselves. A reasonable internal debt will not impoverish our children or put the nation into bankruptcy" (p. 351). Indeed, others maintain that Roosevelt's emphasis on internal debts misguided, as an external debt owed to foreigners need not reduce savings or hurt future generations. Thus, economists espousing the idea of *Ricardian equivalence* claim that rational expectations eliminate the presumed harmful effects of deficits.[39]

To illustrate the theoretical argument, consider the implications of financing a fixed expenditure level by borrowing instead of by taxing. Intuitively, budget deficits increase interest rates, reduce savings, and reduce investment. Such an inference, however, assumes that consumers are myopic. If they possess foresight and if government spends more than it raises in taxes, consumers may expect that future taxes will be increased. In anticipation of higher future taxes, consumers may save more now than they would have given a balanced budget.[40] Such sophisticated responses may undo the overheating of the economy, the reduction in savings, the heightened interest rates, and the burden on future generations that allegedly are produced by deficit financing. In support of this idea, we note that in the same month (September 1998) that President Clinton announced the first federal surplus (of about $70 billion) in twenty-nine years, personal savings in the United States declined from a positive $11 billion the month before, and from positive values in the preceding years, to a negative $12 billion.

But, not surprisingly, the assumption that consumers are farsighted makes the theory of Ricardian equivalence controversial.[41] Specifically, this assumption contradicts much evidence suggesting some consumer myopia.[42] For example, consumers' implicit discount rates are high and variable, indicating myopic rather than farsighted decisionmaking.[43]

Indeed, data indicate that the bad effects of deficits are tempered, but not nullified, by the anticipatory behavior of consumers. Increased deficits do not consistently induce greater personal savings: in the late 1950s and in the mid-1960s national savings were high and deficits rose moderately, while large deficits coexisted with low national savings in the 1980s.

Similarly, behavior associated with the large trade deficits that appeared during the Reagan administration cast doubt on Ricardian equivalence. The logic of Ricardian equivalence dictates that government deficits should cause consumers to increase savings by the amount that their taxes are reduced, resulting in unchanged consumption and an unchanged trade balance (which follows from the definition of the trade balance as Exports − Imports = Y − C − I − G). If, instead, consumers react by saving little more, as they did during the Reagan years (indeed, savings fell), then spending will exceed the domestic production of goods, necessarily increasing imports, and Ricardian equivalence will not be supported (Feldstein 1994).

Analysis of other choices that are comparable to those underlying Ricardian equivalence yield similar results. One test of rational expectations is to compare peoples' forecasts of inflation, as elicited by surveys, with realized inflation. Rational expectations would assume that these forecasts, though possibly imperfect, do not consistently overestimate or underestimate inflation. Yet an analysis of the responses of persons surveyed between 1978 and 1993 shows that only those with at least a college education exhibit rational expectations (Krause and Granato 1998).[44]

Another test is to consider the anticipatory behavior of taxpayers. Although findings vary, they can be reasonably summarized as showing that, consistent with the aggregate data on savings and deficits, citizen adaptation matters but it is imperfect. One could characterize consumers / taxpayers as "semirational." Consider one nice test by Shapiro and Slemrod (1995) of the underlying rational expectations hypothesis. These authors examine how citizens adjusted their behavior when President Bush manipulated withholding rates in 1992 so that individuals could pay more of their taxes when their returns were due on April 15 of the next year rather than during the previous year, allowing them to earn interest on money held for a longer time. The survey data show that only one-third of taxpayers correctly noted the change in withholding rates a month after its occurrence. Furthermore, many filers seemed to overestimate the extent of this change, underwithheld taxes, and were faced with penalties for late payment (Schmedel 1993).

Consumers appear even less farsighted when comparable behavior over longer time periods is considered. For example, increases of 50 percent in real gasoline prices in the eight years after the 1973 oil embargo did not correspondingly increase the prices of fuel-efficient cars. Even when the first-year benefit alone of purchasing such a car was $1,000, the short-term orientation of auto buyers limited to $500 their willingness to pay a higher up-front price (Kahn 1986).

Thus, because many consumers show less foresight than required for Ricardian equivalence to hold, government can lower interest rates and encourage investment by raising taxes and cutting deficits. One estimate indicates that if the U.S. government had avoided a $3 trillion deficit from fiscal 1982 to 1992 (about one-half a year's output), interest rates would have been lower, investment would have been higher, and, consequently, annual GNP would have been about 3 percent higher (Krugman 1994). Elmendorf and Mankiw (1998) estimate that if the United States had no debt at all, or equivalently if cumulative deficits were zero, output would have been about 3.5 percent higher, that is, about the equivalent of three to four years of productivity growth. Such results imply that the nation's standard of living would have increased nontrivially, but not massively, over the long haul with deficit reduction.

In summary, the bad effects of budget deficits are partially checked by rational expectations. However, because consumers rather than only farsighted economic agents among firms, large investors, or unions determine savings, offsetting behavior is smaller than implied by Ricardian equivalence, and governments that run budget deficits may harm the economy.

Can Government Control the Economy?

When viewed in its totality, our findings suggest that government can partially manage the macroeconomy. This ability, however, to guide economic outcomes—which, it should be highlighted, is modest but consequential—and the specific manner in which government can shape economic forces are influenced by the economic constraints highlighted throughout our analysis.

Thus, although monetary policy can stimulate the economy over the short run, rational expectations limit its long-term efficacy. The popular attention given to decisions by central banks, such as to the Federal Reserve Board in the United States, seems out of proportion to their ability to manipulate economic activity.

Fiscal policy may increase growth or reduce unemployment, but its stimulative effects are greater when increased government spending does not immediately reduce private spending via crowding. In practice, fiscal stimulus packages appear roughly consistent with what theory suggests they should look like, although timing such stimuli properly, not to mention justifying such spending politically, is problematic.

Exhortation may be important when several patterns of behavior would result in equilibria. Though quantifying the aggregate effects of such exhortation on the economy is difficult, the effects at times appear large.

Lastly, the incompleteness of offsetting behavior allows government to stimulate long-run economic growth by running balanced budgets. Since some consumers are myopic, the government can significantly, but not dramatically, increase growth by eliminating deficits. Conversely, though not ruinous, budget deficits do lower economic growth over the long run.

For a concluding note, we emphasize that most of these inferences derive from our conceptual apparatus linking economic constraints with politics. Sometimes such features suggest that small government actions can have large effects (for example, with exhortation), sometimes they imply that government behavior that intuitively appears significant is not (for example, fiscal policy in many instances). But, almost always, these constraints are important.

2

Redistribution: A Success Story?

Concerns about the government's ability to manage the macroeconomy are common. But the question "Can government redistribute wealth?" may at first appear trivial. Is not the answer obviously "Yes"? All that government need do is tax some persons or firms and transfer the money to recipients. From this perspective government functions as little more than a broker.[1]

Cursory examination of the evidence indicates that redistributive programs are successful in just this sense. Consider Table 2.1, which displays the poverty rates (defined as the proportion of the population with an income less than 40 percent of the national median), incorporating taxes and cash transfers, in selected countries. A straightforward, albeit naive, interpretation of these data is that government programs reduce poverty, on average, by nearly ten percentage points.[2]

Table 2.1, however, is little more than an accounting sheet that details outcomes in a world with tax and transfer programs. Proper interpretation of these data requires a behavioral underpinning examining how people respond to programs and policies that are nominally redistributive; the world is likely to be more complex and subtle than a static accounting perspective depicts. Most important, crowding out can occur if people with rational expectations adjust their behavior in reaction to public policies: consideration of crowding out is necessary for correctly assessing possibilities for redistribution.

Indeed, although the terminology may vary, conservative critics of the welfare system emphasize the importance of crowding out, pointing out that rational responses to redistributive policies may undercut the intended effects of such efforts (e.g., Murray 1984, Herrnstein and Murray

Table 2.1 Effect of tax and transfer programs on poverty in selected countries
(percentage of population with incomes less than 40 percent of the national income)

Country	Year	Poverty rates (percentage)		Difference
		Pre–tax and transfer	Post–tax and transfer	
United Kingdom	1986	27.9	7.4	−20.5
France	1984	21.1	4.6	−16.5
Netherlands	1987	14.1	3.8	−10.3
Australia	1985	16.4	9.0	−7.4
Canada	1987	15.7	9.3	−6.4
Sweden	1987	7.9	1.6	−6.3
West Germany	1984	8.4	2.8	−5.6
United States	1986	22.3	20.4	−1.9
Average		16.7	7.4	−9.3

Source: U.S. Congress, House Committee on Ways and Means (1992 Green Book). U.S.
Government Printing Office.

1994). For instance, they maintain that persons who are certain that government will aid them will choose to work less.

Such critiques generally assume, however, at least implicitly, that government is committed to continued redistribution. Alternatively, crowding-out behavior by recipients can be small if they fear that future governments will reduce welfare benefits. Similar to the role that surprise plays in
macroeconomics, imperfect commitment to redistribution would make
policy more effective. The behavior limiting redistributive efforts that program critics focus on would then be overstated.

Thus, were there no current or prospective redistributive programs, the
fraction of persons who would be poor in those countries included in
Table 2.1 could have been less than the average of 16.7 percent reported.
Persons who realized that they must fend for themselves could have invested more in their education or have worked additional hours or engaged in other activities to raise their incomes. The inference that transfer
and tax policies reduce poverty rates by almost 10 percent would then
be wrong. If, instead, recipients would have earned no more in a world
without redistribution, the redistributive effects of governmental policies

would have been at least as much as the accounting viewpoint implies and, if high tax rates induce the rich to earn less, could have been greater.

Put another way, proper interpretation of the data in Table 2.1 requires a model of individual behavior. At most, differences between pre-transfer and post-transfer poverty rates give empirical bounds for evaluating the effects of the redistributive policies in question.

Economic Constraints and Redistribution

The previous discussion suggests that economic constraints are important in considering whether government can redistribute. In particular, three related issues are fundamental for determining how much redistribution is possible:[3]

1. Whether government is viewed as committed to redistribution.
2. Whether redistribution crowds out other sources of income among its beneficiaries.
3. Whether people are myopic or are guided by rational expectations.

As implied above, crucial to government's success in redistribution is the credibility of its policy. Understanding the full implications of credibility, however, requires highlighting a potential irony already mentioned: public policies that are the *least* credible may, under specific circumstances, be the *most* effective. When future income is thought to be guaranteed, re-distribution may be undermined by the reactions of the beneficiaries. Redistributive policy may therefore be more effective if its continuance is doubted.

The extent of crowding out—by how much people substitute govern-ment transfers for other potential income sources—also looms large for redistribution. If transfer programs induce recipients to work less or to train less, then the income of recipients may increase little. As will be dis-cussed in more detail, crowding out may take diverse forms, including fewer hours of work, less investment in education, and bigger bequests to children. Finally, whether people behave myopically or have rational ex-pectations is an important consideration for redistribution. But in contrast to macroeconomic policy, where persons with the greatest foresight will have the most influence on the economy, persons who fail to plan ahead may be disproportionately recipients of transfers, as they may be the ones most needing redistributive assistance. As remarked earlier, depending on how it affects credibility and crowding out, the existence of rational expectations or of myopia may either impede or assist redistributive efforts.

Though we lack a direct measure of the relation between the credibility of redistributive policy, the crowding out of transfers, and recipient myopia, we do have evidence–and corroborating economic theory–that crowding out is limited, that government is often viewed as uncommitted to redistribution, and that many people are myopic. The rest of this chapter examines government redistribution with these considerations in mind. We conclude that, despite obstacles, government can redistribute. Redistributive effects, however, cannot be revealed by mere accounting exercises. Rather, a behavioral view, structured by the previously enumerated economic constraints, is necessary to understand policy effectiveness.

Before proceeding, we must clarify the scope of our analysis. Redistribution can take many forms, including progressive income taxes, welfare programs, and retirement programs. Many other policies may also affect the incomes of different groups. For example, policies designed to stimulate or to dampen production, such as agricultural subsidies or oil depletion allowances, may distribute wealth. So can governmental efforts to strengthen or to weaken unions, such as Ronald Reagan's defeat of the air traffic controllers' union, PATCO, in the early 1980s.[4] Also, broad macroeconomic policy may affect income inequality (see, e.g., Hibbs and Dennis 1988). For instance, policies lowering unemployment reduce poverty, and deflationary policies favor creditors over debtors (Blank and Blinder 1986);[5] similarly, a restrictive monetary policy, which increases the trade deficit in durable goods, may redistribute by reducing the number of low-skilled, high-paying jobs (Borjas and Ramey 1994).

Nevertheless, we focus our discussion by considering programs that are more directly redistributive, that is, where the government raises money from some people and gives it more or less directly to others. This limits our discussion principally to three types of policies: (1) social welfare; (2) retirement benefits; and (3) taxation.

Additionally, and in contrast to our discussion of macroeconomics, we pay little attention to partisan effects on redistribution.[6] We disregard partisanship because the evidence uncovering partisan effects is slim. For example, the president's party in the United States explains neither the ratio of white to African-American income nor the share of income earned by the poorest 20 percent of the population.[7]

Similarly, the main United States welfare program until 1996, Aid to Families with Dependent Children (AFDC), appeared unaffected by partisan forces.[8] Federal spending on social programs such as AFDC was similar under different parties and, if anything, the data contradict standard beliefs about partisanship. For example, AFDC grew at an average real annual rate of 7.9 percent during the Democratic Kennedy-Johnson years and at a 9.7 percent rate during the Republican Nixon-Ford years (Danziger, Haveman, and Plotnick 1986). The program's largest growth in beneficiaries occurred over the decade 1965–1975, a period where the Republicans controlled the presidency for six of the ten years. The partisan exception occurs during the Reagan presidency: excluding spending on health, federal spending for social welfare programs declined by about 3 percent between fiscal years 1981 and 1985 (Danziger and Gottschalk 1995). Neither did AFDC benefits display a partisan pattern. Adjusted for inflation, benefits rose gradually over the 1950s, accelerated slightly in the early 1960s, peaked around 1967, and declined thereafter.[9] Welfare reform in the 1990s was itself overtly bipartisan, enacted by a Republican Congress but signed and supported by a Democratic president.

Although the Reagan administration (1981–1989) might seem to offer one exception to the claim that party is irrelevant (the income distribution both before and after taxes and transfers showed higher inequality than in previous years),[10] such an inference would be wrong. Rather, the sharp increase in earnings inequality, particularly among men, began in 1979, two years before Reagan entered office (Levy and Murnane 1992).[11] Despite their obvious incentive to blame the Republicans, even the Democratic staff of the House Ways and Means Committee, writing in their *Green Book* (1992), concur: "The earnings trends appear to have little to do with demographic or cyclical economic factors. Nor can they be attributed, for better or for worse, to policies enacted during the Reagan presidency, since they began several years before Reagan's election and similar changes have taken place in Canada and Europe" (pp. 1465–1466).

Does the absence of partisan effects reflect political preferences or the inherent difficulty of redistribution? In other words, is redistribution possible, even if its pattern is not structured by partisan forces, or is it infeasible? For answers we turn to examining how economic constraints influence social welfare programs, Social Security, and taxation.

Uncertainty and Redistribution: Data

Although we concentrate on what government can accomplish rather than on evaluating existing programs, examining additional descriptive data provides insight into the possibilities for redistribution by providing information about uncertainty and, hence, credibility. We discuss the United States, although most results should apply generally. We will see that the two groups that have been principally targeted as recipients, the poor and the elderly, differ in their behavior and in the government's commitment to aid them. Government commitment to assisting the elderly through programs such as Social Security (if not to the maintenance of specific benefit levels) is stronger than its commitment to a variety of welfare policies—where the elimination of some or all from government rolls is a real, if sporadic, possibility. In both instances, however, government's ability and resolve to continue its redistributive programs are uncertain.

Assorted data highlight this point. Consider Figure 2.1, which shows the percentage of Americans officially defined to be poor from 1965 to 1983 with and without transfer payments taken into account.[12] Transfer pay-

Figure 2.1 U.S. poverty rates (with and without transfer payments). *Source:* Danziger, Haveman, and Plotnick (1986).

ments and their impacts clearly vary over time. In some years, they reduce the post-transfer poverty rate by almost half, while in other years the reduction in poverty is less than one-quarter. Similarly, in absolute terms, poverty reduction from transfer programs ranges from 4 percent to almost 10 percent of the population.

These data seem to support the widespread belief that neither the extent nor the existence of the social safety net is agreed upon. Fiscal constraints, disagreements about the efficacy of transfer programs, ideological schisms, and the vagaries of democratic policymaking have combined to make predictions about government's resolve to aid the poor uncertain.

Other data underscore the point that transfer spending for the poor is erratic. For example, from 1968 to 1973 means-tested spending increased at an average rate of 12.9 percent per year, whereas growth in such spending was less than 1 percent a year from 1978 to 1983. Even with the increased needs in a recession, in 1981–1982 such spending declined by 3.1 percent (Marmor, Mashaw, and Harvey 1990).

Similarly, welfare policy has varied over time in ways that change its value to recipients. For example, the implicit tax rate on income from work, in the form of reduced welfare benefits, dropped from 100 percent in 1967 to 67 percent in 1981, and increased to 100 percent afterwards. Even more dramatically, the 1996 welfare reform contains two provisions that reduce the commitment to welfare payments. First, the federal government no longer defines welfare as an entitlement—states are largely free to set their own eligibility criteria. Second, able-bodied welfare recipients are required to find work within two years after their state program takes effect or face a loss of their benefits, and may not obtain benefits for more than five years over their lifetimes.

Data on intergenerational redistribution lead to comparable inferences about uncertainty concerning the extent and existence of government's commitment. As it is by far the most important governmental transfer to the elderly in the United States, we will focus on Social Security. The uncertainty about future benefits that is part of much public discussion is reinforced by the variance in past government performance. Table 2.2 compares changes in Social Security benefits to changes in wage rates over a thirty-two-year period, 1965 to 1997. Clearly, the differential between the two has varied substantially. Though in some years Social Security benefits rose twice as much as wages (1970), in other years they rose less than half as much (1997).

Table 2.2 Social Security benefit increases

Year	Wage increase (percentage)	Benefit increase (percentage)	Difference
1965	1.8	7.0	5.2
1966	6.0	0.0	−6.0
1967	5.6	0.0	−5.6
1968	6.9	13.0	6.1
1969	5.8	0.0	−5.8
1970	5.0	15.0	10.0
1971	5.0	10.0	5.0
1972	9.8	20.0	10.2
1973	6.3	0.0	−6.3
1974	5.9	11.0	5.1
1975	7.5	8.0	0.5
1976	6.9	6.4	−0.5
1977	6.0	5.9	−0.1
1978	7.9	6.5	−1.4
1979	8.7	9.9	1.2
1980	9.0	14.3	5.3
1981	10.1	11.2	1.1
1982	5.5	7.4	1.9
1983	4.9	3.5	−1.4
1984	5.9	3.5	−2.4
1985	4.3	3.1	−1.2
1986	3.0	1.3	−1.7
1987	6.4	4.2	−2.2
1988	4.9	4.0	−0.9
1989	4.0	4.7	0.7
1990	4.6	5.4	0.8
1991	4.4	3.7	−0.7
1992	5.2	3.0	−2.2
1993	0.9	2.6	1.7
1994	2.7	2.8	−0.1
1995	4.0	2.6	−1.4
1996	4.9	2.9	−2.0
1997	5.8	2.1	3.7

Source: 1965–1991: U.S. Congress, House Committee on Ways and Means (1992 *Green Book*), U.S. Government Printing Office. 1992–1997: Social Security Administration; for benefit increases, http://www.ssa.gov/OACT/COLA/COLA.misc.html#TimeSeries, and for wage increases, http://www.ssa.gov/OACT/COLA/AWIdevelop.html

Furthermore, recent government actions, many of which have yet to affect current Social Security recipients, have likely heightened uncertainty about the program. Indeed, despite repeated pledges that benefit cuts are "off limits" and that the program has been made fiscally responsible, policy changes during the past two decades should give citizens reason to worry about their future benefits. After a large rise in payments in 1972 (as reported in Table 2.2), Congress reduced the growth in initial benefits in 1977 by basing them only on changes in the average wage rather than on changes in prices. Six years later, Congress increased the retirement age from 65 to 67 by the year 2027, lowered the proportion of benefits paid to persons retiring at age 62 in 2009 from 80 percent to 75 percent, delayed cost of living adjustments by six months (effectively reducing long-run benefits by roughly 2 percent), and taxed some Social Security benefits for the first time—at a fixed income level unadjusted for inflation, promising to bring increasing numbers under the taxation umbrella over time (Bernstein and Brodshaug 1988). In 1993 the tax on the highest-earning Social Security recipients was increased further, from 50 to 85 percent of the standard tax rates.

Not only does experience suggest that citizens should be unsure about future Social Security benefits, regardless of government's pledges, but the current political environment reinforces this fear. Cries to cut entitlement and deficit spending and to cut taxes, and statements that Social Security is actuarially unsound, routinely contrast with pronouncements that the program is sacrosanct. As one popular account (Kramer 1996) puts it: "The gene that causes otherwise normal people to seek elective office is encoded with a warning: Don't mess with Social Security. Now, suddenly, the opposite is becoming true. So many average citizens are aware that the system could be bankrupt within 25 years that politicians who deny the problem could risk losing their credibility" (p. 38).

Doubts about the future of Social Security appear in survey data indicating that Americans are divided or pessimistic about whether they will receive benefits. For example, 28 percent of persons questioned in 1985 who were not retired believed that the program would not benefit them when they became eligible; 35 percent of persons aged 25–34 had this opinion (Marmor, Mashaw, and Harvey 1990). More recent data suggest that people have become increasingly skeptical. For instance, a 1994 national poll found that more Americans aged 18–34 believe in UFOs than in the likelihood that Social Security will support their retirement (Wallace 1994).[13]

Government Commitment to Future Redistribution

The data presented above refer to the credibility of observed government policy. They speak only indirectly to whether government could find ways of making strong commitments.

Close examination suggests that government may be unable to make a long-run commitment to redistribution. Though the ability to generate endogenous political support to assure policy longevity exists, it is incomplete. Not only does the essence of democracy preclude such strong commitments for extended periods,[14] but redistributive policies, by their very nature, create animosities over the long haul, making such programs especially susceptible to cuts. It is not surprising that governments adopt methods such as indexing to buffer redistributive programs, shielding such political hot potatoes from continued public scrutiny (see Weaver 1988). Although mechanisms of this sort may furnish wary politicians with cover, credibility will remain problematic.

Nevertheless, different redistributive policies are associated with varying levels of credibility. Some of these discrepancies may arise from differences in public opinion that are fairly consistent in democracies. For example, attitudes toward the elderly are routinely more favorable than attitudes toward the poor.[15] Conversely, the homogeneity of preferences among citizens may vary from country to country. Some nations may have strong, durable agreements among their citizenry on the desirability of redistribution; in other countries, redistributive policies may be more vulnerable as the population is split and the voters are easily swayed.

Some arrangements may build political coalitions that insulate programs from shifting political tides. Redistributive programs that are comparatively inclusive, that benefit persons most likely to mobilize politically, and that foster a sense of entitlement among recipients can have greater credibility. Since government can manipulate these features, at least for some redistributive programs, it can make some efforts to redistribute more credible than others.

The contrast between welfare policy and programs designed to aid the elderly such as Social Security illustrates this distinction. Welfare aids a limited group of persons who are difficult to mobilize and who are not viewed as having paid for the program that supports them. By comparison, Social Security was designed to benefit a far wider group of recipients who are politically powerful, and who, having contributed to the program, are likely to view benefits as an entitlement. Such factors should give Social Security greater permanence (although even social security programs in Australia and Sweden have been substantially reformed in recent years).[16]

Lastly, credibility may also be affected by political institutions. For instance, redistributive policies may be more likely to change in countries with parliamentary systems, where policy can be quickly changed by a simple majority, than in countries like the United States, where power is separated.[17]

In short, a democratic government often has trouble making credible promises for long-term redistribution. Assuring durability is likely to be problematic. Although several factors, mechanisms, and institutions may increase credibility, it seems unreasonable for potential recipients to rely on continuation of current redistributive programs. Such political commitments are hard for democracies to make.

Implications for Redistribution

So far we have established that governments have difficulty committing to long-term redistributive policies. But we have yet to examine whether redistributive programs increase the incomes of recipients or, instead, whether such income transfers merely crowd out income that would otherwise be earned.

In earlier chapters we argued that the effectiveness of some policies increases when people believe government is committed to them. Here we will explain how the opposite can happen for redistribution.

If individuals have foresight, redistributive policies expected to be continued for many years will discourage investments and actions that will reduce future reliance on transfer payments. Potential recipients may leave school earlier than they would otherwise or reject an unpleasant job that provides valuable experience, which they would accept in different circumstances. Rather than investing in the future, these persons can always count on the government assuring them a basic standard of living. Similarly, confident that retirement benefits will be available, they may save less. Alternatively, if redistribution is (appropriately) viewed as not credible, the disincentives to invest are mitigated. A young adult may, for example, enter the labor force because he anticipates cuts in welfare payments. Analogously, a middle-aged worker may save more if he fears that promised Social Security payments will be cut.[18]

To reiterate, the irony of this conclusion is that the more likely a government is to pursue redistribution (for example, because of its political institutions or because its population strongly supports redistribution), the less effective redistributive policy may be. On average, the crowding-out effect witnessed per dollar spent on redistribution will be greater.

Of course, individuals, especially many who may be eligible for redistribution, might be more myopic than this picture suggests. Individuals with imperfect foresight may still respond to noncredible redistributive efforts by increasing reliance on public transfers. For instance, myopic welfare recipients might behave as if their income from government assistance is assured for perpetuity.[19]

To investigate our propositions further, we return in the next section to actual attempts at redistribution. We caution, however, that the inferences that we can draw are inherently asymmetric. Although we may find no redistribution even when government can effect such a policy, finding that redistribution occurs proves that the polity can transfer wealth despite the obvious obstacles.

Effectiveness of Redistributive Policy

As mentioned, we principally consider programs that directly redistribute income across class or generational lines. In other words, we evaluate policies that raise money from some people and try to give it more or less immediately to others. Specifically, we concentrate our attention on the effects of the two major redistributive programs in the United States, welfare and Social Security.

Welfare Programs

Perhaps no issue in American politics is more sensitive than welfare policy. Many object that the welfare system has done little more than create a culture of dependency, encouraging people to rely on government support from the cradle to the grave. Murray (1984; see also Herrnstein and Murray 1994) contends that social welfare programs are bound to fail because transfers conditioned on some particular behavior of the recipient reinforce such negative behavior.[20] Forty-four percent of respondents in the 1984 General Social Survey agreed that social welfare benefits such as disability, unemployment compensation, and early retirement pensions make people not want to work anymore.[21] Others maintain that welfare provides a safety net for well-meaning people who suffer unusual need or misfortune. Rephrased without much of the broader sociological nuance, some claim that government assistance crowds out work effort while others disagree.

As discussed earlier, the evidence might be interpreted as proving that transfers redistribute income. Indeed, the President's Council of Economic Advisors estimates that the officially reported poverty rate of 13.8 percent in 1995 would have been 21.9 percent if cash transfers were not included in income (see the *Economic Report of the President* 1997).[22] Moreover, with a comprehensive measure of income, including all taxes, the earned income tax credit, and the valuation of in-kind transfers, the poverty rate is only 10.3 percent. Thus, transfer programs appear to have reduced the poverty rate by about half. But, we reiterate, this interpretation is an accounting exercise. The argument voiced by critics that these programs discourage desirable behavior must be considered.

Consistent, however, with the hypothesis that many, if not all, persons fear cuts in welfare benefits, analysis of the data suggests that crowding out is far from complete. Crowding increases the cost of redistribution but still allows it to be effective.

Given that welfare programs have been subject to the most scrutiny, their effects on work effort or on labor supply provide the strongest support for this claim. Overall, studies find that adjusting the implicit tax on recipients in the form of the benefit reduction rate (the extent to which benefits are reduced as earnings increase) causes little change in the number of hours worked. Instead, varying this rate has two opposing effects. Allowing welfare recipients to keep more of their earned income simultaneously increases work effort by persons already on welfare and induces others in the labor force to work less by joining welfare programs. Empirically, these two effects roughly cancel each other out, meaning that raising welfare benefits in this way has no net effect on aggregate labor supply (Moffitt 1992). Danziger et al. (1981), in a well-cited study that considered the overall effect of the welfare program, estimated that the reduction in work effort was in the range of 10 to 50 percent of what labor supply would have been in the absence of welfare payments.

Table 2.3 provides another perspective on work effort reduction by summarizing the effect on labor supply for the entire U.S. population (rather than only for welfare recipients) of the most important social insurance and public assistance programs. Although the total effect is nontrivial, the

Table 2.3 Labor supply reduction from social insurance and public assistance (percentage reduction in total labor supply by program)

Type of program	Percentage reduction
Social insurance programs	
Old age and survivors insurance	1.20
Disability insurance	1.20
Unemployment insurance	0.30
Workers' compensation and black lung	0.70
Railroad retirement	Under 0.05
Veterans' disability compensation	0.40
Medicare	Under 0.05
Public assistance programs	
AFDC	0.60
Supplemental security income and veterans' pensions	0.10
Food stamps and housing assistance	0.30
Medicaid	Under 0.05
Total (all programs)	4.80

Source: Danziger, Haveman, and Plotnick (1981).

joint effect of these social insurance and public assistance programs remains below 5 percent.

For another measure that leads to inferences that are roughly comparable, consider the "leaky bucket" approach—when money is poured into the buckets of the poor, how much is captured and how much leaks out (Okun 1975)? The bucket appears to be cracked but serviceable. If welfare programs reduce work effort of recipients by about 30 percent (the midpoint of the 10 to 50 percent estimated above), then for every dollar transferred to an AFDC family about 37 percent leaks out in the form of reduced earnings. Put differently, roughly $1.60 must be spent for a $1.00 increase in recipients' incomes (Moffitt 1992). Not cheap, but also not outrageous.

Estimates of how welfare affects work are also found by comparing behavior in states with different welfare benefits. For instance, higher-range estimates suggest that women will work two hours less per month for every $100 increase in monthly benefits. Thus, the $200 per month difference in AFDC benefit levels between Indiana and Mississippi led AFDC recipients in Indiana to work about forty-eight hours less on average over the year, which is about 5 percent of hours on a half-time job (Blank 1997a).

Although results are preliminary, experience following the Welfare Reform Act of 1996 is broadly consistent with incomplete crowding and effective redistribution. Persons who left welfare in the wake of reform report employment rates of over 50 percent, which are higher than the 28 percent employment rate for persons who continued to receive welfare benefits. But former welfare recipients are not out of poverty. For example, one analysis of former Wisconsin recipients calculated that less than half of them earned enough to put them above the poverty level (Brauner and Loprest 1999). This indicates that the lure of AFDC and other related benefits had pulled few persons with the capacity to earn a substantial living out of the labor force; instead, it was mostly people with only marginal earning potential who were on the welfare rolls.

International comparisons find even less displacement of work by assistance. Consider single-mother families on welfare in Canada and in the United States. Calculating poverty rates in Canada using the U.S. definition of poverty shows poverty in Canada to be about one-third lower than in the United States. This difference is entirely attributable to public assistance: in the mid-1980s, a low-income Canadian single mother received about twice as much in cash transfers as in the United States.[23] Despite these larger benefits, work behavior among poor single-mother families in the two countries is highly similar. The earnings among this group (adjusted for differences in the value of the dollar between the two countries) are also similar (Blank 1997a, p. 142).

Therefore, although crowding out is not trivial when it comes to welfare, redistribution is possible.[24] The evidence shows that at least some welfare recipients anticipate government cuts in welfare, making employment and investment a wise choice. In determining whether it is possible to redistribute to the poor, our response is "Yes, even if it is not cheap."[25]

Social Security and Transfers to the Elderly

Social Security is the largest redistributive program in the United States. In 1995 spending on Social Security was 3.6 percent of GDP and 22 percent of the federal budget, compared with less than 1 percent of GDP spent on AFDC and food stamps combined; those elderly living alone received 48 percent of their income from Social Security and had a median Social

Security income more than double their median income from all other sources (House Committee on Ways and Means 1998).

Befitting Social Security's classification as a redistributive program, the elderly receive more in benefits than they paid in Social Security taxes. Table 2.4, which summarizes estimates by Boskin and Shoven (1988) of the net effects of Social Security for persons of different ages and incomes, provides evidence to this effect. These data indicate that, although they paid Social Security taxes when they worked, the benefits older recipients receive will far exceed the present value of the taxes they paid.[26] Also, given that benefits vary little with contributions, the working poor gain relatively more from Social Security. Regardless of birth year, a person who earned $10,000 in 1985 would get more in Social Security benefits than he paid in Social Security taxes. By contrast, a person who earned $30,000 in 1985 would benefit from the Social Security system only if he were more than forty years old in 1985.

For more detail on transfers by age, consider Table 2.5, which offers a generational accounting perspective.[27] The first column in the table lists the present values of taxes (in thousands of dollars) that the average male of the age in question will pay for the rest of his expected life; the next column shows comparable data for transfers (disability, health, welfare, and Social Security). When this information is used to calculate net payments

Table 2.4 Estimated benefits and costs of Social Security by age and earnings, 1985 (single-earner couples)

Birth year	Transfers received, taxes paid, and net effects	1985 Income		
		$10,000	$20,000	$30,000
1915	Social Security wealth	92,277	144,845	133,969
	Lifetime payroll taxes	36,280	68,340	72,205
	Net gain	55,997	76,505	61,764
1945	Social Security wealth	62,679	109,128	100,503
	Lifetime payroll taxes	48,951	136,498	140,253
	Net gain	13,727	−27,370	−39,750
1975	Social Security wealth	37,774	67,464	63,051
	Lifetime payroll taxes	33,273	99,819	112,081
	Net gain	4,501	−32,355	−49,030

Source: Boskin and Shoven (1988).

Table 2.5 Male generational accounts by age, 1991 (thousands of dollars)

Age in 1991	Tax payments	Transfer receipts	Net payments
0	99.3	20.4	78.9
10	155.3	30.3	125.0
20	229.6	42.5	187.1
30	258.5	53.0	205.5
40	250.0	69.9	180.1
50	193.8	96.6	97.2
60	112.1	135.1	−23.0
70	56.3	137.0	−80.7

Source: Auerbach, Gokhale, and Kotlikoff (1994).

(the third column), we see that the elderly in 1991 receive large transfers, at least in an accounting sense, while all others are worse off.

Although such data are suggestive, as should be readily apparent from our previous discussions, evaluating the effects of Social Security requires consideration of behavior. Consistent with the logic used in analyzing the actions of welfare recipients (for example, if higher taxes reduce take-home pay, the absolute amount saved likely declines), the savings rates of myopic citizens should be unaffected by the program's existence except to the extent that additional taxes crowd out their savings.

When citizens instead anticipate future benefits, crowding out can offset the effects of Social Security on income of the elderly. Such crowding out, however, may be more varied and complicated than occurs with welfare. Individuals with foresight may respond to a retirement program by either earning less or by spending more. Or, in the spirit of Ricardian equivalence (recall our discussion of budget deficits in Chapter 1), parents expecting Social Security benefits may save more to provide bequests to their children who will pay higher taxes (Barro 1974)—that is, the purpose of saving changes from retirement to bequests. Symmetrically, crowding out may be small if otherwise needy parents rely on retirement benefits to replace support previously expected from their children.[28]

In short, if people are myopic, crowding out will occur only because of taxation. If citizens have rational expectations and believe that programs such as Social Security will support them, several mechanisms, in addition to reduced savings, may lead to crowding out. Such crowding out may reduce the effectiveness of transfer programs to the elderly.[29]

It is often assumed that many people are indeed myopic—which, to reiterate, would promote Social Security's success. Certainly, the standard textbook justification for the program is that persons are too shortsighted to save for their old age.[30] For example, Rosen (1988) notes that "the usual argument is that individuals are not farsighted enough to buy enough insurance for their own good and therefore the government must force them to . . . it is popularly believed that in the absence of Social Security, most people would not accumulate enough assets to finance an adequate level of consumption during their retirement" (p. 195).[31]

Indeed, as in our discussion of budget deficits in Chapter 1, the evidence suggests that many persons are myopic. Analyses of redistribution further support this proposition. For example, Social Security recipients increase consumption only in response to actual changes in benefits rather than to announced increases (Wilcox 1989; see also Reimers and Honig 1996). If beneficiaries fail to react to payments due in a few months, why would we expect workers to offset benefits they may receive in twenty years?[32]

Given this description and our view of the world, findings regarding the redistributive effects of Social Security make sense. In the aggregate, these results suggest that various crowding-out problems make the government's ability to transfer income to the elderly more costly but that they do not negate the possibility.

For example, cross-sectional studies estimate that a one dollar increase in Social Security *taxes* reduces savings by about 70 cents, but that increases in expected Social Security *benefits* barely reduce private savings (Kotlikoff 1979).[33] Although some early time-series estimates of the effects of Social Security benefits on savings found substitution effects of about 40 percent (Feldstein 1974; this estimate is revised in Feldstein 1982), later work incorporating the effects of unemployment on savings finds effects ranging from roughly one-tenth the previous estimates (Munnell 1977) to none at all (Leimer and Lesnoy 1982). Inferences from survey data echo the finding that substitution effects are small. Thus, when the Retirement History Survey[34] asked respondents what Social Security benefits they expected to receive in the future and contrasted these responses with savings rates, the results suggested that Social Security depresses personal saving roughly dollar for dollar for single persons, but not at all for the much larger group of married couples (a contrast the authors, Bernheim and Levin 1989, leave unexplained).[35]

Crowding out thus appears modest. Our interpretation is that distrust that government will meet all its obligations, coupled with myopic behavior by some citizens, undermines credibility and makes redistribution possible.

Overcoming Moral Stigma: The Importance of Multiple Equilibria

Beyond reducing credibility, the absence of a sense of entitlement may create multiple equilibria and crowding effects that can influence the effectiveness of redistribution. In particular, programs that stigmatize recipients may undermine redistribution, whereas programs that destigmatize participation may strengthen redistributive efforts. The result may be the realization of one equilibrium rather than another.

Of fundamental importance is that transfer programs require recipients to apply for benefits. Persons believing that they will be stigmatized by receiving aid may choose to forgo such assistance. When some people decline benefits, others may also be induced to avoid participating.

Certainly, the data demonstrate that take-up rates (that is, the fraction of eligible persons who apply for benefits and who then receive them) for the programs likely associated with stigma are often far below 100 percent. Roughly half of the aged poor in the United States eligible for Supplementary Security Income fail to apply.[36] The take-up rate for food stamps is around 40 percent, and the take-up rate in the AFDC unemployed parent program even lower.[37] Take-up rates for AFDC itself, between 62 and 70 percent, were the highest for such redistribution programs (Bishop 1982, Blank and Ruggles 1996, McGarry 1996). And sometimes take-up rates decline: the percent of eligible recipients who received AFDC declined beginning in 1994 (Blank 1997b), and the fraction of unemployed workers receiving regular unemployment insurance payments fell from 75 percent in 1977–1980 to 67 percent after 1982. The failure to accept benefits also appears outside the United States. In Britain, for example, some of the main income-related benefits go unclaimed by up to one-half of those eligible (Craig 1991).

One explanation for these results may be informational, having nothing to do with stigma. Potential recipients may be unaware of the programs, their eligibility, or how to apply. Findings that networks of contacts are important for employment success (Osterman 1991) suggest that factors such as the type of community a potential recipient lives in may have informational effects on participation rates. Yet evidence that more education and higher IQs are associated with *lower* take-up rates, even after controlling for income or family status (McDonald 1977), indicates that low participation is not due solely, or even mostly, to poor information. So does recent evidence that, even among the poor, it is the most needy who apply for benefits (McGarry 1996).

Rather, stigma appears important in reducing take-up rates for redistributive programs. Such stigmatization is well illustrated in one study of welfare participation in a rural town (Rank and Hirschl 1988): "Across the street [from the social service agency] was a tavern. The case workers detailed how men would often sit and gaze out the window of the tavern to observe people going into the office. They would then gossip and joke about who was on welfare, what their situations were, and so on. Potential welfare recipients entering the office were generally aware of this" (p. 201). The resulting feelings of stigmatization are also nicely captured by a food stamp recipient (ibid., 1988), who recounts, "Well, when I went grocery shopping, I usually went to Ceders (a supermarket). Because I figured a lot of people go in there and use 'em, you know, so I wouldn't feel out of place. Otherwise, it would look bad, and I still felt stupid" (pp. 198, 200). More systematic findings, such as those produced by Moffitt's (1983) investigation of the 1976 Michigan Panel Study on Income Dynamics, echo such anecdotal accounts by showing that stigma does, indeed, reduce welfare participation.[38]

Put another way, society may value some personal attributes, such as self-reliance and a willingness to work hard, and transfer recipients may worry about being viewed as lacking these characteristics. As a result, persons may fear that applying for programs such as welfare sends an unfavorable signal to others (Besley and Coate 1992).

Crucially, the view persons may have of someone who accepts government assistance should depend on the average characteristics of beneficiaries—if only the very poor receive assistance, then any one person will be reluctant to be lumped into that category. But if recipients have more varied qualities, the disincentive, and hence the stigma, will be less as recipients in redistributive programs will reveal little about themselves.

Since any one person's behavior depends on the behavior of others, multiple equilibria and crowding in can appear the same way that strategic complementarities appear in investment. In other words, crowding in appears when the choice of some persons to receive assistance induces others to apply: either high-usage or low-usage equilibria may be realized. The likelihood that multiple equilibria, augmented by crowding in, exists may be increased by suppliers' behavior. For example, supermarkets may decide to incur the fixed costs of training or accounting required to process food stamps only if many customers are recipients. If few potential recipients accept food stamps, most stores will find redeeming them unprofitable, and the inconvenience of redemption may deter more persons from applying.

In brief, stigma and the multiple equilibria created by its effects, coupled with crowding in and investment activity, may undermine or support redistribution. Redistributive programs can fail when a low-participation equilibrium is settled upon or succeed when enough people sign up to induce crowding in. Not only do such results suggest when redistribution may succeed or fail, but they indicate that, as in macroeconomic jawboning, if exhortation by public officials or if program design reduces stigma and induces even a few additional persons to participate, the impact may be large as crowding in occurs, the high-participation equilibrium is realized, and participation rates rise.

Why Not Taxes?

So far we have focused on programs that give money to citizens. But since government raises revenue to provide services (such as defense and education) to much of the population, would not taxes alone suffice to redistribute incomes? Or could not the need for transfers be reduced by imposing lower taxes on the poor? Is it inadequate political will, or is redistribution not feasible even under the most favorable political circumstances?

One obvious difficulty with a reliance on taxation is that redistribution often requires payments to the poor. Whereas a regressive tax can hurt welfare recipients, a progressive tax[39] cannot by itself increase the incomes of the poor. Similarly, although some Social Security recipients have high taxable incomes, many others are poor. Progressive taxation will not much benefit such retirees.[40]

Nevertheless, taxation might be progressive or regressive. The substantive concern is whether such taxation can actually redistribute income.

The issue most important for our discussion is the degree to which economic actors anticipate and avoid the effect of taxes nominally intended for redistribution. A related issue is the extent to which, if redistributive taxation is credible over the long term, activities that generate pre-tax income may be crowded out by other behavior such as leisure.

Thus, understanding the effects of taxes on different groups of taxpayers, or of *tax incidence*, is necessary for determining the effectiveness of redistribution by taxation. If such levies are easily avoided, little redistribution will occur. If tax evasion is difficult, then politics is more important in explaining the degree of redistribution.[41]

Economists who study tax incidence in a given year and consider effective rather than nominal taxes largely conclude that what redistribution results from the federal tax system is small. As shown in Table 2.6, in 1966 the poorest tenth of the population paid a federal tax rate that was about half the rate paid by the highest income group (11 percent of their income compared to 20 percent). Tax rates, however, did not vary with income for the 60 percent of the population within the fourth through ninth income deciles. In 1985 differences in tax rates were generally even smaller.

Analyses that consider lifetime incomes rather than short-term effects find redistribution of roughly the same size.[42] For example, in their study of lifetime tax burdens, Fullerton and Rogers (1993) find that the personal income tax burden is somewhat progressive. People with little lifetime income pay about 5 percent of their total earnings in taxes, whereas people with the highest income pay roughly 19 percent.

Accounting tabulations, as illustrated by Table 2.7, show some redistribution—the distribution of post-tax income is more equal than the distribution of pre-tax income. For instance, in 1997 the pre-tax income of the poorest 20 percent of the population was 3.6 percent of national income, while their after-tax share was modestly higher, at 4.4 percent.

Hence, it appears that to at least some extent taxes *can* redistribute in-

Table 2.6 Effective rates of federal taxes (rate by income decile and year for U.S. population)

Income decile	1966	1985
Lowest income decile	10.8	15.4
Second	12.0	15.6
Third	14.7	15.9
Fourth	16.0	16.7
Fifth	16.7	17.2
Sixth	16.8	17.4
Seventh	16.9	17.4
Eighth	17.2	18.2
Ninth	17.2	18.2
Highest income decile	20.2	16.8

Source: Pechman (1985), Table 7-1, average of variants 1c and 3b.

Table 2.7 Share of before-tax and after-tax income in the United States (percentage by income group)

Year	Poorest 20 percent		Middle 60 percent		Richest 5 percent	
	Before tax	After tax	Before tax	After tax	Before tax	After tax
1980	4.2	4.9	51.8	54.6	16.5	14.1
1981	4.1	4.9	51.6	54.3	16.5	14.2
1982	4.0	4.7	51.0	53.6	17.0	14.8
1983	4.0	4.7	50.9	53.3	17.1	15.0
1984	4.0	4.7	50.8	53.0	17.1	15.2
1985	3.9	4.6	50.4	52.9	17.6	15.4
1986	3.8	4.4	50.2	52.9	18.0	15.3
1987	3.8	4.5	50.0	52.9	18.2	15.4
1988	3.8	4.5	49.9	52.6	18.3	15.8
1989	3.8	4.6	49.3	52.1	18.9	16.2
1990	3.8	4.5	49.5	52.0	18.6	16.5
1991	3.8	4.5	49.7	52.3	18.1	16.0
1992	3.7	4.4	49.4	51.9	18.6	16.5
1993	3.6	4.3	47.6	50.7	21.0	18.1
1994	3.6	4.4	47.3	50.6	21.2	18.1
1995	3.7	4.5	47.7	50.8	21.0	17.9
1996	3.7	4.5	47.3	50.8	21.4	17.9
1997	3.6	4.4	47.1	50.8	21.7	18.0

Source: Income Statistics Branch / HHES Division, United States Bureau of the Census, United States Department of Commerce, Table RDI-3, http://www.census.gov/hhes/income/histinc/index.html

come. It is therefore surprising that redistribution is so commonly done by other means. Two political considerations may be important. First, administrative programs, unlike tax policies, let politicians claim credit for helping constituents with the bureaucracy (Fiorina 1989). Second, programs like Social Security and welfare, notwithstanding recent welfare reform in the United States, may be more difficult to change than a tax system. As mentioned, policies can be made more credible by designing them to create significant interests and constituencies who will fight to maintain them. Although subject to credibility problems (as well, of course, to crowding out to the degree that they are credible), programs with identified beneficiaries can be more durable than tax policies. Thus, the voters who at one time favored redistribution may have wished to make it more durable by using entitlement programs and means-based programs instead of sharply progressive tax systems. As we saw, however, such success in durability can also reduce the effectiveness of the program in question.

Conclusions: Redistributive Possibilities

The issue of whether government can redistribute income or wealth has been examined from several angles. When all is said and done, the conclusions are, at least, fourfold.

1. An accounting perspective on redistribution is incorrect and misleading. Only behavioral models provide a correct view of redistribution.
2. Redistribution across generations and social classes is possible. Indeed, of all the policy areas that we survey, redistribution seems to allow for the most effective government action. Low levels of redistribution are primarily due to political preference.
3. As people react to redistribution, they generate additional social costs. Both persons who pay the taxes and persons who get the benefits may work less or save less. Recipients may suffer from the stigma of requesting governmental assistance, leading to an equilibrium with low redistribution.
4. The economic constraints that have been the primary features of our analysis—credibility, crowding out, rational expectations, and multiple equilibria—are important for understanding the possibility for redistribution, the additional costs associated with such policies, and the ways by which redistribution operates.

Two related points should be highlighted. One is the tension associated with credibility. Most notably, the more difficult it is for government to commit to redistributive policies, the more effective such policies may be. A government devoted to redistribution may, therefore, deliberately hide its devotion. Put another way, although redistribution is possible, there are trade-offs between developing a credible program that has a long life and a program that is effective.

The other point is that the hurtful effects of rational expectations and rational reactions on future policy are likely weak. Unlike for many other types of policies, the behavior of myopic persons can make redistribution feasible.

3

When Can Government Regulate?

Governments go beyond increasing and redistributing wealth. They also care about production of outputs more or less directly (the subject of the next chapter) and the regulation of specific behaviors of firms and individuals (the subject of this chapter).

This specificity of regulation presents both obstacles and opportunities for governmental action. Given such precise targets, credibility, as well as its interaction with other economic constraints, is especially important. On the one hand, specific regulation may require that firms (especially) and consumers make large investments designed to meet government goals. As regulation-specific investments would otherwise be valueless, government needs to persuade subjects of regulation of its commitment to relevant policies. To return, however, to a point that we have repeatedly made, establishing the durability of a policy is frequently difficult when political leaders are subject to the whims of the electorate. Weak credibility can lead to an avoidance of large capital outlays by regulatees, presenting a challenge to governmental intervention.

On the other hand, once large, irreversible investments are made, the credibility of policy and the likelihood of successful regulation increase. Investments by firms and individuals increase credibility by reducing the costs of continuing compliance. Not only will the additional costs imposed by continuing the regulation be small,[1] but economic agents who previously invested may now favor the regulation. Crowding in may further buttress policy effectiveness as others, expecting policy regulation to be permanent, also invest. A high-investment equilibrium may then be realized.

Such dynamics can prove crucial for regulatory success. Government may have difficulty inducing those with rational expectations to make investments that lower their future costs of meeting regulatory standards, render continuation of the policy credible, induce crowding in, and move the economy to an equilibrium that government favors. But a regulation's continued enforcement and ultimate success are higher when economic agents make such investments.

Whereas credibility, crowding in, and the selection of some equilibria may lead to the success of policies, in some circumstances, even given credibility, crowding out or the selection of unfavorable equilibria could undermine policy. Such costly crowding out is likely to be most common and damaging for efforts to regulate the behavior of individuals, who may adjust their behavior in ways that largely offset their anticipation of government policy. Also, particularly with regulation of personal behavior, government actions may lead to the establishment of an equilibrium that causes a regulation to fail rather than of the equilibrium that best fulfills policy goals.

We will see that, although the relevance of different constraints varies with the type of regulation addressed, economic constraints are generally important for understanding how effectively government can regulate. Overall, our analysis suggests that regulation is possible—particularly when credibility problems can be overcome—but it will be more circumscribed and less efficient than in an idealized world. Furthermore, beyond success or failure, the choice of regulatory tools may be heavily shaped by economic constraints.

The Scope of Regulation

Before proceeding with our analysis of economic constraints on regulation, it helps to elaborate on our view of regulation. Many important texts covering regulatory behavior lack clear definitions of what the subject covers (e.g., Wilson 1980, Breyer 1982, Reagan 1987, Viscusi, Vernon, and Harrington 1995). Rather, they assume that people recognize regulatory activity intuitively, or that what constitutes regulation is common knowledge. Authors more commonly concentrate on laying out positive or normative rationales for intervention, such as overcoming market failures, and on indicating why such reasons insufficiently explain or justify regulatory activity.

Implicit in most discussions are narrow and broad definitions of regulation. Restrictive definitions typically include laundry lists of agencies engaged in economic and social regulation (such a list for the United States is shown in Table 3.1). Economic regulation generally refers to controls over prices, entry and exit in an industry, and mergers between competitors. Such regulations were particularly popular in the United States in the late nineteenth and early twentieth centuries but have declined in recent years. Social regulation commonly refers to protecting health and safety, reducing energy use, or protecting the environment, and have become especially prominent over the last several decades.

More legalistic and popular discussions of regulation frequently adopt a broader definition, incorporating behavior some view as generating bad externalities or as just evil. For example, pundits often discuss whether efforts to regulate morality—personal speech, expression, or behavior—are desirable. Thus, a broad definition of regulatory activities includes social policy regarding activities such as hate speech, pornography, and abortion.

Table 3.1 U.S. regulatory agencies

Major agencies	Other agencies
Consumer Product Safety Commission	Architectural and Transportation Barriers Compliance Board
Environmental Protection Agency	Commodity Futures Trading Commission
Equal Employment Opportunity Commission	Farm Credit Administration
Federal Communications Commission	Federal Election Commission
Federal Deposit Insurance Commission	Federal Housing Finance Board
Federal Energy Regulatory Commission	Federal Maritime Commission
Federal Reserve System	National Credit Union Administration
Federal Trade Commission	National Mediation Board
Food and Drug Administration	National Transportation Safety Board
National Labor Relations Board	Nuclear Regulatory Commission
Occupational Safety and Health Administration	Pension Benefit Guaranty Corporation
Securities and Exchange Commission	Postal Rate Commission
	Resolution Trust Corporation
	Social Security Administration
	Small Business Administration
	U.S. International Trade Commission
	U.S. Postal Service

Source: Congressional Quarterly, Inc. (1997).

Note: Excludes the roughly eighty departmental agencies and offices with functions classified as regulatory.

For expository convenience and for analytic reasons, we adopt an expansive view of regulation. Although we focus on policies regulating firms, we also refer to policies affecting consumers; not only are consumers important in their own right, but the similarities and the contrasts between these two types of actors and related policies give general insights into regulation. For our purposes, therefore, we define policies designed to direct the production choices of firms or the consumption choices of individuals as regulatory (the distinction between firms and individuals is, for our purposes, more useful than that between economic and social regulation). Although regulation overlaps with the other types of policies that we investigate, regulation has more specific targets than macroeconomic and redistributive policy. And though regulations may be specific, the control government exerts is less direct than when government itself produces a good.

Regulating Firms: Possibilities and Pitfalls

As stated, much economic and social regulation aims to make firms behave in a specific manner. In doing so, the nominal purpose of such policy is to influence the outputs of firms or the way that they produce their goods and services.

We will now elaborate how, and under what conditions, economic constraints are crucial for determining success in regulating such firms' behavior. Specifically, our analysis implies that these constraints are generally important and that their effects may by conditioned both by the market in which firms operate and by the instruments that politicians have to increase credibility, to manipulate crowding behavior, and to establish particular equilibria. It also indicates that, although regulations that employ market-based regulatory instruments will often work well, they are subject to many of the obstacles that have hindered conventional regulatory efforts and that, indeed, such problems may be even more severe.[2]

Implications of Economic Constraints

As stated above, although several economic constraints are relevant for regulating firms, credibility is especially important for understanding what government can and cannot accomplish with regulations. Credibility issues also suggest why we may observe seemingly inefficient regulatory arrangements even without opportunistic behavior by elected officials or without pressures by organized interests. Furthermore, as also briefly discussed, credibility is a dual-edged sword for the regulation of firms. The push and the pull of credibility both lie in what they imply about investment. Although credibility problems can hurt efforts to encourage investment, government may nevertheless adopt regulations requiring irreversible investments in the hopes that it can demonstrate its commitment to a policy, induce investment, and, in the process, reinforce the policy's credibility.

Thus, since changes in what, how, or how much firms produce often require capital outlays, one reason why credibility looms so large is that much economic and social regulation must induce economic agents to make irreversible, durable, investments. For instance, economic regulation, such as the regulation of railroad charges, can only work if producers make the requisite investment to produce the regulated goods and services. When they do not (for example, when railroads in the United States let their trackbeds deteriorate), ill consequences may result (such as the collapse of the Pennsylvania Central railroad in the 1960s). Similarly, social regulation, such as policies with the stated goals of protecting the environment or protecting worker health, often demand large investments.

When asked to make costly investments to meet regulations, firms, however, may fear that a government will later change its policies, or even that it has little intention of enforcing the policy.[3] Government officials, in turn, may worry that investors will either doubt the government's resolve to punish firms not making the requisite investments, or skeptically view government's willingness to continue its policy and to provide the promised return on investments.[4]

Moreover, a regulated firm, or an industry acting in concert, may attempt to reverse government policies by refusing to invest. For example, American automobile companies have repeatedly used brinkmanship in dealing with regulation. These manufacturers often disregarded government regulations to reduce the emissions, increase the fuel efficiency, and improve the safety of their products (e.g., on safety, see Mashaw and Harfst 1990). As deadlines approached, the manufacturers' typical response was that meeting mandated goals was either technologically or financially infeasible and that, without a postponement, they would reduce production and throw thousands out of work. (We will elaborate on this example later.)

The other side of credibility is that, when choosing between regulations requiring little investment but high continuing costs of compliance and regulations requiring a one-time costly investment but little continuing costs, government may favor investment. Assuming that investment can be induced, such one-time costs will make policy reversal less attractive and will encourage crowding in; once investment is made, support for a policy will grow, making it more credible, and firms that had avoided investment, believing penalties for noncompliance will be small, will find investment increasingly profitable.

As will be discussed in more depth below, this logic implies that government may favor command-and-control regulation for reasons related to investment (or, at least, that better credibility will be a by product of such regulation). Government may, for reasons unrelated to electoral politics, reject market-based solutions.

In other words, politicians and their supporters may choose regulations requiring large investments even when, in an idealized world, such investment would be inefficient. The bias toward investment should be particularly strong when expectations are that a change in power from the current government to another with widely divergent preferences about policies is likely (Glazer 1989). Minimally, an unintended consequence of investment-intensive regulations selected for other reasons may be improved credibility.

Governments often choose durable yet inefficient policies. For instance, in regulating cotton dust, the U.S. Congress required expensive ventilation equipment though inexpensive masks were cost-effective substitutes. These alternatives may differ, however, in their allocational implications and in their total costs. Ventilation equipment has a high fixed cost but low marginal costs, whereas use of masks has low fixed costs but high marginal costs. Whereas a future government that favored reducing regulatory costs could cancel regulations requiring protective gear to the benefit of the firms involved, the same government and firms would gain little by allowing the removal of ventilation equipment. Consistent with this view, in his analysis of the seemingly odd regulatory choices made regarding cotton dust, Viscusi (1985) notes:

> The evidence indicates that the [cotton dust] standard has had the expected beneficial effect on worker health, and at a cost much lower than originally anticipated. Nevertheless, the costs still remain very high, far higher than estimates of the value of the results they achieve or of the

value that workers place on them. Moreover, much more efficient ways of achieving comparable results are available. Nevertheless, large firms in the industry now appear to have a vested interest in maintaining the standard in its original form and are unlikely to constitute a force for change. (p. 325)

Or, for another example, to the dismay of many studying cost-effectiveness (e.g., Ackerman and Hassler 1981), in the 1970s Congress required power plants to install smokestack scrubbers rather than to burn low-sulfur coal. For environmental advocates, one potential appeal of scrubbers is their permanence. Burning costly low-sulfur coal instead of cheap high-sulfur coal raises costs each time the substitution is made but (as power plants require no retrofitting) does not appreciably raise fixed costs.[5] This may provide firms that can use cheap high-sulfur coal with an incentive to lobby for reversing the regulation. By contrast, as constructing a scrubber increases fixed costs but makes costs of future compliance low, firms initially opposed have little reason to advocate deregulation once scrubbers have been installed.

Determining when economic constraints permit, or even assist, regulation of firms thus largely translates into determining whether, or under what conditions, investment may be induced; investment, in turn, is induced when credible policy encourages crowding in and influences the move to a high-investment equilibrium. Otherwise, regulation is unlikely to be effective, as even well-meaning political officials will face industry brinkmanship.

The Importance of Market Structure

An important determinant of successful regulation of firms is market structure, in particular whether an industry is economically concentrated and its firms are vertically integrated.[6] Firms in industries that are monopolistic or oligopolistic and firms that are vertically integrated have a greater incentive than others to disobey regulations. Conversely, firms in competitive markets with third parties supplying critical inputs will be more easily regulated.

For several reasons credibility problems appear when government attempts to regulate firms in concentrated markets. First, the ease of collusion in a concentrated industry can produce noncompliance with regulations and a corresponding belief among firms that policy can be undermined. Second, since any one of a few firms constitutes a large part of the market, noncompliance by any one firm may disrupt policy and cause government to reverse regulation. As such, firms in concentrated industries may view policies as noncredible.

By contrast, firms in a competitive industry are more likely to consider policy as credible and to comply with regulations in response. Collusion for such firms is difficult, and the refusal of any single firm to comply will little affect governmental resolve. Noncompliance may also be undermined by crowding in, with one firm breaking rank and making the requisite investment, leading the next to do the same, and so on. Such crowding may induce political pressure and greater support for enforcing a regulation; recognizing this, other firms may also invest, further strengthening support for regulatory enforcement and making the government's credibility and its stated willingness to employ sanctions that much stronger.[7]

Thus, the effectiveness of regulation can vary with the market structure of the regulated industry. A low regulation / low investment equilibrium is more likely to appear than a high regulation / high investment equilibrium in concentrated than in competitive markets.

Additionally, for reasons comparable to concentration, firms that are vertically integrated may more easily thwart regulation than can firms that buy most of their inputs. If investment is needed to comply with a regulation, then an obstructionist, vertically integrated, firm can more easily assure that no such investment is made. By contrast, a downstream producer (the producer making the finished good) that is not vertically integrated and that initially refuses to make the investments needed for regulatory compliance has to worry that one of its suppliers will make the required investment. Similarly, suppliers may worry about the actions of their upstream clients.

In other words, the credibility of regulations affecting concentrated industries may be higher when other firms can profit from taking the initiative. For example, a regulation that increases the price of one firm's output or reduces its demand for inputs may induce the firm's consumers and suppliers to make investments to cushion the effects of regulation on them. If, as a by-product, these investments lower the costs of regulation, government may be more willing to regulate. Hence, credibility is increased, and the original target of regulation will be more likely to invest to reduce the costs of the policy once imposed, further lowering the costs and increasing the credibility of the regulatory policy.

Predictions about the effects of concentration and vertical integration are borne out in practice. To follow up an earlier example, regulation of American automobile companies has repeatedly proven problematic. An important explanation lies, it appears, in the trouble government has had dealing with a concentrated industry where the Big Three (General Motors, Ford, and Chrysler) followed a strategy of brinkmanship and behaved as if they expected regulators to back down. Faced with government regulations to reduce emissions, increase fuel economy, and improve safety, auto producers dragged their feet and stuck to their own lengthy timetables. As regulatory deadlines loomed, manufacturers claimed that meeting the specified standards was impossible and that, without additional time, they would be forced to cut production and lay off thousands of workers.[8] Illustratively, during the 1992 vice presidential debate, Dan Quayle, in voicing his opposition to more stringent corporate average fuel economy (CAFE) standards by environmentalists, repeated industry claims that 300,000 jobs would be lost (Gates 1992).[9]

Industry recalcitrance was especially evident after enactment of the Clean Air Act of 1970, which required firms to produce automobiles with much lower emissions. As it set a goal not achievable with 1970 technology, the original legislation's stipulation for 90 percent emission reductions by 1975 was explicitly technology-forcing. Costly research and development, car redesign, and factory modifications were needed to produce required new equipment such as catalytic converters. Presumably, if firms expected the standards to be enforced with their substantial penalties, they would have invested to meet them. Alternatively, if firms believed that standards would be readily waived, they would have invested little.[10] Faced with a unified and resistant industry, the federal government postponed enforcing the standards. Most dramatically, responding to producers' claims that the enforcement of current emission standards would close factories (which, given the limited investment by the auto producers, seemed plausible), Congress weakened requirements or postponed deadlines in 1977 and in 1988 (Bailey 1998).

A similar pattern is found in efforts to make manufacturers install passive restraints, such as automatic seat belts or air bags, which require no actions by drivers and passengers. Efforts to mandate passenger restraints reflected a reaction to the limited use of nonpassive restraints such as conventional seat belts—drivers and passengers preferred to drive without such protection (driver use reached 15 percent in the United States only in 1984). To safety advocates, this recklessness argued for requiring passive restraints that could not be avoided. Although regulations for installing passive restraint systems were supposed to be enforced in the 1970s, deadlines were postponed for one year in 1975 and the requirements were suspended twice (although later reinstituted) in the next seven years. Not until model year 1990 did a phase-in begin (see Donohue 1989, Cook 1995). In surveying the history of passive restraints (with special emphasis on air bags, which have become the restraint system of choice), one commentator (Kelly 1992) notes how tortuous and lengthy the process has been: "The air bag, arguably the single most important crash-protection device yet developed, was a proven technology in 1971 and ready for the marketplace in 1974. Yet its protective benefits were denied to motorists for fifteen years by the auto industry's unyielding opposition" (p. 51).

Lastly, credibility was also imperfect in enforcing automobile fuel economy standards. Following the 1973 energy crisis, Congress adopted CAFE standards for all new light-duty passenger vehicles sold in the United States. Fleets were to average 18.5 miles per gallon (mpg) for model year 1978, 21 mpg for 1980, and 27.5 mpg for 1986. Cries of infeasibility, however, similar to those voiced regarding emissions requirements and passive restraint systems, were heard, and standards were relaxed three times by the secretary of transportation so that only for the 1989 model year was the standard to rise to 26.5 mpg. Later efforts to raise requirements above 27.5 mpg, such as calls by environmentalists for a 45 mpg standard, have floundered (see, e.g., Bergman 1996 on the position of the Sierra Club).

In fairness, safety restraints are now widely installed, auto emissions have been reduced by about 90 percent, and fuel efficiency of cars has risen. Although these changes have not occurred solely because of regulations, such policies were effective in the long run. But economic constraints contributed to making change painfully slow and expensive.

And the progress that was made may have arisen from the absence of vertical integration. Notably, third parties were willing and able to break rank with automakers. In other words, the extent to which automotive manufacturers obeyed regulations may largely have depended on how other firms behaved.

A nice example of this process—and one that helps explain why manufacturers may impede but not defeat regulations—is found in the early history of regulating emissions (White 1982). When southern California politicians became concerned about automobile exhausts in the early 1950s, car producers responded by claiming that more research was needed. Predictably, these companies did little and instead in 1955 entered into a cross-licensing agreement for sharing patents on emissions equipment that strongly discouraged any company to invest: why invest when one can free ride on the work of the other producers? However, after California adopted a rule stating that regulations would be implemented if two practical devices were developed at reasonable cost, equipment manufacturers who supplied the automobile industry undermined producer solidarity by developing the necessary technology.[11] The automobile manufacturers responded by introducing devices of their own.

Comparable explanations focusing on vertical integration apply to two of the more successful regulatory policies in the United States in recent years: the elimination of lead from gasoline and the reduction in chlorofluorocarbon (CFC) production.[12] Both policies affected firms that produced inputs for firms in other industries, and the actions of one set of firms undermined the ability of the other set of firms to hold out and not meet regulatory standards.

Consider regulations to limit the use of leaded gasoline. Soon after establishment of the Environmental Protection Agency in 1970, regulators addressed the dangers of lead exposure from automobile emissions. Initial regulations, issued in 1973, ensured the availability of unleaded gasoline for use in vehicles equipped with catalytic converters. Later regulations then limited the use of lead in gasoline. In 1982 the allowable lead per gallon of gasoline dropped from 4.0 grams (2.5 was generally used) to 1.1 grams. Allowable levels were then reduced to 0.5 grams in 1985 and, finally, to 0.1 grams the next year. As a result, total lead emissions by highway vehicles declined from 171,960 short tons in 1970, to 130,210 in 1975, to 1,380 in 1993, and to 19in 1998 (Davis 1995, U.S. Environmental Protection Agency 2000).

Why the success in reducing use of lead? Lead pollution and air pollution were joined as political issues, with refiners and automobile producers supporting different alternatives. Refiners wanted to invest as little as possible, to continue to produce leaded gasoline, and to force the adoption of leaded gasoline technologies by car manufacturers to reduce emissions. Auto producers preferred catalytic converters, which required unleaded gasoline, over emissions systems burning leaded gasoline, and so wanted refineries to produce unleaded gasoline. Thus, at least two equilibria could appear: leaded gasoline / no catalytic converter and unleaded gasoline / catalytic converter. Consequently, a policy influencing either refiners or car builders—or altering expectations of what government policy would be—promised to be self-reinforcing. In the United States, auto companies invested in catalytic converters and became advocates for unleaded fuel. Once investments in catalytic converters were made, oil companies, recognizing increased political support and a market for unleaded fuel, transformed their refineries. Credibility, changed expectations, and crowding in combined to establish an equilibrium with dramatically lower lead production and emissions.[13]

A similar story appears with CFC production. Believing that the long-term prospects for the chemical's production were slim, manufacturers of products that used CFCs invested in technology to allow substitutes (Benedick 1991). This undermined claims that firms using CFCs had no alternative. Given reduced demand for their product and an incentive to invest in goods that manufacturers wanted, CFC capacity and opposition to restricting the chemical by their producers also declined. Production of CFCs fell from about 1 million tons in 1986 to about 200,000 tons in 1995.[14] Thus, one equilibrium may have had no investment in CFC substitutes and its continued production and use; the other equilibrium had investment in the production of less harmful chemicals and a drastic reduction in CFC use. A lack of vertical integration allowed attainment of the latter equilibrium and the achievement of regulatory goals.

In brief, industry structure may be important to the success of regulation. An industry with most firms viewing regulation as not credible will invest little because of their anticipations and will induce an equilibrium with low investment. The result may be a slowing of regulatory compliance, which is frequently seen as lengthy regardless of industry structure, because policymakers will find imposing mandated regulation too costly. In contrast, third party involvement in the absence of vertical integration may promote regulatory success. Credible regulation may lead to crowding in and increased investment. Opposition to regulation will then decline and regulations can be effective once they are adopted.

Delegation and Appointments

So far, we have surveyed the inherent possibilities and problems associated with regulation and how, in turn, market structure may constrain or promote policy. Politicians, however, also have tools that can help regulations succeed.[15] Typically, each of these alternatives comes with a cost and imperfectly assures regulation, particularly given the endogeneity of political choices and the short time horizons of many politicians.

For example, politicians may delegate power in ways that increase the credibility and the durability of policy and thereby induce the crowding in already discussed. They may commit policy by limiting an agency's freedom of action, particularly if the politicians fear that future bureaucrats will have preferences different from those of the current government (McCubbins, Noll, and Weingast 1987, 1989; Calvert, McCubbins, and Weingast 1989); by creating administrative procedures that limit flexibility and political responsiveness (Bawn 1995); or by delegating authority to an agency known to support the desired policy or that benefits from its continuation (Kunioka and Rothenberg 1993).

The logic behind such reasoning is easily illustrated. Suppose the issue in question is enforcing CAFE standards and that the choice lies between two alternative implementation methods. The first delegates enforcement to a pro-business agency, whose leaders are replaced frequently, and where standing to appeal decisions to the courts is restricted to groups with large vested interests (for example, producers or labor unions). The other delegates authority to a pro-consumer agency, with appointees insulated from frequent review, and with standing broadly defined so that consumer advocates (for example, Ralph Nader and his allies) can easily participate. Even for regulations specifying the same fuel economy standards, credibility may be higher, investment will be greater, crowding in will be stronger, and an equilibrium with higher investment will more likely be established when delegation gives voice to groups that favor rather than oppose the regulation. Additionally, even if current regulators and legislators hold the same preferences, a legislative coalition worried about losing power may set future policy by specifying exact standards rather than vague provisions that let the agency choose rules at its discretion.

Yet delegation is no panacea. Though delegation can overcome some credibility problems, the ability to insulate agencies is inherently limited. Even if regulatory capture by organized interests can be avoided, attempts by legislators to shield agencies can also be undone. So, for example, regardless of the protections built into legislation such as the 1990 Clean Air Act Amendments (for instance, via extraordinarily detailed instructions), policies may be reversed statutorily or administratively by a new political majority (on the 1990 clean air legislation, see Bryner 1995).[16]

Appointments have many of the same strengths and weaknesses as delegation in increasing the credibility of policies. Proper selection of regulators may make policy more credible; appointees, however, can be undermined and eventually replaced. Furthermore, since appointments usually last for less time than do most delegation decisions, the ability of such regulators to commit has additional limits (on the transience of American political appointees, see Heclo 1977).

Nonetheless, some appointments do seem to overcome credibility problems by leading to changed expectations. For example, recalling our discussion of macroeconomics, the selection of Paul Volcker in 1979 as chairman of the Federal Reserve Board was largely motivated by credibility concerns. In the late 1970s inflation was running at double-digit rates and expectations for future inflation were high (reflecting expectations, short-term rates were around 10 percent a year). In response, President Carter appointed Volcker, who was both rigidly conservative and known as an individualist, to fight inflation. Expectations changed in the financial markets, leading to years of low inflation, which continued under Volcker's successor, the highly credible Alan Greenspan.[17]

Similarly, Ronald Reagan's appointment of William Ruckelshaus to head the Environmental Protection Agency (EPA) in 1983 was designed to change expectations. President Reagan's original EPA appointments had proven unpopular and scandal-prone, prompting Reagan to demonstrate that his administration would indeed enforce environmental laws. He appointed Ruckelshaus, who was an advocate of environmental policy and had been the agency's first head in its promising early days. Having been fired by Richard Nixon in the legendary Saturday Night Massacre (where the attorney general was asked to fire the special Watergate prosecutor), Ruckelshaus had a reputation for integrity and independence (Landy, Roberts, and Thomas 1994). Indeed, the EPA subsequently became more active, as measured by large increases in referrals to the Department of Justice and in administrative actions against polluters (Viscusi 1994).

More generally, appointments may be used to vary agency outputs in predictable ways (Wood and Waterman 1994). Thus, the choice of a particular regulator may lead rational economic agents to change their expectations about future policy in a way that induces them to make the investments necessary for policy success. However, although some appointments can encourage compliance with regulations, appointments are unlikely to suffice if long-term credibility is needed. After all, to recall another prominent example, the liberal Michael Pertschuk may have dominated the Federal Trade Commission (FTC) in the second half of the 1970s, but it was clear that any Republican president would replace him.[18]

Related to delegation and appointments, regulators may try to foster credibility, crowding in, and the like by developing a reputation as strong-willed.[19] Not only may regulators want to acquire a firm reputation for enforcing a given policy, but other regulatees may take this behavior as a general signal of toughness. For example, if regulators enforce a CAFE standard in one period, firms may anticipate enforcement of high standards in later periods. Though there are theoretical reasons to be cautious—a regulator's limited time in office or his high valuation on present relative to future returns may reduce his incentive to make short-term sacrifices for long-term rewards—reputation may nevertheless be significant.[20]

Several factors may enhance the potential importance of reputation. Regulators worried that their successors will be more lenient may be exceptionally harsh in order to make policy more durable: paradoxically, this implies that possible changes in power can increase their ability to regulate. The effects of reputation will also be enhanced, and the incentive to act tough will be stronger, if firms are initially uncertain about a regulator's preferences, as regulators may correctly believe that a tough stand now induces beliefs that they will be tough later.

Given its subtlety, discussion of reputation and uncertainty may benefit from a numerical example.[21] Consider a two-period game, where firms are uncertain about how much an administrator cares about a policy (say, emissions and the environment) and regulations must be issued in both periods. In period one the regulator must decide whether to reduce emissions at a cost of $900 million. At the end of period one, firms observe the regulator's behavior and decide whether to invest in abatement. The cost of the investment is positive but small, say $10 million. In period two, the same regulator must choose whether to impose additional regulation to reduce emissions, at a cost of $100 million if firms invested in period one and at a cost of $500 million if they had not. The regulator is of one of three possible types, valuing emissions reductions at either $1 billion, $700 million, or $0.

At the beginning of period one, firms do not know his type, but think it equally likely that he is of any one of the three types. A regulator failing to adopt the regulation in period one clearly values emission reduction at less than $900 million, that is, at either $700 million or $0. Firms thinking it likely that this administrator places little value on emissions reductions will not invest. But if the regulation is adopted in period one, then firms will know the regulator values emission reduction at either $1 billion or $700 million. (A regulator with valuation of $1 billion clearly favors the regulation, whereas, as will be seen, one with a valuation of $700 million adopts the regulation for reputational reasons.) Firms will therefore know that the regulator will impose emission standards in period two; the firms minimize their costs by investing in period one. The $400 million savings in period two more than compensates the regulator for the costly regulation in period one (viewed as providing a net benefit of either $1 billion − $900 million = $100 million or of $700 million − $900 million − −$200 million). Note that, in the absence of reputational considerations, a regulator who values emissions reductions at $700 million would not impose the regulation in period one but, given such reputational concerns, the possible existence of a regulator placing no value on emissions reductions can cause the imposition of costly regulations in period one.

The general point is that reputational considerations can make policy credible and garner political support. Although there are theoretical and practical limits to reputation's usefulness, it is at least one more reason to believe that government can regulate.

In summary, politicians have several tools that can make regulation effective. Nonetheless, the benefits of molding delegation, making appointments, or cultivating a reputation are subject to limits. The very nature of democracies makes it possible to undo such features in ways that undermine regulatory credibility and effectiveness.

Are Markets the Answer?

An alternative to the command-and-control regulations we have considered are market mechanisms.[22] Are they the answer?

Our previous discussion should have made it clear that, although regulation through the market has advantages, this approach cannot solve all regulatory problems. Indeed, the efficiencies of market mechanisms may be undermined by greater difficulties in dealing with economic constraints. These difficulties appear both when regulators change incentives to engage in relevant activities by taxing or subsidizing them and when regulators create markets where none previously existed by setting aggregate limits on some harmful activity and allowing firms to trade in rights to engage in that activity.[23]

Credibility is a major pitfall in applying such market mechanisms. Markets that are created can be destroyed. Will a market system continue once it is adopted, especially when it does not mandate investment? Put another way, can regulators be excluded from the regulatory market?

For example, assume that a market for pollution allowances is promulgated by a free-market Republican administration. Instead of dictating that all polluters must use a specified technology, the market allows firms that can most efficiently lower their emissions by any means to do so.

Such a system will work only if some potential polluters make investments to reduce emissions. But firms will invest in emissions reductions only if they anticipate that emissions will continue to be restricted. With such beliefs, investments will be made, political support for regulation will increase, crowding in will take place, and an equilibrium with welfare-improving trades will be attained. By contrast, the market will function poorly if firms believe government will change policy. Support for continuing the system will be weak, no crowding in will take place, and an equilibrium with few trades in permits and little investment will be realized. Ultimately, with little endogenous political support and few trades, changing political fortunes may lead the market to disappear.

Indeed, in Western Europe—where green taxes are more popular than in the United States—experience indicates that concerns about future policy may be important for explaining the uneven experiences with market mechanisms. For example, in his in-depth study of effluent charges in four European countries, Mikael Anderson (1994; see also Weale 1992) concludes:

> It was initially expected to find three cases of success and one of failure, reflecting the three countries having economic instruments and the one without [Netherlands, France, and Germany on the one hand and Denmark on the other]. The case studies indeed confirmed the case of failure in Denmark, but on the other hand failed to support our initial hypothesis that the use of the effluent charge policy instruments ensured similar degrees of successful pollution control in all three of the remaining cases. In fact, only the Dutch programme proved to be successful, in terms of both emissions, costs and technological responses. (pp. 199–200)

In Anderson's view, market solutions often fail because countries proud of their consensual policymaking have difficulty ensuring political support for the policy. Rephrased for our analysis, these policies were viewed as not credible even in nations with institutions thought to foster consensus.

Experiences with American market permits for clean air allowances designed to reduce acid rain as part of the Clean Air Act Amendment of 1990 also underscore the importance of credibility.[24] Earlier experience with the program was discouraging. Utilities hesitated to trade pollution rights because they feared that government would change the rules. For instance, utilities worried that state-level regulators might not let them recover the costs of the pollution permits that they bought, while still demanding that income from sales of pollution rights be rebated to consumers. The result was a stagnant market (Klebnikov 1993; see also Foster and Hahn 1995). As the years passed, however, and politicians of different ideologies demonstrated no inclination to change the program, the market has worked more efficiently and become more vigorous (Joskow, Schmalensee, and Bailey 1998). Thus, by 1994, outcomes began to improve noticeably and the current evaluation of the tradable permit scheme is more positive.

In other words, market mechanisms are subject to many of the economic constraints that limit other efforts to regulate firms. Completely and categorically removing regulators from the process and allowing free markets to operate prove difficult. Experience suggests that democracies have difficulty in providing the requisite assurances, with programs often updated or refocused (Carson 1994). If credibility can be assured, market mechanisms do offer hope that government can reach its goals more effectively and efficiently.

Regulating Consumer Behavior

As mentioned, the regulation of personal behavior spans many activities. Rather than providing a detailed inventory, we emphasize two related differences that distinguish regulation of people from regulation of firms.

- *Offsetting behavior, crowding out the effects of regulation, appears more important for persons than for firms.* The goals of regulations on individual behavior are often deflected, as the targets of policy can engage in compensating activities.
- *Possibilities for using crowding in to guide equilibrium selection are greater for individuals than for firms.* Policies that change the behavior

of some persons may create social pressures that change the behavior of many others, thereby also increasing political credibility.

Both points are intuitive. Concerning offsetting behavior and crowding out, individuals can engage in a wide range of harmful or morally suspect activities. If government aims to stop citizens from engaging in one bad behavior, some of these persons will find a substitute or another way of satisfying their taste for the discouraged activity. Particularly given the many consumers affected, it may be difficult to design policies that a creative regulatee cannot circumvent. To anticipate an example we extend later, forcing automobile drivers and passengers to wear seat beats, or requiring that cars be equipped with antilock brakes and other safety equipment, may only induce more risk taking on the road. Safe actions may be offset by reckless reactions.

By contrast, crowding in should more effectively select among multiple equilibria for personal behavior than for firm behavior because social conformity is more important to a person than to a firm. In general, any one firm will change its actions in response to the changed behavior by other firms only if it is profitable (recall the discussion of the economics of agglomeration in our analysis of multiple equilibria in macroeconomics). People, in contrast, are social animals who may conform to the behavior of others, allowing richer opportunities for crowding in or crowding out to lead to a desired equilibrium. That is, since social pressures may work better on people than on firms, there are more opportunities in changing one person's behavior to set off chain reactions in which others follow suit. Consequently, government may more easily establish a desired equilibrium when individuals are the target of regulation than when firms are.

As illustration, and to follow up on the example developed in our Introduction, cigarette smoking may be reduced by convincing some persons, say middle-aged men, that smoking is bad. If enough of these persons stop smoking, potential smokers in this peer group are likely to avoid the habit and other current smokers may be induced to make the requisite investments to quit. In both instances, such persons may be motivated by a desire to conform to the new norm or by an anticipation that smoking will become expensive or inconvenient. This decline in smoking may be accentuated by investments that make a renewal of customer or employee smoking expensive and that lead firms to support, or at least to tolerate, antismoking policies. A low-smoking equilibrium will be observed. Alternatively, the opposite processes may be realized, leading to the appearance in other groups (or in entire countries) of a high-smoking equilibrium. We suggest that the existence of multiple equilibria provides insight into why smoking is pervasive and socially acceptable in some wealthy and highly educated nations but not in others.

Crowding Out Regulatory Policies

Obviously, problems of crowding out cripple many regulatory programs directed at firms and individuals alike. Firms routinely substitute one damaging activity for another in response to government regulations. For example, polluters have found that they can meet regulatory mandates to lower measured emission levels in surrounding areas by constructing tall smokestacks that disperse the pollution further afield.

Yet regulation of personal behavior is especially constrained by crowding out. The flexibility of many persons in responding to government efforts to control their activities, the wide variety of tastes that citizens hold, and the sheer number of persons who may be the subject of a regulation combine to make crowding out a particularly vexing problem. Although crowding out does not assure failure (and in some instances may even facilitate success), it generally set limits on, and raises the costs of, regulatory policies.

Consider an issue that we discussed when referring to firms: the use of safety equipment in automobiles (principally seat belts, air bags, and antilock brakes). When it comes to getting manufacturers to install safety features in their cars, the starkest regulatory hurdle is establishing a commitment to a policy. But when the focus shifts to drivers, the fundamental issue is encouraging people with safer cars to act with the same care that they had previously. Otherwise, the effects of more investment in automobile safety are crowded out by individual choices about driving.

Such offsetting behavior is important when assessing policies for improving the safety features of cars (Lave and Weber 1970). The most extensively studied issue of this kind concerns seat belts. Do drivers wearing seat belts drive more recklessly? Although some claim that seat belts and mandatory seat belt laws caused no reduction in occupant fatalities, and others claim that fatalities were reduced by less than predicted by naive analysis, the consensus is that offsetting behavior is substantial and that the increase in reckless driving has endangered pedestrians (Peltzman 1975, Blomquist

1988, Keeler 1994). Similarly, and although investigated in less depth, some evidence suggests that air bags have also reduced injuries less than hoped. Not only does the evidence, analogous to the findings for seat belts, show that air bags cause more reckless driving (Peterson, Hoffer, and Millner 1995), but the data indicate that air bags may also induce other types of hazardous behavior that offset some of their benefits. For example, the National Highway Traffic Safety Administration is worried about the dangers of placing children in car seats that face air bags (U.S. Department of Health and Human Services 1995, Reed 1996). Specifically, it appears that the benefits of air bags are reduced if parents place their children in the front seat (which is presumably more convenient) rather than in the back where they are safer. Thus, if parents ignore the dangers of air bags by placing their children in front seats, safety may little improve.

Data on antilock brakes are also corroborative.[25] For example, a German study of taxicab crashes in 1981–1983 showed similar accident rates with and without antilock brakes. Taxi drivers with antilock brakes were "less accommodating about getting into the correct lanes, cut curves closer, held less to their own traffic lane, took risks more frequently, and paid less attention to traffic situations ahead of them than did drivers of normal vehicles" ("Antilock Brakes," 1994, p. 4).

Auto safety is a nice example because systematic investigation is generally straightforward. But the logic of crowding often applies when people can change their behavior. For example, on a different topic, efforts to reduce unintended pregnancies by increasing the use of birth control may be less successful than hoped because sexual activity may increase and, assuming some failures of birth control devices, the number of pregnancies will be greater than if there was no offsetting behavior. Policies designed to reduce unwanted births by encouraging investment in abortion clinics may also be less effective if more women become accidentally pregnant on the ground that abortion is an option but some subsequently decide against abortions. Similarly, because narcotics and alcohol are substitutes, policies that reduce alcohol use may unintentionally increase drug use. For instance, DiNardo and Lemieux (1992) find that a higher legal minimum drinking age increases the consumption of marijuana.

Social Pressures and Equilibrium Selection

Whereas much of the previous discussion concentrated on the constraints that hurt regulatory policy, in other circumstances such constraints can make regulation more effective. Specifically, an activist government may be able to guide which policy outcome is realized when multiple equilibria exist and when social pressures influence behavior.

This possibility was illustrated in the Introduction when we compared smoking with automobile emissions. For smoking, multiple equilibria exist and social pressures are present. Crowding in is thus possible and policy becomes increasingly credible. For automobile emissions, the equilibrium is unique and social pressures do not push citizens to conform. Crowding in is limited and credibility is weak. The key distinctions are the existence of multiple equilibria and the likelihood that people know and care whether others conform.

The potential interaction of multiple equilibria and social pressures, in conjunction with other economic constraints, suggests that government may sometimes achieve regulatory goals by taking advantage of multiple equilibria and by making the public feel that some behavior is good or bad. Given multiple equilibria, political suasion may result in social pressures, crowding in, revised expectations of credibility, and movements toward the desired equilibrium. To return to examples related to the automobile, suppose government wants to discourage drunk driving. If, through moral suasion or stiff penalties, government induces some persons who would otherwise drive drunk not to (Chaloupka, Saffer, and Grossman 1993), peer pressure may cause others to drink less. Consistent with this perspective on crowding in, shame and embarrassment, as well as legal sanctions, appear to lower drunk driving (Grasmick, Bursik, and Arneklev 1993). Reduced drinking can then generate additional political support and make policy yet more credible. Firms that rely on selling alcohol will adapt in ways that can reduce their opposition to programs discouraging drunk driving. Bars, for example, may encourage designated drivers not to drink, arrange transportation home for drunk customers, switch to nonalcohol sales, and so on (U.S. Department of Health and Human Services 1988a). Or automobile companies may invest in ignition interlock systems that prevent inebriated drivers from starting their autos. Alternatively, drunk driving may become widely accepted, and another set of attitudes, expectations, and investments, all part of a different equilibrium, is realized.

Again, such possibilities for government action to move behavior from one equilibrium to another may be relevant for any policy where social pressure can be brought to bear. For instance, liberalized divorce laws may cause crowding in as other couples consider divorce more acceptable (on the effects of divorce legislation, see Kidd 1995).[26] Once divorce becomes more acceptable, institutions may emerge catering to singles who were formerly married, assisting the children of single parents, and creating expectations that a liberal policy will continue. A high-divorce equilibrium may emerge. This general story seems consistent with both the dramatic increase in divorce in the United States (from roughly 4 percent to 16 percent of marriages from 1970 to 1990), the wide variation in divorce rates among subgroups, and a growing movement to reform divorce laws and to reduce the social acceptability of divorce (on the reform movement, see Gallagher 1996, Schoenfeld 1996).

Conditions for Regulatory Success

We have demonstrated that regulations can succeed. But obstacles related to credibility, expectations, equilibrium selection, and crowding out restrict which objectives are likely attainable, influence the type of regulatory instruments that will be effective, and raise the costs of success even under the best conditions.

As mentioned, credibility and its interaction with other economic constraints appear especially crucial. Whereas weak credibility may undermine regulatory initiatives, policy established as credible may induce investment and promote the success of regulations. After such investments are made, expectations may be revised, political support may increase, crowding in may take place, and a preferred equilibrium may be attained.

Other factors may mediate this process. Within limits, market structure can influence the effectiveness of regulations. Although politicians control powerful tools, democratic procedures impose constraints; in particular, the inability to commit directly may lead the current government to favor policies that require firms to make irreversible investments.

Regulating personal behavior, as we broadly defined it, also has its own opportunities and obstacles. Although credibility is less relevant than it is for firms, crowding in and equilibrium selection are probably more important. People may behave in ways that negate the goals of public policies. But when individuals' behavior is subject to social pressure, government may exploit crowding in and make regulation effective.

In short, regulation is more likely to succeed in some definable circumstances than in others, although usually economic constraints such as credibility are important. Regulatory success is likely when government tries to control firms in a diversified industry, where regulation is less subject to threats of noncompliance. Regulations directed at people will more likely succeed when changing the actions of a few persons is likely to persuade others to behave similarly. Where conditions differ, regulation will prove more difficult.

4

Producing Goods and Services:
Getting the Right Mix

Outside of paying taxes, the primary interaction of many people with government is in consuming the services that government directly or indirectly produces. Citizens may send their children to taxpayer-supported schools, enjoy government-provided parks, commute to work on publicly built and publicly maintained roads, and receive medical care at publicly financed hospitals. When a personal or a national crisis arises, citizens may also depend on police, fire-fighting, and military protection produced with their tax dollars. For instance, in the United States government spent 4.8 percent of the nation's 1993 GDP on defense, 4.5 percent on medical care, and 4.9 percent on police and corrections (Dawson and Stan 1995).

Yet despite popular reliance on such goods and services—what for our purposes we label *production* (and what political scientists typically call distribution)—governments often fail to furnish the right mix and amount of outputs. Although, to paraphrase comments made in our Introduction, government sometimes succeeds, the overall picture has created dismay. Not only is the ability to produce the outputs desired by citizens questioned, but in other instances politicians fail to limit production of goods and services to predetermined levels. Curiously, though government often appears unable to produce (consider the embarrassment created by the inability of the United States Federal Aviation Administration (FAA) to develop a new air traffic control system over the course of a decade), in other situations it appears subject to inexorable creep, with small, manageable policies expanding into out-of-control behemoths (Model Cities is a classic example that is often cited).[1]

Doubts about the government's efficiency in producing some outputs, and skepticism about its ability to limit provision of other goods or services, have some solid theoretical justification. We shall see that production raises problems similar to those associated with the regulation of firms, stemming from imperfect credibility, crowding out, and rational expectations. Concerning production, these factors may hinder government efforts both to induce production *and* to limit outputs.[2]

Production of some goods and services may face three difficulties:

1. Government output may merely supplant production that would otherwise occur. As a result, crowding out can reduce or eliminate the aggregate effect of government efforts to produce additional goods or services.

2. Citizens or firms who doubt that government will continue to provide a good or a service may reject making investments necessary for production. Achieving production goals is then likely to be difficult.

3. Government may be unable to restrict output if it cannot refuse providing a good or service and if crowding out is small. When juxtaposed against the difficulty of inducing investment, this suggests that government must often trade one credibility problem—the belief that it may repudiate its plans to produce—for another problem—doubts about the credibility of its policies to limit eligibility. Put differently, the very investments that can induce consumers and firms to believe that government will produce or buy some goods or services may be the actions that impede limiting consumption.

Thus, problems of crowding out, credibility, and expectations may sometimes stop government from reaching its production goals. Also, when the credibility difficulties that make limiting production problematic are overcome, another credibility problem is created as those actions facilitating production undermine the limitation of outputs.

Also, just as constraints such as commitment can influence the effectiveness of different regulatory instruments, such constraints may also affect how successful some means of producing goods and services are compared to others. Types of investment and methods of production that are otherwise undesirable may become more attractive. Most notably, where credibility problems of inducing or limiting production are severe, government may have reason to arrange production in a manner that would seem inefficient. When aiming to increase production, government may want to invest in large capacity, which makes cutting production save little in costs. And when attempting to limit production, government may want to furnish goods directly, rather than design goods or services in a way that would later allow the private sector to increase production.

In other words, although government may successfully produce many goods and services, arriving at the preferred mix will be difficult and the optimal production methods may appear strange. The analysis of production is particularly notable for a series of trade-offs that must be made even by well-meaning politicians trying to establish the right mix and levels of outputs.

What Is Production?

Governmental production, for our purposes, is the direct or the indirect manufacturing of goods or provision of services by government. As implied above, direct and indirect production may be substitutes. For instance, whether government should produce outputs or instead have the private market furnish these goods and services under contractual agreement ("contracting out") is hotly debated (Kettl 1993).[3] Thus, government can directly control housing, run a school district, and collect trash, or it can provide people with vouchers to receive the same level of housing or education and contract with private concerns for trash collection.

Although related to, and overlapping with, regulation and redistribution, production's focus on government's supply of goods and services makes it qualitatively and conceptually distinct. For example, pharmaceutical regulation may have government decide which drugs private firms can produce, but the central exchange is between firms and consumers; by contrast, presuming government leaves development and production of pharmaceuticals to others, at the heart of government production may lie which products government purchases for the medical care that it provides. Similarly, regulation may specify entry barriers in the form of teacher qualifications even if all schools are private, whereas production may entail educating students in government-run schools or paying private providers through vouchers.[4] In the same spirit, whereas redistribution transfers wealth or income, production creates goods (for example, housing) that are frequently part of redistributive efforts.[5]

This description of production leads to three questions:

1. Can government increase aggregate provision of a good also produced by the private sector, or does crowding out undermine such efforts?
2. Can government produce goods that require private investments, or do concerns about changes in policy thwart such endeavors?
3. Can government effectively and credibly limit production despite inevitable pressures to loosen eligibility standards and to increase the amount that it provides?

Together, these questions embody much of what makes the analysis of government production intriguing. As mentioned, government production often aims to augment existing private production of a good or service. An obvious, but hardly the only, example of such activity is governmental attempts to supplement existing charitable or philanthropic activities, ranging from feeding the poor to subsidizing the arts. Although programs to aid the poor and to support the arts exist even in the absence of government production or subsidization, such efforts may be viewed as insufficient without additional government support.

A naive approach of the sort that we discussed (and rejected) in previous chapters would suggest that government's ability to augment private production is beyond debate. Government need merely produce more, with total output equal to the sum of the new public and the previous private production.

As already foreshadowed, several pitfalls can undermine such efforts. First, government programs may merely crowd out private actions, with public production replacing all or some of the previous private production. The greater the initial private production, the more likely increased output will be problematic. Second, when production requires investment, increased provision may be thwarted if the long-term commitment of government to providing additional goods is questioned. The more private investment that is required from economic actors with foresight, the greater the obstacle that credibility problems will pose for increasing production.

As also indicated earlier, the credibility problem has another side. A government that can produce a good or a service but cannot commit to denying service to some persons may be unable to constrain program growth. This inability to deny service may make public programs expensive and ineffective. Government may therefore reject the program in the first place or it may use production methods that limit expansion.

Clearly, obstacles to successful government production created by the reduction of private efforts, the undermining of necessary investment, and difficulties in limiting program size are interrelated. Nevertheless, for analytic convenience we will examine them sequentially.

Crowding Out Private Provision

Although much of the underlying logic is comparable, goods prone to crowding out may be categorized into those mostly produced for sale by firms and those provided by nonprofit organizations financed by philanthropic contributions. The main difference between the two is that profit motives drive market production, whereas free riding (where some avoid contributing in the hope that others will) is central when crowding out interacts with philanthropy (for a classic discussion of free riding, see Olson 1965).

Crowding Out Market Goods

When a product is sold on the market, increased government production of the good or service can reduce private output in two ways. First, large governmental provision may reduce the market price, making private production less profitable.[6] Second, increased government production increases demand for the inputs used by producers (such as specialized labor, machinery, and raw materials), thereby raising the prices of these inputs and reducing the profitability of private production. Both reductions in market prices and increases in input costs have the same result: greater provision of a good or service by government may reduce private provision.[7] Indeed, empirically, crowding out as a result of government production is likely more severe than when private firms, even large corporations, expand output, because increased government activity will less typically be a response to heightened demand.

As an example of such government production, consider the Strategic Petroleum Reserve (SPR) in the United States (see Weimer 1982). Between 1970 and 1990, the U.S. government accumulated nearly 600 million barrels of petroleum in the SPR (stored physically in salt domes in Louisiana and Texas) with the stated purpose of providing a hedge against cuts in world supply. The effectiveness of these reserves in reducing American vulnerability to an oil embargo or to other reduction in oil supplies was, however, mitigated by crowding out. As the SPR grew, the value of petroleum reserves to private holders correspondingly dropped. Moreover, to the extent that the SPR program raised the cost of stockpiling petroleum (for example, by increasing the price of the best sites for storage, the wages of petroleum engineers, or the price of oil), investing in private stockpiles became more expensive. Thus, private inventories started declining when the SPR's effects began to be felt in the late 1970s (Nivola and Crandall 1995).

Such crowding out, however, need not be great under all conditions and at all times. Rather, in several circumstances crowding out can be small:

1. *When the economy has idle workers and factories.* Similar to a point that we made regarding fiscal policy, increasing production of some good will be easier, and the inflationary effects of government production will be smaller, if much labor and capital are initially idle.

For a dramatic illustration, consider production in the United States during World War II. Despite the war fears in Europe and in the Far East, only 2 percent of total national output in 1939 consisted of military production. Were the economy at full capacity, increased military production would have necessarily displaced production elsewhere in the economy. Firms would have found producing military goods more profitable than staying in their present lines of business, and inputs for many activities would have become more expensive. Given, however, that the United States was just emerging from the Depression, the country's large untapped economic resources (for example, labor was readily available as the unemployment rate in 1939 was 17 percent) were mobilized for the war effort without reducing other production. Even as the United States rapidly mobilized—by 1943, 40 percent of output was directed toward war production[8]—total production expanded so much that during the five war years consumers' purchases of goods and services also increased by 12 percent (Milward 1977).

2. *When government is expected to reverse policy.* If government commitment to a policy is weak, private economic actors engage in few actions that undermine effectiveness.

Suppose, for example, that a government decides to open public beaches. If government commitment to providing such services is strong, private beach clubs may exit as their input prices increase and the price they can charge declines. Alternatively, if these private firms believe that the government's desire to maintain public facilities will quickly wane (for example, that government inattention will lead to dirty public beaches without lifeguards and other amenities), then these private clubs may remain in business to retain their clientele and to later attract dissatisfied consumers who turn to the market.[9] Similarly, holders of petroleum reserves may not divest (or divest less than they would have otherwise) if they believe that the government will stop adding to, or begin subtracting from, the reserves. For example, in 1996 President Clinton ordered the SPR to sell 12 million barrels of crude oil, with the goal of reducing gasoline prices, although the SPR was never intended to deal with such changes; even before this price rise, Republican senators had proposed selling 15–17 billion barrels to reduce oil prices and raise revenue.

3. *When short-run effects are considered.* For reasons roughly parallel to our earlier discussion of how monetary policy is more effective over the short run than over the long run, crowding out is likely a less severe problem in the short run. It will take time for the full effects of crowding out to be felt.

Two main reasons account for the difference between short-run and long-run effects. First, when input prices are sticky, firms profit little from reducing production quickly. Second, given significant investment, it will take time to shut down or to shift production to other outputs even if costs unexpectedly increase.

Consequently, increased government output may little reduce private production over a short period. But over longer periods (and, again, assuming credibility and assuming firms can enter and exit with ease), as government production reduces output prices and increases production costs, the production of private goods and services will decline and crowding out will become more severe.

In short, crowding out of market production can severely limit the extent and the effectiveness of government production: it can both reduce demand directly and increase input prices for private production, raising the cost of outputs in the process.

Crowding Out Private Philanthropy

As foreshadowed, the story is roughly analogous when we turn our attention away from services by the market and toward services produced by nonprofits. Crowding-out problems similar to those impairing efforts to supplement production of market goods and services may arise when government tries to produce services also financed by private philanthropy.

More specifically, just as increasing government output of a good or service previously provided by the market results in lower prices and higher production costs, comparable provision of a good or service where philanthropy is important reduces benefits from additional nonprofit provision and raises input prices. Consequently, when government furnishes more of a good or a service that is also financed by private contributions, philanthropists may contribute less. For instance, supporters of symphony orchestras may believe that their contributions do little to increase the quality and the availability of performances when government also funds the arts. Conversely, when the U.S. government reduces funding for such organizations as the Public Broadcasting System, private contributors may make up some of the shortfall. That effect is reflected in the statement by the head of marketing for the Public Broadcast System that "corporations seem to be more than willing to make up the money that is [being] taken away by the government" (Brunelli 1995, p. 12).[10]

Such experience is consistent with theoretical analyses concluding that government supply of public goods crowds out private supply, as contributors free ride at government expense. Indeed, according to such analyses, crowding out is complete if all persons initially donate and government then provides the public good (Warr 1982, Bergstrom, Blume, and Varian 1986, Bernheim 1986).

To illustrate, suppose that each of 1,000 consumers with a pre-tax income of $50,000 pays $1,000 in taxes, donates $300 for a public good such as educational television, and uses the remaining $48,700 to spend on himself. The total contribution for the public good is thus $300,000. Now suppose that government wishes to see $400,000 worth of the public good provided and increases taxes by $100 per capita for this purpose. Consumers preferring the previous allocation need only reduce their contributions by $100 each to retain it. The $100 in increased government spending will be matched by a $100 decline in private spending, rendering government policy ineffective.

For further illustration, consider a two-player game, with one player the government and the other player a consumer, where each player must decide whether to contribute. Assume, as before, that a consumer's additional benefit from the good is smaller the higher its provision. Specifically, suppose a consumer values one unit at four dollars and values two units at six dollars. Let both the government and a consumer provide either one or zero units of the good and let the cost to a consumer of providing a unit of the good be three dollars. Table 4.1, which lists assumed gross payoffs to the consumer from taking an action given the action of the government, shows that the consumer has an incentive to free ride if the government provides the good in question.

Specifically, if government provides one unit of the good, the consumer will wish to provide nothing (net benefits when abstaining are 4 instead of $6 - 3 = 3$ when contributing). If the government provides nothing, the consumer will choose to provide one unit (with a net benefit of $4 - 3 = 1$ instead of 0). The incentive to free ride results in government provision crowding out private activities.

Parenthetically, the same logic applies for a federal government that funds production at the state and local levels. When the federal government funds local spending on some activity, although crowding out is incomplete rather than one-for-one and total spending does increase, local governments reduce their own spending.[11]

Comparable empirical evidence about crowding out of philanthropy is mixed. Roberts (1984) finds much crowding out, claiming that government subsidies for the poor in the United States have largely displaced private assistance. Though individuals once contributed substantially to assist the poor, philanthropy to the needy began to decline in the 1930s with the rise of the New Deal welfare state; almost none of the $50 billion donated to private charity in 1981 was for the poor. Crowding out is virtually complete, as one dollar of private support evaporated for each dollar the U.S. government gave to aid the poor. Similar results are reported by Thorpe and Phelps (1991) regarding the private provision of medical care. At one time, private hospitals provided medical services to those who were unable to pay. But as public hospitals increasingly treated indigents, private hospitals showed increasing reluctance to provide such charitable service.

Table 4.1 A private contribution game (consumer payoffs according to contribution level)

Players		Government	
	Amount of good provided (units)	One	Zero
Consumer	One	6	4
	Zero	4	0

Others studying charity generally discover less crowding out (Steinberg 1989). For example, Abrams and Schmitz (1978) estimate that crowding out in the Unites States is 28 percent. Posnett and Sandler (1989) uncover no crowding out in their study of 300 British charities. Results finding such incomplete crowding out are descriptively consistent with contributors getting direct pleasure from giving[12] or signaling the high quality of a project (or signaling that government supervision will assure a good product).[13]

Crowding out may be limited by several factors:

1. *Low initial support.* It seems simplistic to say that there will be little to crowd out if initial production without governmental intervention is small. But what makes this observation notable for goods and services financed by philanthropy is the implication that government may be especially successful at producing outputs that generate little private support (interestingly, for reasons similar to why fiscal policy works best when government spending is on goods in low demand). For example, because contributors are unlikely to donate to assist drug addicts or to produce national defense privately, these services can be more effectively supplied than "popular" commodities such as research for cures to childhood diseases. This, of course, ignores the likelihood that many programs that cannot draw donations, such as aid to drug addicts, are also politically unpopular.

2. *Provision by government that exceeds what persons initially contributed.* Closely related to the first point, crowding out will be incomplete if government provides more of the good than was initially available. Alternatively, when government contributions are smaller than what donors would provide without public support—aid to educational television, symphony orchestras, or museums—crowding out may be severe.

3. *Expectations that government will reverse policy.* Analogous to consumers of market goods, philanthropists may continue to contribute if they believe that government commitment is weak. In turn, the decision by private actors to continue contributing may weaken political pressure for maintaining public provision, which may make expectations about government's lack of credibility self-fulfilling.

4. *Provision by government of an input used to produce the good.* Re-

lated to the idea that government is successful when private contributions are small, it is possible that the public provision of inputs used by charitable organizations can complement rather than substitute for other production. Indeed, crowding in may replace crowding out.

To illustrate this last factor, suppose that production of a good requires capital and a variable input and that the greater the amount of capital, the greater the additional output from the variable input. With abundant capital, increased use of the variable input greatly increases output, inducing individuals to increase their contributions of that input.[14] This process may, for example, explain why little crowding out is seen in higher education—government support complements private support. Government funding may help, along with tuition and other revenue sources, to buy inputs for which private donors find contributing unappealing (for example, building maintenance, library books), while restricted gifts from individuals and firms pay for high-profile endeavors (for example, laboratories for applied research, sports facilities). Similarly, besides its validation effect, the Corporation for Public Broadcasting may need governmental funding for essential infrastructure that is unattractive for private donors. Such contributors may, for example, be interested only in underwriting specific programs and want overhead to be covered from other sources.

Thus, as with goods produced by the market, crowding out can be a serious problem for goods and services whose funding otherwise heavily relies on philanthropy. Where firms may reduce production of goods they sell on the market because government outputs reduce profits, each donor may free ride by letting others pay the bill, and so reducing total contributions. Ironically, unless donors contribute because they value the sheer act of giving, crowding out is likely to be large except for those services or commodities for which philanthropists contribute little in the first place or where the government is seen as having little commitment.

Credibility as an Obstacle to Inducing Production

Not only may crowding out offset public production, but government also faces a credibility problem when trying to increase the output of a good or a service in its role as a direct or an indirect producer. Inducing workers and firms to invest can be problematic, making production difficult or impossible.[15]

Analogous to regulation, this credibility problem arises from at least two related behaviors:

1. *Firms and potential workers may anticipate that government will stop purchasing their goods or services.* Consequently, private economic actors will hesitate to make the initial investments needed for production.
2. *Firms and workers may fear that, although purchases and employment will continue, government will abandon programs that would make investments profitable.* Of particular concern is that government will renege on financial promises—the hold-up problem discussed previously—offering to pay only low prices after firms make costly investments.

There should be a strong relationship between these two considerations. On the one hand, investments by the government itself or by relevant workers and firms make continuation of relevant public programs more likely. On the other hand, firms or workers that invest subject themselves to future hold-up when government repudiates its agreements and reduces the prices it pays; the government can make the production unprofitable, ex post, by refusing to compensate for fixed investments. Anticipating hold-up by not having capital costs covered makes investment less likely, which results in a greater likelihood of program termination.

The picture, however, is not totally bleak: under specified conditions, government can explicitly make policy more credible or can reduce the cost to firms and workers of investing (indirectly making policy more credible in the process).

The first credibility problem, that the government will reduce its purchases after private investments are made, may be ameliorated when government makes investments that have few alternative uses. In other words, rather than plan for flexibility should external conditions change, government can do the opposite. For instance, the credibility of support for military installations can be increased by situating them in remote areas with limited alternative uses of the land or facilities. That would assure firms asked to make complementary investments that the government would gain little by closing the installation. Private investment would then become less risky.[16]

Similarly, government has reason to structure the investments asked of private actors (as compared with its own investments) so that they have many alternative uses. This suggests that purchasing goods not specifically designed to meet unique government specifications is desirable, both because such products may be cheaper to produce and because these goods can be redirected toward the private sector if government withdraws from the market.[17]

Credibility can also be enhanced by government compensating investors earlier rather than later (or even by directly paying for investments). Government thereby increases the incentives of firms and workers to invest. Not only is the risk to investors associated with future program cancellation reduced but, as such up-front expenditures lower the government's cost of continuing the program, the risk that policy will be abandoned declines.

For instance, government may subsidize the training of future military officers by such programs as the Reserve Officer Training Corps or by offering free education at government-run military academies. This may be in the government's interest because subsidizing the cost of a person's military education instead of promising high salaries may better aid military recruitment by reducing the risk to those contemplating a military career. Given the government's initial investment and low payroll costs, potential recruits will have more confidence that they will be able to have a long career in the military than if they had paid for their own education with the expectation of higher compensation. In turn, because subsidizing educational expenses reduces the marginal costs of manning the military, the credibility needed to induce additional investment is more likely to exist; for example, by having trained a large corps of military officers, government reduces the future costs of defense, encouraging expectations that government is committed to the military, and making the private investments needed for maintaining large armed forces more attractive.

Analogously, government may establish credibility and counter fears of a hold-up by building facilities to produce goods or by assuming an equity stake (see Rogerson 1994 for a discussion related to military procurement). Doing so reduces the risk assumed by private producers—mitigating the downside of government reneging—and increases credibility by lowering future costs of continuing the government's program. Given this logic, when credibility issues are severe, government may want to build its own production facilities.

Government can also allay the fears of firms and workers that they will be held up by putting itself in a similar position, for example, by creating a bilateral monopoly where it puts itself in a position of having only one supplier. Simply put, firms may be more willing to invest if they can also hold up government.[18] For example, during the World Wars firms knew that government would pay a premium for tanks, airplanes, and other military equipment; such firms did not need to refuse delivery overtly to hold up the military but could instead claim delays, refuse to modify designs of goods produced, or pay less attention to quality.[19]

Government may achieve the same objective by creating institutional restrictions. Requirements such as due process or multiple layers of review, with each layer given veto power, may make it more difficult for government to repudiate agreements, thus encouraging needed investments (Levy and Spiller 1996).

Lastly, government may enhance credibility by relying on political endogeneity. For example, political support for program continuation is likely to be stronger when an identified group of workers, either in government or in a few firms, relies on the program for their jobs. The increased support, in turn, gives more incentive for firms to make the requisite investments. This credibility effect is likely to be especially strong when labor is unionized (on public sector unions, see Stieber 1972, Babcock, Engberg, and Glazer 1997). Though, like many of the actions discussed, significant costs may be attached, increased power of unions can buttress credibility.

In short, credibility is a dual-edged sword. Many actions that better commit government to continued production may also produce fears of hold-up. Although these difficulties can be ameliorated, even a well-meaning and adroit democratic government will inevitably find itself making trade-offs.

Credibility as an Obstacle to Restricting Production

Producing goods and services is not the only challenge that governments face in their provision. Another problem that they confront is restraining the quantity produced. Failure to restrain provision can result in large program expansion, with output levels that far exceed those that politicians with the ability to commit would choose.

The difficulty of limiting service follows straightforwardly from our earlier emphasis on inducing investment to increase production. Government may find it difficult to refuse to furnish a good or a service if the costs of additional provision are low (and investment often makes them low), even if the marginal costs exceed the benefits and despite *ex ante* rules restricting eligibility. As a result, credible enforcement of rules limiting eligibility to receive goods produced directly or indirectly by government is likely most effective when costs of additional production are high. And such costs should be especially high when capacity is restricted. Thus, a government may want to ensure that investment does not create excess capacity. Limits on capacity could be desirable even if additional investment is optimal—for example, to handle surges in demand—given credible commitment.

Put differently, government may be unable to deny specific persons a good or service while maintaining the capacity to provide it for others. Elsewhere we label denial of such consumption as *specific rationing* (Glazer and Rothenberg 1999). Although civil servants are often viewed as constrained by rules to the point of letting common sense go unheeded (Bardach and Kagan 1982), even well-meaning officials can fall prey to the converse, as it can be impossible to follow rules that are actually quite reasonable.

Consequently, one way of limiting aggregate consumption, setting rules on eligibility via specific rationing, can be unenforceable. Moreover, this credibility problem has some intriguing implications for how consumption might be limited.

Notably, a result of weak credibility given capacity is that effective rationing must be indirect, requiring what we call *abstract rationing*. Abstract rationing is rationing out of necessity based on limited capacity; some consumers are denied a good or a service when capacity is insufficient to serve everyone.

To reiterate, abstract rationing can be desirable for reasons of commitment. Whereas rules designed explicitly to deny eligibility to identified persons lack credibility, a policy that makes it difficult to furnish a good or a service to all who desire it necessarily denies service to some. Such implicit rationing, achieved by limiting how much can be produced, may be feasible. In this context, rationing decisions take on a less personal, less politically volatile, tone than when specific rationing choices are made.

A disadvantage of abstract rationing lies in the delays imposed, for essentially political reasons, on those served. In theory, capacity to provide a good or service could exist but remain generally unused. People denied service, however, could point to the existence of idle capacity and argue that they should be served as well. Waits should be particularly long when much physical capacity or specialized labor is required in production. And though production delays of government outputs are typically attributed to bureaucratic ineptitude, the logic of abstract rationing virtually requires that a well-functioning system has lengthy queues (on waiting and rationing, see Barzel 1974, Lindsay and Feigenbaum 1984).

Consider the provision of medical care. Credibility problems imply that specific rationing of health services—where consequences of denying care can be severe—is likely difficult. Abstract rationing is more feasible.

Indeed, experience suggests that abstract rationing has been more successful at restricting access to health care than has specific rationing. Certainly, successful attempts at specific rationing in the United States are rare (Baily 1993).[20] Although no constitutional provisions prevent rationing of goods such as medical care, examination of federal and state laws, in conjunction with judicial and administrative rulings, shows a system heavily biased against denying care where capacity exists.

Illustrative of the dominant legislative response to specific rationing is the 1986 Consolidated Omnibus Budget Reconciliation Act (COBRA), which mandates that any hospital with a Medicare provider agreement must, regardless of a patient's ability to pay, screen and stabilize any patient with an emergency condition. This obligation falls on the hospital and on all physicians providing on-call services at the hospital. Thus, COBRA largely forbids specific rationing.

The courts have reinforced this bias against specific rationing. For instance, they are reluctant to enforce contracts that ration service to consenting consumers (for example, by restricting costly procedures in the last months of life). More generally, an expectation has developed that care, once begun, will be provided for as long as needed and will continue even for patients who cannot pay and for treatments that are exorbitantly expensive.[21]

Administrative reactions have also made specific rationing less credible. Even state governments exploring specific rationing have met federal resistance. In one highly publicized decision, the Bush administration refused to allow the state of Oregon to deny care for some illnesses although only the most marginal medical services were to be restricted (Janofsky 1994). Not only have physicians circumvented the state's rules on treatments by creative diagnoses, but the federal Health Care Finance Administration, which oversees Medicaid, has continued to restrict Oregon's ability to deny treatments (Kilborn 1999). Similarly, Medicare administrators have extended care to include several previously excluded procedures such as kidney dialysis and heart transplants, at great financial cost. Such experiences show that governments (in these cases, state and federal) cannot easily resist pressures to provide services to people with diseases who, by the rules, must be allowed to suffer or die.

Perhaps, one might respond, countries with national health insurance impose specific rationing because they have more credibility in implementing specific service limits. But the evidence suggests that, regardless of their health care system, governments generally serve citizens when the capacity exists to treat them. If anything, data indicate that other nations are better than the United States at abstract rationing: the main policy tool that these nations use is limiting consumption via capacity constraints.

A look at Great Britain demonstrates abstract rationing in practice.[22] As suggested, abstract rationing is particularly effective when large capital expenditures or investments in training highly specialized staff must be made.[23] Thus, dialysis is limited in Britain because the requisite equipment purchases are constrained, as are investments in training qualified nurses and technicians; admission to intensive care units for all but the most severe cases is difficult because facilities are scarce; and CAT scans are used at 20 percent of the U.S. rate. Generally, procedures that demand much time from specialized personnel or claim much scarce physical plant (for example, surgery requiring operating room time) are hard to obtain. By contrast, abstract rationing is, predictably, ineffective when capacity is hard to restrict. Thus, care that can be furnished by regular medical personnel or from ordinary drugs and supplies is plentiful. For example, in contrast to the United States, Britain spends as much on total parenteral nutrition (nutrition bypassing the digestive tract) as it spends on CAT scans. This would seem to reflect that, of the two procedures, only total parenteral nutrition requires no appreciable capital outlay and can be ordered by physicians on a case-by-case basis.

Also reflecting the interaction of abstract rationing and issues of credibility are the delays for which the British and other national health systems are notorious. In Britain, for example, one-third of all admitted patients must wait three months or more for hospital treatment and 6 percent must wait for a year.

Such delays are rare in the United States. The reason for this discrepancy is straightforward. With its reliance on private markets to provide health care, the United States stands in marked contrast to other wealthy countries. The United States has expanded rather than constrained capacity. Diverse policy choices—from the availability of Medicare reimbursement to the issuance of tax-exempt bonds—have all been credited with fueling big capital projects that expand capacity (Stevens 1989). Reflecting the large capital stock in the United States, American physicians have been less likely than physicians in other countries to complain of poorly equipped medical facilities (Blendon et al. 1993).[24] Also, illustratively, as shown in Table 4.2, the United States has spent far more on medical care than have other countries.

While the United States spent about 14 percent of its 1995 GDP on

Table 4.2 Per capita health spending and total health expenditures as a percentage of gross domestic product

Country	1970	1980	1990	1995	Per capita expenditures in 1995 ($)
Turkey	NA	4.0	4.0	5.2	272
Greece	4.0	4.3	5.3	5.5	634
Luxembourg	4.1	6.8	7.2	6.5	1,962
Denmark	6.1	6.8	6.3	6.6	1,344
Japan	4.6	6.6	6.6	6.9	1,454
United Kingdom	4.5	5.8	6.2	6.9	1,213
New Zealand	5.2	7.2	7.3	7.1	1,151
Spain	3.7	5.6	6.6	7.3	992
Ireland	5.6	9.2	7.0	7.6	1,201
Sweden	7.2	9.4	8.6	7.6	1,339
Austria	5.4	7.9	8.4	7.8	1,573
Portugal	3.1	5.9	5.4	7.8	939
Finland	5.7	6.5	8.0	7.9	1,289
Norway	5.0	6.6	7.5	8.0	1,754
Belgium	4.1	6.6	7.6	8.1	1,653
Iceland	5.2	6.4	8.2	8.1	1,571
Australia	5.7	7.3	8.2	8.4	1,609
Italy	5.2	6.9	8.1	8.4	1,559
Netherlands	6.0	8.0	8.2	8.8	1,643
Switzerland	5.2	7.3	8.4	9.5	2,280
France	5.8	7.6	8.9	9.7	1,868
Canada	7.1	7.4	9.4	9.9	2,005
Germany	5.9	8.4	8.3	10.3	2,020
United States	7.4	9.2	12.6	14.1	3,462

Source: U.S. Congress, House Committee on Ways and Means (1998 *Green Book)*, Table C-31. U.S. Government Printing Office.

medical care, no other nation significantly exceeded 10 percent of its GDP. Over the period 1970–1995, growth of medical spending as a share of GDP in the United States was 90 percent. Only three countries (Belgium, Portugal, and Turkey) had higher growth rates. The United Kingdom increased its share by 53 percent, about half the U.S. increase, and Sweden and Denmark raised their shares by less than 10 percent.

Admittedly, and as foreshadowed, the one widespread attempt in the United States to restrict capacity via abstract rationing failed because of excessive incentives for investment.[25] In the late 1970s and the early 1980s, the federal government required states to prevent duplication of medical facilities. In response, all states but Louisiana required health care providers to obtain a "certificate of need" (CON) from a public agency before making a capital expenditure larger than $100,000 or $150,000. Failure to obtain a CON could result in disqualification for Medicaid and Medicare reimbursement.

Weak incentives, however, caused the CON program to limit hospital construction mostly in states with excess capacity, to have no effect on hospital investments, and to shift investment from hospital beds to more loosely regulated hospital equipment (Feldstein 1993). All the CON program proves is that abstract rationing that disregards issues of credibility and investment will fail.

The evidence therefore suggests that attempts at specific rationing of medical care have failed. What rationing exists is via capacity constraints, which generate queues and delay.

Lessons generated from the study of medical care apply to many goods and services that government supplies. For example, public universities can more successfully limit enrollment by restricting construction of campuses or essential facilities on existing campuses (for example, dormitories) rather than by issuing rules detailing how many, or what quality, students will be admitted.[26] Similarly, communities may best control development by limiting sewer and water capacity rather than by issuing rules about allowable growth.[27]

Even more important than presenting a litany of examples are general implications, several counterintuitive, stemming from credibility issues related to limiting production. First, *what often appear as barriers to the production of services may help limit the amount of services provided.* As seems to be reflected with national health care, government may wish to provide services directly—even if private firms could produce them more cheaply—as a means of restricting physical capacity when specific rationing is not possible. Government may prefer public housing to rental subsidies because it can thereby better restrict the number of persons assisted; it may choose to run job training programs itself rather than contract out to limit how many spots are available; and it may insist that government workers rather than private firms clean up toxic waste if the number of civil servants is seen as fixed for political reasons. Only when government aims to fill all demand, as for pre-college education, will such barriers be undesirable.[28]

Similarly, if we view limited personnel as constraining capacity, apparently arcane work rules (for example, rules forbidding nurses from administering procedures or rules preventing attorneys' legal assistants from processing legal documents) may efficiently limit production. The existence of such restraints may at least not create as much inefficiency as feared. Analogously, bureaucratic rules, such as rules requiring high-level approvals for small expenditures, can be efficient because they restrict the volume of production.

The ramifications of production barriers may explain some political structures, employment restrictions, and administrative rules that often typify public policy. We do not claim that the only reason for government to reserve functions for itself that would seem best left to the private sector is to restrict capacity. Nor do we assert that the only motive for personnel restrictions such as licensing professionals is service rationing. We do not assert that the motive for byzantine bureaucratic procedures is always the desire to increase waiting times. Nonetheless, at least one by-product of such activities may be a form of abstract rationing.

Also, *increasing effective capacity by reducing the services provided each recipient may increase costs.* This is essentially the obverse of the previous point and is conveyed by illustration. Suppose the average length of a patient's stay in a hospital is shortened. The part of the stay that is eliminated, however, is likely the least expensive for the hospital to provide, for example, rest after expensive surgery. The increase in the number of patients per bed may thus increase total costs for the beds in question.

It should be pointed out that this rise in costs appears only when commitment is difficult. In the hospital example, patients could be discharged and beds could be left unoccupied were commitment possible. But if commitment is difficult and the number of beds can be reduced, then the bed immediately gets filled for another costly procedure and costs rise.

Such implications are not exhaustive. But they do demonstrate that the combined effects of credibility, limits on investment in capacity, and rationing may create difficulties for limiting production and may make apparently inefficient choices more desirable.

Production Is Difficult

The above discussion should make it clear that even competent, well-meaning politicians will often find producing the right mix of goods and services impossible and that the types of government investments and the forms of production that they sometimes use are surprising. At the heart of such difficulties are factors related to credibility, crowding out, and expectations. Though politicians can engage in an intricate juggling act to reduce these effects, overcoming one obstacle often creates another. Government may therefore choose investments and production techniques that appear inefficient.

For instance, worries about crowding out may induce weakened government commitment—perhaps by avoiding large capital investments or by contracting out. Providers, whether market-driven firms or public-minded philanthropists, who believe that government is not committed may continue to supply the goods or services in question. In not committing to provide such products or services, however, government creates other problems. If required private investments, either by firms or by workers, are not forthcoming, government may fail in its production efforts. Or if private investments are unnecessary and government can cheaply produce additional units, the government may find expenses spiraling out of control because potential consumers view its rules on eligibility as not credible.

If the government reverses course and makes large investments on its own, crowding out can be a problem. Additionally, private investors may worry that the government will renege and not compensate them for their investments, which may necessitate another set of awkward institutional arrangements. And if government builds too much capacity to deal with legitimate demand fluctuations and the like, it may still find production levels far exceeding pre-set limits. Of course, if government reduces its own investment, it induces less private investment and less private production.

Although not the only cause for government's trouble in increasing production or for government's choice of some production arrangements over others, such effects are important and may help explain why government production of goods and services often appears an impenetrable morass. Certainly, they demonstrate that, compared with private production, economic constraints in the form of crowding out, credibility, and expectations make government production qualitatively different and more problematic.

CHAPTER

5

Economic Constraints
and Political Institutions

So far we have emphasized how credibility, expectations, crowding, and multiple equilibria relate to the effectiveness of public policies. For our purposes, we could mostly abstract away from the rules and the details of political institutions and from the differences in political systems. An idealized view of politics sufficed for making generic inferences about economic constraints on policy.

Yet issues of institutional design are hotly debated in popular and scholarly political discourse. For instance, calls for "reinventing government" by redesigning institutions have been a hallmark of recent debates about American public management (Osborne and Gaebler 1992, Gore 1994, Kettl 1994, 1998).

Since much of the concern with alternative arrangements relates to the quality of the policy produced, how institutions interact with the constraints that we discuss throughout this book can be important. Indeed, as shown in the following analysis, although factors in addition to credibility, expectations, crowding, and multiple equilibria should be considered in constitutional and institutional design, they have important ramifications for the effects of such designs on policy.

This, our final substantive chapter, though not giving a comprehensive overview, does illustrate how institutional form and constitutional rules may interact with economic constraints in predictable ways that structure policy effectiveness. We focus on three issues that characterize many of the debates in contemporary America about institutional design:

- whether policy outcomes differ under divided government compared with unified government;

- whether policy responsibility should remain at the national level or be devolved to local governments; and
- whether limits on the periods during which politicians serve (term limits) and policies continue (sunset reviews) are desirable.

In all three instances, our basic theme is comparable. Institutional conditions and rules defining government may influence how credibility, expectations, crowding, and multiple equilibria condition public policy. As a result, incorporating such economic constraints into the analysis of rules and institutions may generate insights, often counterintuitive, into the policy implications of different forms of government.

Although all the economic constraints we examine may be crucial for policy effectiveness, we emphasize credibility because it can vary most directly with the design of government. For purposes of the present investigation, credibility is the most direct product of institutional arrangements. Expectations and multiple equilibria are essentially technological givens that policymakers must confront, whereas crowding is a behavioral reaction that may depend on expectations, multiple equilibria, and also credibility.

As policies are generally more effective when they are viewed as credible and when individuals or firms react accordingly (for example, by making investments to comply with regulations), institutional arrangements that create a belief that government will continue a policy often allow such a policy to succeed.[1]

More succinctly, in this chapter politics comes to the forefront of our analysis. We accordingly focus on how political institutions affect credibility, which, in turn, may influence expectations, offsetting behavior, and the selection among multiple equilibria. We then briefly speculate on the extent to which political decisionmakers are aware of how political institutions and economic constraints affect the success of the policies they champion.

Divided Government and the Politics of Gridlock

Institutional and constitutional designs differ in how unified or divided they make government. In the early 1950s, for example, political scientists asked whether "responsible party government," that is, a British-style parliamentary system where parties could enforce policies and be judged by them, was more desirable than the separation of powers found in the United States (American Political Science Association 1950, Ranney 1954). Similarly, recent students of American politics have been fascinated by the causes and the policy impacts of divided government—where branches of government are controlled by opposing political parties or where legislatures consist of two chambers. Such concerns are not surprising since the United States has seen split partisan control for parts of each of the last five decades (Jacobson 1990, Cox and Kernell 1991, Mayhew 1991, Alesina and Rosenthal 1995, Fiorina 1996, Epstein and O'Halloran 1999).[2]

The literature on divided government is multifaceted, as scholars debate both its causes (e.g., Jacobson 1990, Born 1994, Fiorina 1994, 1996) and its implications (e.g., Mayhew 1991, Alt and Lowry 1994, Epstein and O'Halloran 1996, Edwards, Barrett, and Peake 1997). Nonetheless, the conventional wisdom is that split control is bad for public policy: by allowing each side to veto the other's policy proposals, divided government frustrates the adoption of effective policies. McKay (1994; see also Brady 1993, Brady and Volden 1998) illustrates this perspective when he states:

> DG [Divided government] is almost universally perceived as a bad thing. Among other sins, it allegedly undermines coherent and cohesive policy making by removing the vital institutional connective tissue provided by common party control. DG has been invoked, therefore, as the cause of a number of problems, including the budget deficit, difficulties associated with the presidential appointment and treaty-making powers, and a general inability to produce effective domestic policies. (p. 525)

Some are more sanguine, viewing divided government as reflecting voters' beliefs that split tickets will moderate policy (e.g., Fiorina 1996). The typical condemnation of divided government suffers from an additional shortcoming. Although measuring government performance is difficult, some evidence shows that divided governments can perform as well as undivided governments. Most notably, Mayhew's (1991) analysis of important policies enacted in the United States from 1947 to 1990 finds that major legislation is as likely under divided government as under unified regimes (this result is summarized in Table 5.1).[3] Of the 267 laws that Mayhew defines as major, on average 12.8 were enacted during each two-year period of unified control, and on average 13 were enacted during comparable periods of divided control. What makes this finding more surprising is that, with the exception of 1953–1954, all unified governments were under

Table 5.1 Important legislation under divided and unified governments, 1947–1990 (number of enactments per congressional session)

President (year)	Divided government	Unified government
Truman (1947–48)	10	
Truman (1949–50)		12
Truman (1951–52)		6
Eisenhower (1953–54)		9
Eisenhower (1955–56)	6	
Eisenhower (1957–58)	11	
Eisenhower (1959–60)	5	
Kennedy (1961–62)		15
Kennedy / Johnson (1963–64)		13
Johnson (1965–66)		22
Johnson (1967–68)		16
Nixon (1969–70)	22	
Nixon (1971–72)	16	
Nixon / Ford (1973–74)	22	
Ford (1975–76)	14	
Carter (1977–78)		12
Carter (1979–80)		6
Reagan (1981–82)	9	
Reagan (1983–84)	7	
Reagan (1985–86)	9	
Reagan (1987–88)	12	
Bush (1989–90)	9	
Average	13.0	12.8

Source: Mayhew (1991).

Democratic Party control. Since we usually think that Democrats are more favorable than Republicans to governmental action, there could be an artifactual bias in favor of uncovering a difference between divided and unified regimes. The absence of such a difference strengthens the conclusion that institutional structure can be inconsequential.

Mayhew's results are also largely consistent with accepted views of American presidencies. Several presidents with Congresses controlled by their party accomplished little. Truman was besieged in his last years in office. Kennedy was better known for promises than for exceptional accomplishments. Carter had ambitious goals but was unable to follow through.

By contrast, Nixon, a Republican who faced a Democratic Congress, passed many major reforms (other Republican presidents dealing with divided government did not have activist agendas). Certainly, policy accomplishments under unified governments are no more lauded historically than policies made under divided control.[4]

Nor are policies enacted during unified government obviously more effective than those passed under divided government. Anecdotally, some of the more dramatic policy failures of contemporary American politics, such as Superfund (Hird 1994) and banking deregulation (Romer and Weingast 1991) were adopted under unified regimes. Similarly, critics who point to poor "structural choices" of government agencies are equally dismayed with policies passed under unified and divided governments, since they view the separation of powers rather than partisan control as fundamental.[5]

If Mayhew's findings are reliable and if unified governments are not more effective, then the obvious issue is why the expected discrepancy does not appear. One reason may be that, as just stated, institutional differences overwhelm other factors. That is, in textbook fashion, the tension between the parochial incentives of legislators (in alliance with organized interests) and the broader outlook of presidents (not to mention the meddling of the judiciary) may swamp the effects of divided government. Although such varying incentives can dampen the differences between unified and divided government (consider how Presidents Kennedy, Carter, and Clinton were constrained by congressional Democrats), these forces seem unlikely to mask all effects of divided control.

Rather, data such as Mayhew's are consistent with the contention that credibility is essential for policy effectiveness and that policy may be more credible when enacted under divided than under unified government. Policies passed under divided government may be especially effective as they demonstrate a broader political consensus than those produced by a unified regime. Economic actors should form appropriate expectations and be more willing to behave in ways (for example, investment) that make policy succeed. By contrast, economic actors may hesitate in responding to policies passed by unified governments because they may expect large future swings in policy—the stance of different British governments toward industry nationalization, for instance, represents a classic example if we expand our horizon to include parliamentary regimes (as we will shortly).[6] Consequently, all else being equal, the policies of divided governments should be more likely to succeed than policies of their unified counterparts.

If the tortuous routes created by divided government make policy more stable, firms and consumers should view policies passed under divided government as more credible than policies produced by a unified government. Economic agents may therefore behave in ways that aid implementation. Such responses, in turn, will bolster political support, endogenously enhancing credibility, inducing crowding in, and leading to the establishment of equilibria associated with policy success.

This discussion provides insight into why divided governments may enact as many important policies as unified governments. Although differences in policies preferred by competing political parties may make agreement under divided governments difficult, politicians' incentives to pass policies may be greater. Economic actors, seeing a broad consensus, develop expectations that such policies are unlikely to be rescinded and behave accordingly.

Conversely, a unified government may hesitate to approve legislation because skeptical economic agents can make the policy ineffective. For example, political decisions about whether to support the comprehensive health care reform proposed by Bill Clinton to a Democratic Congress in 1993–1994 may have been influenced by a belief that producers would refrain from making costly investments given an expectation that a later Republican Congress or president would dramatically change policies. Certainly, the 1994 Republican landslide reduced political support for reform (Skocpol 1996). The expected ineffectiveness of policy arising from insufficient investment may have reduced political support for the initiative. After all, politicians know that their constituents will disapprove of ineffectual changes, which only raise costs.

Thus, though perhaps counterintuitive, the logic of credibility suggests that the differences in the passage of policies between divided and unified governments should be smaller (or even nonexistent) than might initially be assumed. Although a divided government may have difficulty passing legislation, the bipartisan support for policies that are adopted makes the continuation of the policy under a future government likely and thus makes the policy credible. Mayhew's findings, though not definitive (for example, he might be uncovering only differences in institutional incentives), indicate that credibility is important.

Implications of this view are consistent with analyses of presidential and parliamentary systems—with presidential systems more often having divided governance. Notably, detailed studies by Weaver and Rockman (1993) discover that the unique separation of powers in the United States (the prerequisite for divided government and, as mentioned, the source of much blame for policy failure in its own right) is not the root cause of policy inaction or policy failure. Rather, they maintain that governance problems have a large generic component:

> Most of the governance problems of the United States are shared by all industrial democracies, most of which have similar difficulties in addressing those problems. Few countries succeed in targeting resources on behalf of an effective industrial policy, for example. Problems with balancing budgets are ubiquitous. All elected (and most unelected) governments are reluctant to impose losses on pensioners. Ethnic, racial, and linguistic conflict is all too common. Particular institutional arrangements do not cause these governance problems; they are inherent in complex societies and in democratic government. Groups inevitably want more from government than government is able to provide, and they want above all else to be protected from losing ground. Therefore, policy failings in the United States should not be blamed exclusively, or perhaps even mainly, on the structure of American political institutions. (p. 445)

Additionally, the authors find that parliamentary systems with party governments (rather than with coalition governments consisting of multiple parties) exhibit more policy instability (but see Moe and Caldwell 1994). Put another way, a higher probability that a government with much different preferences may soon come to power is likely to disrupt implementation. This is especially true in sectors where clear and consistent long-term signals and incentives are necessary to encourage private investment. Economic agents will be reluctant to invest when policies, and, hence, long-term payoffs, may change.

In summary, unified government is routinely assumed to lead to more and better policy. Yet the data imply that the performance of divided government is better than is conventionally suggested. This assertion is supported both by historical American data and by comparisons of the United States with parliamentary regimes where party government is the rule.

One explanation for these results is that policies produced by divided government are more credible, with economic agents reacting accordingly.

If firms and consumers anticipate large policy changes under unified governments, then the effectiveness of the new policies is undermined by the expectations that future governments will reverse them. Even if an unconscious choice, perhaps American voters have been wise to accept the tensions created by dividing authority between competing political parties.[7]

Federalism and the Devolution of Authority

Just as the consequences of separation of powers have spurred debate, so has the division of authority between levels of government in a federal structure.[8] Contemporary America has seen debate, for instance, about whether a "new federalism" is a desirable way to structure policy (Galston and Tibbetts 1994, Conlan 1988, 1998). Certainly, as we illustrated in several of our earlier discussions, some local policies do succeed. The issue is whether control over policy should generally be local or national.

Advocates of federalism maintain that a greater sensitivity to local conditions and preferences, a better matching of individuals with localities that provide public goods, and opportunities for innovation, experimentation, and learning will make delegated policy in a federal system more successful.[9] Critics contend that federalism makes the provision of certain public goods difficult because of competition from other jurisdictions, and that under federalism one jurisdiction may saddle another with such problems as pollution or poverty.[10] Stewart (1977) gives a clear statement of the argument as applied to environmental policy:

> Given the mobility of industry and commerce, any individual state or community may rationally decline unilaterally to adopt high environment standards that entail substantial costs for industry and obstacles to economic development for fear that the resulting environmental gains will be more than offset by movement of capital to other areas with lower standards. If each locality reasons in the same way, all will adopt lower standards of environmental quality than they would prefer if there were some binding mechanism that enabled them simultaneously to enact higher standards, thus eliminating the threatened loss of industry or development.

Others question whether trade and mobility necessarily weaken local regulations. Increased trade may give new prominence to consumer and environmental groups and their demands for regulation (Vogel 1995). Or a state seeing increased pollution from new plants may increase its own regulatory standards, thereby inhibiting mobility of industry and leading to the efficiency of local regulation (Oates and Schwab 1988, Levinson 1997, Besley and Coate 1999).[11]

This criticism focusing on competition can also be questioned on empirical grounds roughly analogous to those mentioned in our discussion of divided government. Descriptively, local governments vary greatly in the types and amounts of public goods they provide; local provision of public goods beyond minimum levels is possible. For example, Table 5.2 displays differences in 1991 spending on the environment and natural resources both in per capita terms and as a percentage of state spending. Even ignoring two dramatic outliers (Alaska and Wyoming), these expenditures vary from roughly $14 to $90 per capita, and from 0.62 percent of the state budget to 3.55 percent. Some states spent much more than others in protecting the environment—and more than dictated by national statutes.

These variations in environmental policies are frequent. States have often been more stringent than the national government in regulating cigarette smoking, in protecting safety and health, in licensing myriad professions, and in setting minimum wages. Indeed, scholars claim that the 1990s have been marked by a resurgence in state governing capacity (e.g., Grady and Chi 1994).

Such discrepancies may be explained as reflecting differences in voters' preferences (Erikson, Wright, and McIver 1993) or in the power of interest groups (Lowery and Gray 1995). But differences in political pressures would matter little if competition across jurisdictions forced them into a "race to the bottom" where none adopted strict regulations, provided many services, or redistributed much.

The economic constraints that we emphasize may provide additional explanation for how federalism allows diversity in state policies and permits states to set standards exceeding national mandates.[12] Although they are not the only explanation, we believe thinking in terms of such constraints provides some interesting insight and intuition.

Consider the credibility of policies enacted at the local and national levels. For statistical reasons, local support for policies may, on average, be more stable over time than support for corresponding national policies. For instance, following our discussion of divided government, the longevity of a policy may be questionable if it is initiated at the national level as a result of a landslide favoring one legislative party or as a result of a sudden

Table 5.2 Spending on environmental and natural resources in U.S. states (fiscal year 1991)

State	Per capita spending (dollars)	Percentage of budget	State	Per capita spending (dollars)	Percentage of budget
Alabama	22.43	1.02	Montana	72.32	2.42
Alaska	519.83	5.79	Nebraska	27.89	1.35
Arizona	15.63	0.73	Nevada	46.17	1.61
Arkansas	25.66	1.29	New Hampshire	39.50	2.05
California	68.44	2.38	New Jersey	51.85	1.70
Colorado	68.41	3.22	New Mexico	35.62	1.19
Connecticut	20.98	0.62	New York	32.08	0.90
Delaware	63.70	1.83	North Carolina	16.96	0.75
Florida	29.29	1.51	North Dakota	79.48	2.83
Georgia	21.69	1.06	Ohio	16.26	0.64
Hawaii	34.00	0.84	Oklahoma	19.00	0.83
Idaho	81.22	3.55	Oregon	60.79	2.28
Illinois	35.17	1.63	Pennsylvania	24.13	1.17
Indiana	13.98	0.67	Rhode Island	40.38	1.17
Iowa	23.74	0.97	South Carolina	32.63	1.27
Kansas	23.16	1.12	South Dakota	45.02	2.21
Kentucky	28.38	1.16	Tennessee	22.04	0.88
Louisiana	49.16	1.97	Texas	18.36	1.06
Maine	47.35	1.66	Utah	43.95	1.84
Maryland	31.98	1.22	Vermont	89.60	2.90
Massachusetts	39.08	1.16	Virginia	29.27	1.31
Michigan	23.56	0.91	Washington	78.45	1.58
Minnesota	50.50	1.74	West Virginia	21.01	0.79
Mississippi	30.41	1.51	Wisconsin	36.75	1.44
Missouri	50.31	2.78	Wyoming	221.10	5.53

Source: Council of State Governments (1994).

upsurge in presidential popularity. As comparable idiosyncrasies at the local level may work in opposite directions, they may cancel one another and lead to little change over time in the aggregate effects of such policies. Firms operating in many localities may expect the actions of various localities to lead to a stable demand for their services. Put another way, whereas national firms may prefer national policies that last for a long time, in practice local policies may be more reliable in the aggregate and, given that such expectations may make policies more successful, such reliability allows local governments to succeed with policies that would fail for the national government.

To elaborate, local leaders who wish to make a policy more credible will encourage firms and individuals to make the investments that are necessary for policies to succeed. Investors with a stake in such policies should then support continuation of that policy. That is, endogenously generated support strengthened by crowding in should further stabilize policy and allow attainment of the desired equilibrium. For similar reasons, programs affecting only a small, geographically concentrated population may be more credible at the local level, as political support created endogenously may be stronger locally than nationally. As a result, local leaders may better establish credibility and induce behavior that makes policy effective.

Thus, the expectations, credibility, crowding, and equilibrium selection that aid policy effectiveness may be easier to produce locally than nationally. Given that such forces may contribute to policy effectiveness, they can motivate local officials to adopt tougher policies and even to adopt policies that the national government may dismiss as extreme.

A hypothetical example sheds light on this process. Suppose that government subsidizes bus service in Pittsburgh to increase the use of mass transit and to reduce dependency on automobiles. It is, therefore, essential that government persuade citizens to move downtown, induce builders to construct fewer parking spots, persuade consumers to buy fewer automobiles, and so on. If, however, people will change their behavior only when persuaded that subsidized bus service will continue in the long term, and if potential bus riders and investors believe that national support will evaporate but that local support will remain firm, then federal policies will be less effective than local policies. For example, the investments that government wants to encourage will not be made if people see obstacles to the program's continuation and if such hurdles—possible loss of power by local members of Congress championing subsidies, effective lobbying by other cities for the funds allocated for subsidies, and a variety of other factors—are more problematic nationally than locally. If local programs are considered more credible, firms and citizens may change their behavior when subsidies are local and not national. Furthermore, support by persons who altered their behavior, and later crowding in, should matter much more at the local than at the national level. Hence, local policy may be more effective.

The skeptical reader may believe that our analysis is one-sided by implying that the instability of central government may only weaken policy. If such instability at the national level eventually results in revisions that strengthen rather than weaken legislation, might the initial adoption of weaker policies be more successful than first thought?

As was foreshadowed in our discussions of regulation and production, such anticipation of tougher policies need not increase investment. Specifically, firms (especially) and individuals may delay investing if they anticipate a policy change, even if it means that policy will get stronger. Under many circumstances, they require a stable policy. More precisely, three conditions, which apply to many important public policies, particularly at the national level, may make delaying any investment profitable:[13]

1. The investment entails sunk costs that cannot be recouped if policy is later changed.
2. The decisionmaker is uncertain about future economic (or political) conditions and gains additional information only gradually.
3. An investment not made now can be made later.

To illustrate how even instability that would seem to aid national policy success can lead to failure, suppose the national government adopts pollution standards for electric utilities. Utilities may invest little to meet the current standards if they fear that such rules will later be strengthened, as they will wait until more stringent regulations are adopted (a reasonable description of the history of policy toward utilities in the United States during the last third of the twentieth century). In the interim, compliance with current standards may be expensive or incomplete. In contrast, if several states adopt some set of standards, and if no one state is expected to later adopt more stringent ones because each state fears losing business to other states, then the utilities can find it profitable to invest in equipment that meets these standards immediately.

Similarly, delegation of authority to subnational units under federalism may more effectively lead economic agents to develop strong beliefs on which to act. Such delegation will produce numerous readings for interested parties about policy, giving firms and consumers increased confidence about future policy and about how they should respond.

Federalism, of course, has its drawbacks. For instance, mobility may interact with expectations and credibility in ways that undermine policy success. We must consider not only whether the policy will stay in force but also whether firms or households will stay put.

Redistribution, for example, may be influenced by such factors. If mobility is easy and if policies vary across localities, then recipients of redistribution such as welfare will avoid costly activities that could reduce their need for public assistance. They may hesitate to acquire work experience or education as long as they expect that a desirable benefit will be offered by some other locality.[14] By contrast, if redistribution is controlled at the national level, recipients cannot count on moving from one locality to another to get better benefits. Thus, particularly when national policy is not considered credible, desirable behavior can be induced.

An analogous story may be told for the regulation of firms. Those firms that are potentially mobile may ignore local regulations because they may consider moving to a state with weaker policies. Such a disincentive to comply can arise even if firms relocate primarily for reasons unrelated to government policy, such as for low wages. The possibility of mobility therefore reduces incentives to make investments that meet policy requirements, even if local policies are deemed credible, and suggests that policies might be less successful than if they are implemented nationally. Local regulation will thus be particularly ineffective if it requires investments (for example, in physical plant) that become worthless if the firm moves.

In the spirit of our discussion of the regulation of firms, how much more effective local policy can be than centralized policy can also depend on industry structure. Recall that government may be held up by a monopolistic firm that refuses to make an investment necessary to meet a regulation because the firm can thereby induce the government to repeal the policy. An equilibrium requiring private investments will more likely be established if a policy affects multiple firms, as each firm may invest since it expects others to do so and because getting some firms to invest initially may crowd in others. Consequently, the absence of monopoly, the mobility of firms, and the existence of policies that allow more firms to compete in markets (for example, reduced barriers to trade) can all make regulation by a single state more credible and effective.

To recapitulate: whereas federalism has many advocates, others believe it undermines policy initiatives and success. Although our analysis covers only a few facets of federalism, it suggests that under a variety of conditions local governments may have advantages, often unrecognized, in implementing policies. Most notably, local policy may be more credible, and thus more effective in exploiting crowding in to induce firms and consumers to make investments needed for policy success. The improbability of all local governments abandoning a policy and wiping out an investment can also improve credibility, as can the more restricted choices that local officials face compared with national officials. Although factors such as mobility may make local policy success more difficult, incorporating economic constraints gives insight into why local governments can have differing policies from one another and the national government, why lowest common denominator standards are not universal, and how resurgences of local government capacity are possible.

Political and Policy Reform

Another set of issues that routinely generates heated debate in both scholarly and popular quarters concerns reforms of the political and policy systems. Much of the discussion concentrates on a common question: how desirable is it to revise policies and to change the elected politicians who enact them?

In the United States these efforts take several forms. Many states have sunset provisions terminating agencies or policies unless the legislature later votes to extend them. Sunset laws were a policy innovation that spread wildly in the 1970s. For example, twenty-five states adopted such provisions between 1975 and 1976, with the number rising to thirty-six by 1982—although eleven would eventually repeal them—and other states have written them into specific statutes. Table 5.3, which gives more detail on past and current sunset programs, shows that sunset rules vary widely in the scope of policies and agencies they cover and in the number of years between review. Although less successful on the national level, the sunset movement has strong advocates, as typified by the efforts of Vice President Albert Gore when he headed the highly publicized National Performance Review (1994).

Concerning elected officials, proposals for change appear in two principal types: campaign finance reform and term limits. In both instances, a stated goal of reformers is to increase the turnover of elected officials: term limits do it mechanically; campaign finance reforms do it by reducing the electoral advantages of incumbency, perhaps thereby attracting better challengers.

The first national finance reform in the United States with any enforcement was passed in the 1970s and spread in different forms to most states (Alexander 1991). "Good government" advocates, however, are still concerned that the policies adopted protect incumbents rather than encourage turnover. On the national level, reform efforts by such groups as Common

Table 5.3 Sunset review in U.S. states

State	Years to review	Comment
Alabama	—	Terminated
Alaska	Usually four	Comprehensive
Arizona	Ten	Selective
Arkansas	—	Terminated 1983
California	—	Has included sunset for selected programs
Colorado	Ten or less	Regulatory
Connecticut	—	Terminated 1983
Delaware	Four or less	Comprehensive
Florida	Ten	Regulatory
Georgia	One to six	Regulatory
Hawaii	Six to ten	Regulatory
Idaho	—	Has included sunset for selected programs
Illinois	Ten	Regulatory
Indiana	Ten	Comprehensive
Iowa	—	—
Kansas	—	Terminated 1992
Kentucky	—	—
Louisiana	Six or less	Comprehensive
Maine	Ten	Comprehensive
Maryland	Ten	Regulatory
Massachusetts	—	—
Michigan	—	Has included sunset for selected programs
Minnesota	—	Has included sunset for selected programs
Mississippi	—	Terminated 1984
Missouri	—	—
Montana	—	Has included sunset for selected programs
Nebraska	—	Has included sunset for selected programs
Nevada	—	Has included sunset for selected programs
New Hampshire	—	Terminated 1986
New Jersey	—	Has included sunset for selected programs
New Mexico	Five to seven	Regulatory
New York	—	Has included sunset for selected programs
North Carolina	—	Terminated 1981
North Dakota	—	—
Ohio	Four or less	Selective
Oklahoma	Six	Comprehensive
Oregon	—	Terminated 1993
Pennsylvania	—	Has included sunset for selected programs
Rhode Island	—	Terminated 1993

Table 5.3 (continued)

State	Years to review	Comment
South Carolina	Six	Regulatory
South Dakota	—	Terminated 1979
Tennessee	One to eight	Comprehensive
Texas	Twelve	Selective
Utah	Ten or less	Regulatory
Vermont	None specified	Selective—only professions and occupations
Virginia	None specified	Selective
Washington	Varies	Comprehensive
West Virginia	Six	Selective
Wisconsin	—	Has included sunset for selected programs
Wyoming	—	Terminated 1988

Source: Council of State Governments (1998).

Cause have failed (Rothenberg 1992, 2000). Many, in their frustration (joined by others driven by different motives), have turned to term limits to increase turnover (on the electoral effects of term limits, see Gilmour and Rothstein 1993, Reed and Schansberg 1994). Although efforts to enact a national law covering all fifty states have thus far faltered, term limits for members of Congress were adopted in twenty-two states in the years 1990–1994.[15]

It should be clear that these political reforms can affect credibility, expectations, crowding behavior, and the establishment of equilibria. Any increase in the volatility of policy or personnel can reduce credibility, inducing firms and consumers to delay costly investments needed to implement policy, reducing crowding in, and increasing the chance that a suboptimal equilibrium will be established.

Data support our interpretation. Although directly estimating the effects of sunset provisions on actions such as investment is difficult, the provisions have clearly led to instability, which has dismayed even reformers (Kearney 1990). For example, as one observer writes (McNeely 1994; see also Curry 1990), Texas has considered revoking sunset provisions because of the havoc that they have created:[16]

> Several of the officials who had rammed through a process to institutionalize a blitzkrieg assault on waste and inefficiency in state agencies had

arrived at the same conclusion legislators in several other states had—
that the sunset law, originally designed to do something similar, had
evolved from being a solution into being the kind of problem it had been
created to solve . . . the sunset commission [charged with reviewing agen-
cies] had gone beyond simply deciding whether an agency should continue in existence; instead it had become involved in substantive policy
issues. Because a positive vote of the Legislature is needed to continue
an agency, sunset bills are often loaded up with substantive issues. (pp.
17–18)

Indeed, in states that dropped sunset review, the relevant provisions had
caused programs to be terminated or modified. Although sunset policies
worked as expected, these states found it distasteful (Kearney 1990). We see
such provisions as reducing credibility, leading to expectations that would
dissuade compliance by economic actors, and undermining political support for desired policies.

Assuming that they survive constitutional challenges and are effective,
term limits and campaign finance reform appear to be electoral analogues
to sunset laws.[17] If their implementation creates instability or uncertainty
about future policy, they may cause whatever policy that is adopted to be
less effective than it would be otherwise. Ensuring compliance would be
difficult and implementation would be further thwarted by the failure to
create political support for the policy.[18]

But this process may be more subtle and nuanced than the above description implies. Specifically, rather than weakening all policy, political reforms of the sort discussed here may separate policies into two categories:
policies with and without widespread credibility. Analogous to policy created under divided government, if policy remains stable despite reassessment by sunset provisions or heightened electoral turnover, beliefs that
policy will continue may be stronger than if no sunset provisions exist or if
legislative membership is more stable.[19]

In other words, those impacted by new policies may be skeptical that
such programs will continue. Sunset provisions that demand a referendum
on policy thereby provide information about which policies are likely to
persist for long and which will not. Without sunset provisions, such information is more difficult to garner because the political system produces it
less frequently. Similarly, campaign finance reform and term limits that induce electoral change may allow firms and consumers to separate policies
whose passage reflected idiosyncrasies and are subject to change from poli-

cies with firmer political foundation. Consequently, political reforms may increase the credibility of some policies while undermining others.

For instance, if an investment is profitable only if policy is in place for several years, investors may delay acting until they witness a sunset review or an election with significant turnover. The additional information reduces uncertainty, and economic agents will react accordingly. Credibility may be especially enhanced if policy remains intact after intensive reviews or after elections that lead to much legislative turnover.[20]

By similar reasoning, an agency may be viewed as more committed to a policy when few rules dictate its actions. Rather, discretion to follow desired policies may increase credibility because policy is always subject to change and stable policy thereby provides information about commitment.

Consider the German Bundesbank for an example of how discretion may produce credibility. Despite few formal constraints (its charter states a general commitment to price stability but provides no means for enforcement, and the government has significant control over appointment to its governing board (Forder 1998)), the Bundesbank and German politicians enjoyed a strong anti-inflationary reputation. Indeed, it was commonly expected that low inflation would continue precisely because the Bundesbank chose to keep prices low and because German politicians had demonstrated that they would not impose inflationary policies even though they could do so were they sufficiently determined. The world had learned that German central bankers and politicians abhor inflation. Agency discretion, as well as incomplete independence from political control, may strengthen a central bank's credibility and resulting policy success. The continual and recurring decisions made under circumstances of discretion may increase the confidence of investors and other economic agents who are key for much policy implementation.[21] More generally, frequent reviews of programs or short term limits (or other mechanisms enhancing turnover) may increase rather than reduce credibility.[22]

To conclude, changes in rules and institutions intended to increase policy oversight and political turnover will change how economic constraints affect policy. Although reduced discretion may undermine policy by reducing stability, it may also make policy more effective by reducing uncertainty about future policy. Such information may separate policies into two types, those shown to have much credibility and those shown to enjoy little support.

Therefore, though likely important, the way economic constraints interact with political reforms is not cut and dried. Rather, it tends to make distinctions between policies more stark. For instance, the experience with sunset legislation is emblematic of the contrasting undercurrents. On the one hand, even reformers are frustrated by the instability created. On the other hand, some policies are made more legitimate because they have successfully passed review.

What Do Politicians Know?

The above discussion mostly considered how the interaction of economic constraints with key institutional features affects public policy. As an addendum to this analysis, we can speculate about whether, at least intuitively, politicians recognize such interactions. We would expect that successful politicians would indeed be aware of, and act on, such an understanding of the world.

Indeed, the evidence shows that sometimes they do. We have, for example, shown how credibility concerns have entered policy decisions. In Chapter 3 we noted that President Reagan defused a volatile political issue by appointing William Ruckelshaus to head the Environmental Protection Agency, effectively reestablishing the agency's credibility. Since Ruckelshaus had refused to acquiesce to Nixon in the legendary Saturday Night Massacre and had ultimately been fired, the appointment was a credible sign that the agency would be given discretion despite the president's power to interfere; Reagan purposely limited his own power. And, indeed, even Reagan's most vociferous critics noted a change at the agency from this point onward.

Similarly, we discussed how the post–World War II German government kept inflation low by showing its commitment to not interfering with the Bundesbank (which had gained a strong anti-inflationary reputation) despite the government's authority to do so. The success of the resulting monetary policy is exemplified by the observation that in the 1980s several European countries sought to control inflation by joining the European Monetary System, pegging their exchange rates to the German mark and thereby benefiting from the reputation of the Bundesbank (Weber 1991).

Or consider a genius of American politics, Franklin Roosevelt, who understood how credibility could be generated. A management consultant criticized the inefficiency of the new Social Security system in recording the contributions of each worker. Any contributor could request a statement of his total contributions and an estimate of his eventual benefits. Thousands did so and were courteously answered, although the benefits were determined by Congress rather than by any insurance contract. Roosevelt justified the costs of maintaining the individual accounts on policy grounds: "That account is not to determine how much should be paid out, to control what should be paid out. That account is there so those sons of bitches up on the Hill can't ever abandon this system when I'm gone" (quoted in Neustadt and May 1986, p. 102). In other words, even given a unified government with a huge Democratic majority, Roosevelt could not take it for granted that Social Security would continue under changed political circumstances. Therefore, he had to use other means to establish the policy's longevity.

Other presidents were less insightful. For example, in August 1964 Congress passed the Gulf of Tonkin resolution, authorizing American military operations in Vietnam, by a vote of 414–0 in the House and of 88–2 in the Senate. The political power of President Lyndon Johnson before the 1964 election and minimal deliberation weakened the significance of the resolution as a binding commitment. If the vote had taken place under different circumstances—for example, under a president facing a Congress with a strong opposition, making it possible for Congress to have voted otherwise—either the credibility of domestic support for the Vietnam War might have been greater or the decision to go ahead with policies that ultimately proved unpopular might have been avoided.

Indeed, though politicians often consider the interaction of economic constraints and institutional characteristics, at times they do not fully consider, or at least not act on, such interaction. Sometimes these politicians may simply make mistakes, while in other instances they may have little incentive to consider the full implications of their actions. For whereas this book studies long-range consequences, politicians have incentives to adopt a short-term outlook; we inquire into the consequences of policy over ten or twenty years, but most politicians care about short-term impacts. This is another cost of democracy that is difficult to overcome completely.

Institutional Design and Policy Effectiveness

Institutional design and policy effectiveness are intertwined, often in surprising ways. When we examine major debates about the structure of government—whether power should be unified or divided, whether it should be centralized or devolved, whether it should promote change or secure stability—we discover that integrating economic constraints, especially credibility, has implications for policy performance. Thus, the similar policy performance of unified and divided governments may partly result from such constraints. So, too, may such features explain the variation in policies that we observe across states and provide insights into why a resurgence in state capacity is possible. Similarly, the constraints that we highlight here may help explain why sunset laws have proven problematic and may give pause to advocates of term limits and of campaign reform. Although some politicians may poorly integrate the interaction of economic constraints and institutional features, they are likely an important explanation of the policy world.

While our main interest is in positive analysis, we can draw two normative inferences that are the opposite sides of the same coin. One is that assessments of a policy's potential effectiveness should incorporate the institutional context in which it will function. The other is that the adoption of institutional forms and rules should reckon with their impact on policy effectiveness. In both instances, the kinds of economic constraints that we have highlighted should prove essential to the analysis.

6

Final Thoughts

We believe that the analysis presented in the preceding chapters supports the proposition that, although sometimes facilitating success, even in an idealized political situation economic constraints frequently make policy ineffective. Blaming policy failures mostly on the behavior of venal, misleading, or ill-informed politicians, or on the efforts of self-aggrandizing special interests, is incorrect. Attributing policy successes solely to the good behavior of elected officials, bureaucrats, or interest groups is also wrong. Although explicitly political forces certainly cause many policy failures and may account for some successes, the larger economic context in which such outcomes occur must also be incorporated before policy performance can be well understood.[1]

Having made such sweeping assertions, can we make more specific, definite generalizations about the effects of economic constraints? Such statements are difficult since, as demonstrated throughout our investigation, the impact of any given economic constraint is often subtle and frequently intertwined with the impacts of other constraints. For instance, though credible policies may often succeed, the benefits of credibility may be undermined by crowding out, as firms or consumers who believe that government is committed to a policy may make choices and investments that let them reduce the costs that they would otherwise bear. Such crowding-out effects will be especially strong when a new policy is anticipated rather than when it comes as a surprise (but, admittedly, democratic governments are poor at keeping secrets, so a surprise may be uncommon if decisionmakers have rational expectations). Similarly, due to other economic constraints, the existence of multiple equilibria can both lead some policies to be more effective—for example, by taking advantage of crowding in—and may make other policies less successful—for example, as political turnover or lobbyists, which can cause policy reversal, reduce the credibility of policy. Or, to offer a final example, rational expectations may enhance the credibility and the probability of success for time-consistent policies (which, to reiterate, are policies that a government has an incentive to pursue after it announces them and after key economic agents respond), but will create credibility problems and will reduce the likelihood of success for time-inconsistent policies where government has an incentive to reverse course.

Nonetheless, despite the possible differential effects of economic constraints, we can generalize about their overall impacts on policy. Not only does each substantive policy area that we examine reflect such interwoven processes, but it is possible to draw broad inferences about the net effect of economic constraints on policy success.

Thus, we confidently conclude that government's ability to control macroeconomic policy is weaker than is routinely suggested by the popular press or by numerous credit-claiming presidents. Monetary policy, often exalted in popular discussions with each utterance of the head of the U.S. Federal Reserve Board considered an earth-shattering event, is undermined by rational expectations; fiscal policy is limited by crowding out; the effects of exhortation and persuasion, beyond their inherent limits, may be tempered because the existence of multiple equilibria—while providing opportunities for sophisticated politicians to improve the economy by changing expectations, changing behavior, and generating crowding in—may also lead to a policy's undoing; and balanced budgets are not the cure to all of society's ills that many public figures assert because expectations and crowding out mitigate the negative effects of deficits.

Redistribution, by contrast, is easier than is often depicted in public discussion, which often fails to separate clearly economic constraints from political interests. Yes, crowding out, multiple equilibria, credibility, and rational expectations all have important, if sometimes nonintuitive, effects and do indeed raise the cost of redistribution. But these costs are not insurmountable. Economic constraints do not prevent redistribution and sometimes they can aid its success. Thus, small efforts at redistribution likely reflect low political support for redistribution rather than a fear that offsetting behavior by the winners and losers would make redistributive policies ineffective.

By contrast, failed regulation should not be attributed solely to the political ineptitude or the venality so often castigated in popular and scholarly discussions. Though political factors do undermine regulatory efforts, economic constraints can also undermine them. We have seen in particular, that without establishing credibility, even well-meaning governments will discover that regulating firms is difficult. And, unless crowding in can be generated, even determined politicians may be unable to regulate personal behavior.

Conversely, effective production may be as difficult as is frequently depicted in popular discussions. Such discussions, however, tend to ignore the interrelationship between excessive and insufficient production or the key role played by economic constraints. Put differently, economic constraints may explain why popular critics deplore both difficulties in limiting and in stimulating production. Trade-offs that must be made in establishing credibility, inducing crowding in, and molding expectations will frequently impede efforts to increase production or to limit output levels. What is a solution to one problem exacerbates another.

Nor, despite many calls by political reformers, are there easy institutional fixes for governmental failures. Whatever the benefits of market-like reforms, the inherent endogeneity of political institutions and the very nature of democracy make credibility more problematic than in the private sector. Indeed, such difficulties may make the adoption of policy instruments that are prima facie undesirable somewhat less costly.

What Can Government Do?: Five Lessons

Analogous to our ability to draw inferences about different policies despite the fact that economic constraints may have different effects in different circumstances, we also find some essential generalities or what we call policy lessons. When considered in total, we believe that at least five such lessons come out of our analysis and that they offer important, often novel, ways of thinking about public policy. Taken together, they should provide us with a better idea of how to analyze and understand public policy and, perhaps, in some instances craft better policies.

Manipulate the Few

A clear implication of our analysis is that government manipulation of the behavior of a small fraction of firms or persons may lead to effective policy.

At one level, such an assertion is mundane. Obviously, government will be more successful if it can induce some persons or firms to behave in ways consistent with its own interests compared to manipulating none at all. At another level, this statement is deeper. Specifically, manipulating some economic actors may have larger effects than might be expected because crowding responses change the behavior of others. As we saw, in many instances (for example, in stimulating macroeconomic activity, overcoming the stigma of welfare, and reducing observable behavior such as smoking) a government that directly induces some economic actors to comply may generate crowding-in pressures that induce others to change their actions in the way that government wants. Such crowding in can appear for several related reasons: social pressures, strategic complementarities, increased policy credibility, or political endogeneity producing political support.

Thus, one way to distinguish types of issues is by the possibilities for manipulation via crowding. While this may sometimes backfire in the end as other societal interests with preferences antithetical to those of government decisionmakers recognize the same opportunities, it does seem to be an important element for understanding policy processes and outcomes.

The Possibility of Failure May Promote Success

One would think that increased certainty always leads to better public policy and that multiple equilibria are baneful to any program advocate wishing to accomplish policy goals. Yet we often find that the very fragility of decisionmaking offers opportunities for policy success. Although multiple equilibria may reduce credibility and may make the impacts of actions such as lobbying by policy opponents potentially more influential as they can influence which equilibrium results, the existence of many equilibria can also offer opportunities for policymakers. By inducing some people to behave in desired ways, government may exploit crowding in, generate endogenous political support, and increase credibility; without multiple equilibria, such opportunities are absent.

Indeed, we can extend this point to suggest that, given the uncertainty created by multiple equilibria and potential crowding, a government insulated from outside forces (that is, where only it exerts pressure on firms or consumers and is itself immune from pressures) may be less effective than a seemingly more vulnerable regime. In situations of multiple equilibria and potential crowding, a policy can succeed because some persons (rather than just the government) can change the behavior of others and because endogenous political support can increase the credibility of the policy. Under these conditions, government may benefit from crowding in, expectations of a credible policy, and the attainment of an equilibrium that promotes policy success.

Policy Can Benefit from Ignorance

Intuition suggests that the better informed the public the better the public policy outcome. Indeed, a major criticism of democracy is that citizens are disengaged from politics and policy. The implication is that the world would improve if people better understood the intricate workings of government and overcame their ignorance, however rational the basis for it might be.

Although this prescription is often valid (for example, democracy might work better if the behavior of special interests and their political allies were more closely monitored), our analysis also demonstrates how knowledge can undermine policy and how ignorance can promote success. Macroeconomic policy especially works better with surprise; so will aspects of regulation and of redistribution. In these instances, offsetting behavior undermines successful policy outcomes.

For related normative and positive reasons, the inference that ignorance is good may be disheartening. Normatively, as implied, we may object to anything that indicates that keeping the citizenry in the dark makes government work better. For example, should a central bank make decisions in secrecy? Should individuals not be informed about all the implications of programs designed for intergenerational redistribution? Should welfare recipients be misled into believing that their benefits are likely to be terminated?

As mentioned, a democracy may be particularly bad at surprising firms and individuals when they have direct, fundamental, interests at stake. Therefore, while policy can benefit from ignorance, and sometimes ignorance will prevail, the relative openness of democracy compared to other governmental forms, such as more authoritarian regimes, means that this will occur only modestly. Nonetheless, if government decisionmakers care about results rather than about form, they may have incentive to cultivate secrecy and to build complications into the policy process that obscure the impacts of policy choices.

Inefficiency May Be Efficient

Understanding why political institutions, agencies, and policies are set up the way they are is frequently perplexing. One possible insight into such choices, or at least into their consequences, is that seemingly inefficient structural arrangements may be efficient. In our analysis of redistribution, regulation, and production we saw that, mostly for reasons related to credibility, seemingly inefficient institutions may be less costly than is otherwise thought or may even be the best choice. This cost reduction occurs when inefficient methods of allocation make it difficult to change policy. The consequent credibility of policy can induce firms and individuals to invest, thereby making redistribution, regulation, and production effective. For instance, market-based solutions, which represent the most notable alternatives to inefficient allocation methods such as command-and-control regulation or government-controlled production, have many advantages; depending, however, on the context and the extent of the policy's credibility, they may fail to stimulate private investment, to deny the requests of potential claimants, and to limit aggregate costs.

It is important in making these points to reiterate that we are not suggesting that, under all circumstances, designing constitutional systems, agencies, or policies as rigidly as possible is desirable regardless of the inefficiencies that are incorporated as a consequence. But we are implying that there are some conditions, such as the need to induce investment, that make stable structures and policies especially useful. For instance, dramatic swings in policy, such as in public ownership or in price regulation of a capital-intensive industry, are likely to be undesirable. Conversely, in some situations long-term stability is especially harmful, for example, when new knowledge or conditions require policy adaptation. The benefits of stable policy may partly explain why certain forms of economic regulation, such as command-and-control regulation, which were recognized as causing inefficiencies and which were unable to take advantage of technological change, were nevertheless allowed to persist for long.

The Power of Weak Institutions

Related to the above lesson, strong political institutions are typically thought to enhance public policy and, undoubtedly, they frequently do. But because powerful institutions can quickly change policies, they may often suffer from poor credibility. Our analyses of unified versus divided governments and of centralized versus federal governments in particular suggest that unified, parliamentary, or centralized governments that produce dramatic, often pendulum-like, changes undermine policy by deterring compliance. Seemingly weaker institutions may promote stability, compliance (for example, by inducing investment), and, hence, policy success.

Clearly, the importance and the desirability of weak institutions will vary with several characteristics. The most obvious is, once again, the importance of investment to policy success. If much investment is needed, credibility is required, and weak institutions are more likely to provide such assurances. And, similar to what was implied above, weak institutions will work best when the constancy of policy is more important than adapting to changed conditions. Thus, for example, weak institutions may work very well in getting educational institutions to invest in complying with a law such as the Americans with Disabilities Act. But they may deal poorly with an economic sector such as high technology which is constantly reinventing itself and for which current policies may quickly become anachronistic. Nonetheless, while weak institutions may have shortfalls, they may have their benefits too.

Conclusions: The Burden of Government

We intend to redesign, to reinvest, to reinvigorate the entire National Government. (President Bill Clinton, March 3, 1993)

Calls for the reinvention, reform, or reengineering of public policy, such as those made by Bill Clinton early in his presidency, are commonplace. Typically, such advocates go on to argue that government can look like the private sector, with all of its flexibility, cost-consciousness, flexibility, and creativity. All that is needed is some political ingenuity.

Our analysis suggests that the world of politics is more complex and qualitatively different than that of the market. Beyond their obvious political problems, dramatic reform efforts are unlikely to be cure-alls because of the nature of underlying economic processes. Economic constraints will always place limitations and costs on what government can accomplish. Failure to integrate such economic logic into policy analyses will obscure what government can and cannot accomplish.

Put differently, public policy will never be markets writ large. Public and private actions are marked by fundamental economic differences, many of which we have covered in our analysis of credibility, crowding, expectations, and multiple equilibria. While political reorganization and streamlining may have many benefits, attempts to solve the problems of government by merely superimposing the logic of the market on the political system will lead to consequences that are often unintended and frequently undesirable.

Rather, the underlying economic processes that will be crucial for normative and positive analysis must be carefully considered and integrated. Policy will be a function of what is possible—what government can do— the nature of the political system, and the interaction between the two. Since what government can do is not equivalent to what the market can produce, our expectations of and evaluations about the political system must be adjusted accordingly.

NOTES

REFERENCES

INDEX

Notes

Introduction

1. See, however, Wittman (1995), who persuasively argues that government fails no more than do free markets.
2. We use public good in its technical sense: for a public good, the amount that each person can consume equals the amount produced. In contrast, for a private good, the *sum* of the amounts consumed equals the amount produced. Note that some public goods (such as television broadcasts) may be provided by private firms and that some private goods (such as mail service) may be provided by government.
3. Several of these reforms and structural changes are discussed further in Chapter 5.
4. Although economic explanations of policy are common, they are often economic analogues to political explanations. (The notable exception is macroeconomics, which we discuss in depth later.) These are interesting and valuable explanations, but our focus lies elsewhere. For instance, some economic interpretations of policy failures roughly parallel the two political explanations already discussed. Related to the assertion that politicians do not aim to solve social problems, a standard argument is that politicians assure poor outcomes by favoring command-and-control over market-based solutions (that is, defining required behaviors that are punishable over providing incentives that should result in desired results; for a discussion, see Schultze 1977). For example, rather than instructed to use performance-based regulations or liability laws for enforcement, the United States Occupational Safety and Health Administration was directed to write detailed rules on exactly what factories should do (Viscusi, Vernon, and Harrington 1995). Roughly corresponding to the idea that organized interests induce government to help them when the social benefits are small or negative, economists cite examples where government adopted policies to remedy a market failure that never existed in the first place.

For instance, at least before deregulation, entry and exit into transportation industries was restricted when there was no need for any government action (Rothenberg 1994).

5. Notably, although the state of the economy is consistently reported to be crucial in elections, political scientists usually ignore macroeconomics in such overviews of public policy. Also, as we explicitly consider major policy functions in an idealized political setting, we neglect important areas of current research in political science and economics that are relevant to policy. Thus, for example, we largely ignore principal-agent and related informational problems between members of Congress, the president, and the bureaucracy, or between agencies and those they attempt to control (Moe 1984, Horn 1995). Rather, we move a step beyond, generally asking whether even unified and well-informed governments can solve some policy problems but not others.

6. Admittedly, tobacco assistance may lower consumption by limiting production and raising prices. Nonetheless, by reducing risk, such a policy should also encourage tobacco farmers to remain in business.

7. The small drop in U.S. alcohol consumption compared to the drop in the proportion of smokers (only 5 percent compared to almost 30 percent for the period from 1974 to 1991) supports the intuition that concerns in addition to health explain the decline in smoking.

8. The calculation of annual damage uses the assumption that in 1991 the average pollution cost for each mile traveled in automobiles is 3 cents. Cost estimates are from Small and Kazimi 1995; travel data are reported in Table 1040 of the *Statistical Abstract of the United States* (U.S. Bureau of the Census 1993).

9. About 10 percent of the fleet produces half of all automobile-related pollutants, both because older cars pollute more and because a few cars produce most of the pollution within any model year (for a survey, see Glazer, Klein, and Lave 1995).

10. This is not to say that they would be an optimal solution. For example, given the wide variance in how much pollution each car produces, a better approach could be to estimate probabilities that a car's emissions would exceed a threshold (and by how much) and mandate that only those cars where expected returns from testing are positive be examined.

11. Externalities appear when one party hurts another without bearing all the costs.

12. This distinction applies less now than several decades ago. The accumulation of data on secondhand smoke (e.g., U.S. Environment Protection Agency 1993), though contested (Barnes and Bero 1998), shows that cigarette smoking can be a negative externality. Indeed, about 60 percent of Americans favor restricting smoking to designated areas in workplaces and restaurants (Robinson and Speer 1995).

13. On nicotine addiction, see U.S. Department of Health and Human Services 1988a, Orleans and Slade 1993, National Institute on Drug Abuse 1998.

14. As we will see in later chapters, crowding is often especially relevant for efforts to control the behavior of individuals.

15. As the popular press has frequently mentioned (e.g., Hilts 1995), social pressures are strong. For instance, the recent rise in smoking among college students appears to arise largely from social pressures. That smoking is lower at commuter colleges, where students presumably spend less time with their peers than at residential colleges, provides additional evidence that crowding effects are at work (see Wechsler et al. 1998).

16. We should be cautious about this point, since the existence of these multiple equilibria could also make advertising for tobacco highly effective. For instance, cigarette companies that target only some young women may cause others who see their peers smoking to take up the habit. In addition, as will become clearer shortly, individuals may anticipate that government will renege on its policy and act accordingly. Imperfect credibility will lead to low investment and will generally discourage compliance.

17. Becker, Grossman, and Murphy (1994; see also Chaloupka and Warner 1999) find that consumers have rational expectations about cigarette prices (and, as implied before, give evidence that at least some smokers can overcome their addictions). They show that a 10 percent permanent increase in the price of cigarettes reduces current consumption by 4 percent in the short run and by 7.5 percent in the long run. In contrast, a 10 percent increase in price for only one period reduces consumption by only 3 percent. Additionally, this one-period price increase of 10 percent reduces consumption in the *previous* period by 0.6 percent. These intertemporal effects are consistent with the assumption that consumers consider future prices (or future cigarette consumption by others) in deciding whether to become addicted to cigarettes.

1. Macroeconomics

1. For example, the difficulty of isolating political and market influences on the macroeconomy plagues studies attempting to isolate the effects of economic conditions on voting (Kramer 1983).

2. Economic growth also reduces unemployment. By a famous empirical regularity known as Okun's law (Okun 1962), a one percentage point increase in economic growth is associated with a one-half percentage point reduction in the unemployment rate.

3. The evidence that voters care about growth and inflation—though not demonstrating that politicians manipulate these features—is strong. For example, Fair's model of elections correctly predicts whether the Democratic presiden-

tial candidate will win more votes than the Republican in seventeen out of twenty-one elections since 1916, with only four close elections incorrectly predicted (Wilson / Hughes in 1916, Nixon / Kennedy in 1960, Nixon / Humphrey in 1968, and Ford / Carter in 1976). Others employ somewhat different assumptions in estimating election models (and also predict well); the finding that short-term retrospective conditions are crucial in presidential elections is robust.

4. GDP is the total value of goods and services produced in a country. For the Unites States, the GDP is very close to the gross national product (GNP), which excludes the output of foreign-owned business in the country and includes the output of U.S.-owned businesses abroad.

5. Money differs from wealth, as people and firms hold assets besides cash and checking accounts.

6. Strictly speaking, the Federal Reserve Bank buys Treasury bills from a few large dealers. For expository purposes, we speak of direct purchases from consumers. Also, the Bank may pay a premium, for example $9,600 rather than $9,500, to buy the bill. We assume that the bill is bought for $9,500 only for simplicity.

7. In their classic paper, Sargent and Wallace (1981) show conditions that make expansionary monetary policy *reduce* consumption and *reduce* aggregate demand. Specifically, expansionary monetary policy that allows government to print money to cover a portion of its expenses reduces government's need to borrow. This lower level of borrowing allows government to print less money in later periods, reduces future inflation, increases the willingness of economic agents to hold money, and, as a result, increases demand for cash and reduces consumers' incentives to spend. If the increased demand for cash is sufficiently high, prices will decline. The conditions, however, required for expansionary monetary policy to reduce consumption are improbable. For example, Dotsey (1996) shows that, given plausible estimates of demand for money, the required conditions are not met in the United States.

8. The real interest rate is the inflation-adjusted interest rate, roughly equal to the nominal interest rate minus the inflation rate.

9. As this result requires the rates of return (including expected changes in exchange rates) on domestic assets to equal returns on foreign assets, it implies that a policy change may temporarily cause the exchange rate to overshoot its long-run equilibrium value. For example, a short-term increase, say for one year, in the U.S. money supply will lower domestic interest rates for one year. This increased money supply will cause the dollar to trade for less foreign currency, as capital initially flows abroad, and then to appreciate at a rate that makes the rate of return on U.S. assets equal the rate of return on foreign assets. After a year of gradual increases, U.S. interest rates and the dollar's exchange rate will return to their initial levels (Dornbusch 1976).

10. According to Feldstein (1994), the converse was witnessed in the 1980s, as Ronald Reagan's 1980 election reinforced beliefs that the Federal Reserve Bank would fight inflation. Real interest rates, abetted by large budget deficits, rose, increasing the attractiveness of dollar investments and appreciating the dollar.

11. Indeed, maintaining the assumption of imperfect foresight is crucial for finding empirical evidence that monetary policy matters in a manner consistent with the traditional view. For instance, if we do not assume rational expectations, the empirical evidence on the relationship between real interest rates, output, and prices is consistent with that predicted by traditional models in which monetary policy is effective. By contrast, under the assumption of rational expectations the evidence suggests that changes in real interest rates are exogenous and do not produce changes in output or prices; that is, monetary policy is ineffective (Litterman and Weiss 1985).

12. The real price of a good adjusts for inflation; it is the price charged divided by a price index. The change in the real price is approximately equal to the change in the nominal price minus the inflation rate.

13. These data are adapted from Carlton (1986). Similar findings are presented by Blinder (1991) for the Unites States and by Bergeijk, Haffner, and Waasdorp (1993) and Anderson (1994) for Europe and Japan. Gagnon and Knetter (1995) also find comparable price stickiness in response to exchange rate fluctuations.

14. One might maintain that firms anticipating election results would adjust their behavior just before the election (although some important works assume that price rises before an election are little influenced by whether a Republican or a Democrat wins; for a review, see Alesina (1995)). It is hard to believe, however, that elections never surprise, and we would expect rational firms and workers to delay price or wage changes until they see the new monetary policy.

15. These results are based on Garfinkel and Glazer (1994).

16. Though the first few days in November are pre-election, little error is introduced by including them in the post-election quarter.

17. Although we would like to incorporate the value of the wage contracts agreed upon, such data are difficult to obtain.

18. We obtain similar results when examining the proportion of all workers entering into contracts, rather than the proportion of all contracts that are signed.

19. The weak relationship between timing and contract signings might represent rational expectations as politicians, knowing that labor and business will adjust their behavior, will not bother manipulating monetary policy. Such reasoning, however, violates "time consistency." Barro and Gordon (1983) argue that if economic agents anticipate inflation, then government will increase the money supply to generate that inflation. In the United States, this would mean that if Democrats won an election they would still increase the money supply.

If firms did not increase prices (and, presumably, nominal labor costs), then Democrats would be able to stimulate the economy; if prices go up, then Democrats could try to prevent the recession that would otherwise occur.

20. A Chi-square test shows that the difference in the time distribution of contracts in years with and without a presidential election is statistically significant at the 5 percent level; the difference between election and non election years is insignificant.

21. As a further test of the "rational partisan" view combining rational expectations with partisan politics, we examined whether changes in real economic growth and unemployment in the United States from 1952 to 1988 relate to the closeness of electoral outcomes, as measured both by electoral college and popular vote results (on the rational partisan view, see Alesina and Rosenthal (1995); for a critique, see Hibbs (1992)). This test finds no support for the prediction of the rational partisan view that greater surprise leads to larger changes in the economy. Although we are unsure why different measures of surprise should produce different results, Alesina, Roubini, and Cohen (1997) do find a positive relationship between surprise and post-election changes in economic conditions when they use pre-election polls to measure the surprise of an election result. Also finding evidence for the importance of elections (although not measuring surprise per se), Gartner (1986) shows that spot exchange rates change immediately after an election, as they should if the outcomes are surprises and if the identity of the winner affects economic conditions. Similarly, Ellis and Thoma (1995) and Garfinkel, Glazer, and Lee (1999) uncover partisan effects on real exchange rates.

22. Widely cited papers are Alesina (1989) and Cukierman et al. (1992). Recent work that finds that central bank independence lowers the mean and variance of inflation is Eijffinger, Schaling, and Hoeberichts (1998). Forder (1998), however, questions the reliability of measures of central independence and thus the reliability of the results. Also, analyses may be plagued by selection problems, as the relationship between independence and inflation may arise not because of independence per se but because countries that most care about low inflation are those that delegate the most independence to central banks. Our view is that central bank policy does matter, but that the formal independence of the central bank may not be all that important.

23. The desirability of discretion arises from a simple principle—that it is hard to discover information about officials bound by rules. If the rule is ever removed or relaxed, uncertainty about future policy may be greater than if discretion had previously prevailed. In contrast, discretion generates information about the determinants of government policy, such as the types of officials in power, the preferences of voters, or the influence of special interest groups (Cowen, Glazer, and Zajc 2000).

24. Whereas interpreting (1.1) as an accounting identity assumes that goods that firms produce but cannot sell are investments in inventory, interpreting it as reflecting desired spending dictates making the more sensible assumption that excess inventory is unplanned and undesired.

25. By a result known as the balanced budget multiplier, this analysis can be extended to show that the stimulus from fiscal policy will appear even if government increases taxes to pay for increased expenditures. Specifically, the effects of fiscal policy depend not only on the deficit but also on the tax and expenditure *levels*. To see this, let the initial equilibrium have aggregate income Y_0 and taxes T_0; then let government spending and taxes both increase by ΔG. If we suppose that consumption depends only on disposal income, $Y - T$, we can see that when Y also increases by ΔG, disposal income is $(Y_0 + \Delta G) - (T_0 + \Delta G) = Y_0 - T_0$. In other words, consumption remains the same when government spending and taxes increase by ΔG, leading to an increase in aggregate spending so that they now equal $Y_0 + \Delta G$. With slack in the economy, the increased demand can generate increased output, leading to a new equilibrium output, $Y_0 + \Delta G$; that is, a fiscal stimulus is felt even with higher taxes.

26. As we will explain when we discuss budget deficits, this result holds even if government reduces taxes instead of increases spending.

27. Beyond crowding, rational expectations may also limit the long-run effectiveness of fiscal policy in a manner analogous to how they limit monetary policy; that is, rational expectation of a fiscal stimulus may undermine its effectiveness. For instance, a worker expecting that the government will stimulate the economy under the threat of increasing unemployment may be less willing to make wage concessions despite apparently low labor demand or to relocate to a community with higher labor demand. The resulting price rigidity and labor immobility may increase unemployment, and a fiscal stimulus will only mitigate such effects. Evidence for such claims is mixed. Case studies examining Ireland, Italy, and France find that when the government more strongly commits to maintaining fixed exchange rates and thus to limiting its use of fiscal policy, wages and prices are more flexible. But cross-country studies uncover no such effect (Eichengreen 1998).

28. For a nice exposition of cheap talk and its ability to coordinate action, see Farrell and Rabin (1996).

29. Cheap talk is likely to be more effective with consumers than with producers, since producers are typically more sophisticated economic actors than consumers and will want to see costly signals. For example, to fight inflation, President Jimmy Carter appealed to the American people early in 1980 to stop using their credit cards. As a result (aided by some mild consumer credit controls that the Federal Reserve Bank adopted in the hope that they would be ineffective), gross national product shrank at an annual rate of 10 percent within

three months, its sharpest dip in thirty-five years, and within four months unemployment increased from 6.3 percent to 7.8 percent (Greider 1987). By contrast, to the extent that it was directed at producers, the Ford administration's effort to assure voluntary price restraints, to "whip inflation now," failed (Stein 1994).

30. The mechanistic Phillips curve describing the negative relationship between inflation and unemployment represents an older view of the trade-off between the two. This view fell into disrepute with the high inflation and the high unemployment of the 1970s. Rather, as will become clearer shortly, the magnitude of the trade-off between inflation and unemployment is subject to manipulation.

31. Government can punish banks in several ways that may make political threats more credible. One is to impose additional regulation against the wishes of those in the banking industry. Another is to withdraw deposits, for instance, through the U.S. Treasury, from some banks in favor of others. Additionally, banks could be turned away when they seek assistance on one issue or another; for example, many of the nation's largest banks would shortly request assistance in dealing with massive debts owed by the Third World.

32. The following analysis of the partisan business cycle mostly follows Garfinkel and Glazer (1996).

33. A similar self-fulfilling process could occur within an incumbent's term if it is believed that other firms will increase their investment only at some points, such as at the term's beginning.

34. The example given is an application of coordination problems that are studied in game theory under the name of the prisoners' dilemma. For applications of this logic to macroeconomics, see Bryant (1983, 1996).

35. In contrast, productivity may decline when high demand for labor raises wages and workers know that they can easily find new employment.

36. Indicative planning is defined as "the construction of economy wide medium-term economic projections by the government, typically in conjunction with representatives of business and possibly of labor and consumers" (Brada and Estrin 1990, p. 524).

37. The following section ignores stimulative effects of chosen spending levels, since they were covered under fiscal policy. Nor do we discuss whether deficits make it easier to justify higher spending levels, since this is the type of purely political issue that is beyond our purview.

38. Reasoning similar to that about fiscal policy shows that although a stimulus to the economy can do good in a recession, deficits may only raise prices if the economy is running near capacity.

39. Robert Barro's work on Ricardian equivalence is seminal (see especially Barro 1974; for a survey, see Barro 1989).

40. For instance, some evidence indicates that politicians behave as if Ricardian equivalence characterizes their constituents' behavior. In examining congressional voting on a 1972 bill to increase Social Security benefits by 20 percent, Lipford and Dougan (1995) find no evidence that congressmen were influenced by the share of the population in their state or district older than 44 or older than 64. This is consistent with predictions stemming from Ricardian equivalence, as one would expect that the direct benefits to the elderly from Social Security increases would be matched by higher taxes to their children.

41. Some elements of consumer myopia are covered in more depth in the discussion of redistribution in the next chapter.

42. The relevant literature is large, including Diamond 1977; Feldstein 1985, 1987; Atkinson 1987; Kotlikoff 1987; and Blanchard and Fischer 1989.

43. For instance, implicit discount rates for energy-saving consumer durables— space heaters, refrigerators, and water heaters—vary from 2 to 300 percent (Dubin 1992).

44. The authors do not test for "strong rational expectations," which hypothesizes that persons use all available information in forming their expectations. Rather, they test for "weak rational expectations" by estimating an equation of the form: Realized inflation in 12 months $= a + b \times$ Expected inflation + Error. Weak rational expectations imply that $a = 0$ and $b = 1$, and therefore any results to the contrary are inconsistent with this version of rational expectations.

2. Redistribution

1. It is a virtual mantra among political scientists that political opposition to redistribution makes it difficult to implement. In the most widely cited statement of this perspective, Theodore Lowi writes that both regulatory and distributive policies are easier to carry out than are redistributive policies (Lowi 1964, 1972). Although we will not deal with this issue head on, as it largely concerns what government wants to do rather than what it can accomplish, our analysis in this chapter is relevant for inferring whether redistribution is as difficult as claimed.

2. The data in Table 2.1 may underestimate the decline in poverty in the United States, and should be viewed with caution. For example, as we shall see, the effects of transfers appear larger if the nation's official poverty measures are used.

3. As we discuss later, designing policy to nudge behavior toward a particular equilibrium is also important for selected issues of redistribution. For instance, equilibrium selection is relevant for redistribution to groups that have

been historically discriminated against, such as to African-Americans, and in explaining how many people eligible for benefits apply for them.

4. Generally, policies helping or hurting labor unions can have redistributive effects. Thus, the fall in American union density in the 1980s caused about 40 to 50 percent of the increase in the wages of white-collar compared with blue-collar workers (Freeman 1993). Similarly, about 40 percent of the difference in wage inequality between the United States and Canada is explained by Canada's higher rate of unionization (Lemieux 1993).

5. From the 1950s through the 1970s, a 1 percentage point increase in the unemployment rate reduced the income share of the poorest quartile by 0.19 percentage points; a 1 percentage point increase in the inflation rate increased the income share of the poorest quartile by 0.11 percentage points. These relationships weakened in the 1980s but reappeared in the 1990s (Haveman and Schwabish 1999).

6. We also ignore local redistribution. Following the work of Tiebout (1956; for similar statements by a political scientist, see Peterson 1981, 1995), conventional wisdom claims that reactions or threats to move elsewhere by persons who must pay for the redistribution will make such policies nearly impossible. More recent work suggests that such inferences are overstated for reasons that are largely unrelated to those discussed in our analysis (Epple and Romer 1991). To illustrate, suppose that a city raises taxes on the rich to redistribute the poor. Although the rich are made worse off by paying higher taxes, the resulting decline in property values can attract new residents. Some wealthy persons will likely prefer a city with high taxes and low land values rather than vice versa. The little data available to test this assertion lend support to the belief that local redistribution is feasible (Orr 1975).

7. We base this inference on two time-series regressions that we estimated. The dependent variables were white income divided by African-American income, and the income share of the poorest 20 percent of the population. The independent variables were percent unemployment, year, year squared, and presidential party in the current and previous years (indicated by dummy variables equal to 1 for Democratic presidents). In explaining the ratio of African-American to white income, unemployment and year are statistically significant (with the ratio of white to African-American income rising as unemployment rises). Coefficients for presidential party are small and statistically insignificant; these political effects are even smaller for determining the income share of the poorest 20 percent. For contrary evidence, see, however, Hibbs and Dennis (1988).

8. AFDC began as a minor provision in the Social Security program. By 1991 it had become a $20 billion program serving 12 million children and parents (Melnick 1994). In 1996 the Personal Responsibility and Work Opportunity Reconciliation Act reformed U.S. welfare programs (Cammisa 1998).

9. Rather than a product of overt decisions by the federal government, this decline in real benefits was a mechanical result of state legislatures failing to raise
nominal benefits to keep up with inflation (Moffitt 1992).

10. For example, even after adjusting for family size, from 1979 to 1987 real income among the poorest 10 percent of families and unrelated individuals declined by 6 percent, while it increased by 14 percent for the highest-earning 10
percent of families (Karoly 1993).

11. The same pattern appears in several countries. In the 1970s Australia, Canada,
France, Germany, Italy, Japan, Korea, the Netherlands, Sweden, the United
Kingdom, and the United States all exhibited declining differences in earnings
between people with high education or skills and people with low education or
skills. But only Korea and the Netherlands showed continued drops in the
1980s (Freeman and Katz 1994).

12. The official measure of poverty specifies income thresholds that are adjusted
for household size, the age of the head of the household, and the number of
children younger than 18. These thresholds are updated annually in accor-
dance with the Consumer Price Index, so that purchasing power is comparable
over time. Pre-transfer poverty, as shown in Figure 2.1, excludes government
income; post-transfer poverty includes all sources of cash income and of noncash transfers but excludes all other sources of noncash income.

13. One reason for this increased pessimism may lie in the steep decline in the ratio of retirees to workers paying the taxes that support them. This dependency
ratio fell from 177 to 1 in 1940, to 13.8 to 1 in 1950, to 3.5 to 1 in 1970, and is
expected to decline to 2 to 1 by 2030 (*Congressional Quarterly* 1983).

14. To foreshadow our discussion of production, the best-known examples of government reneging on long-term programs involve large military and scientific
projects such as the B-2 bomber and the Supercollider particle accelerator. Although large sunk costs would seem to have made these projects durable, they
were not. Intuitively, it should be even easier to cut redistributive programs,
since they do not require the same investment in research and development
and in physical plant. Indeed, what makes cancellation of these production
programs so extraordinary is the amount of money already invested that could
not be recouped. Such impediments to cancellation are absent for redistributive policies.

15. For instance, the General Social Survey of American public opinion (see also
Page and Shapiro 1992) shows that citizens overwhelmingly support the no-
tion that the government should "provide a decent standard of living for the
old" (87.5 percent of those responding between 1988 and 1991), although 56.5
percent disagree with the claim that governmental responsibility includes efforts to "reduce income differences between the rich and poor."

16. The difficulties of assuring durability will be discussed in more depth when we
cover regulation and production.

17. On the differences between parliamentary systems and systems with separa-tion of powers, see Moe and Caldwell (1994) and our discussion in Chapter 5. The flip side of credibility induced by an institutional separation of powers is that reform may also be difficult. For example (though a bit ironically, given that welfare reform *was* finally adopted in 1996), Hayes (1992, p. 198) be-moaned the inability of the American system to adopt comprehensive welfare reform rather than rely on incremental tinkering to the system, complaining that "sunk costs and vested interests in established policies—expanded and modified incrementally over the years—can make rational reform impossible." As mentioned, although calls for changing Social Security are common (for example, during the 1996 U.S. presidential campaign, Republican aspirant Steve Forbes advocated partial privatization of the retirement system, as did George W. Bush in 2000), its comprehensive reform appears more difficult.

18. Although an individual's decision to save does not influence whether redistri-bution takes place per se, saving can result in a higher retirement income at the expense of present income.

19. The implications of myopia for a program such as Social Security, whose bene-fits are seen only late in life, are a bit more complicated. Presumably, myopic individuals would not reduce savings in anticipation of future Social Security benefits since they behave as if such payments are unexpected (although, as will be discussed, Social Security taxes may reduce their savings by limiting funds available for saving). With some exceptions that will be spelled out shortly, myopia will result in less crowding out.

20. Murray (1984) illustrates the general ineffectiveness of government with the example of antismoking policy. Yet, as already discussed, crowding in (given both credibility and rational expectations) and the existence of multiple equi-libria appear to have allowed some governments to reduce smoking in the population.

21. The wording of the statement evaluated by respondents was "If social welfare benefits such as disability, unemployment compensation, and early retirement pensions are as high as they are now, it only makes people not want to work anymore."

22. Similar in magnitude to the 37 percent reduction in poverty found by the Council, Plotnick et al. (1998) estimate that transfers and taxes moved 47 per-cent of the pre-transfer poor above the poverty line.

23. Canada also provided some national transfers through the tax system for fami-lies with children.

24. Besides welfare, the data indicate that government can effectively redistribute by outlawing discrimination and by mandating affirmative action. For exam-ple, evidence suggests that the wage differential between African-American and white males declined steadily over time. African-American males earned

43.3 percent of what white males earned in 1940, 55.2 percent in 1950, 57.5 percent in 1960, and 72.6 percent in 1990. Although not all of this change arose from antidiscrimination and affirmative action programs (it reflects higher African-American education levels, for example), research shows that these policies worked (Smith and Welch 1989; for a specific discussion of the changes in the 1940s, see Goldin and Margo 1992). Similarly, studies find that affirmative action has raised the occupational levels of nonwhite males (Leonard 1990) and increased employment of African-Americans by requiring firms to submit to compliance reviews (Leonard 1985). During World War II, the Fair Employment Practice Commission, which had no formal powers and operated solely through exhortation, played a key role in opening employment opportunities for African-Americans (Collins 1997). Thus, although individuals and firms may try to evade antidiscrimination and affirmative action laws and undermine their impacts, they have not negated their redistributive effects. One reason such policies may be effective is that they move hiring practices at firms from one of several multiple equilibria to another.

25. To reiterate, this should not be interpreted to imply that welfare policy either succeeded or failed. We are agnostic about the broader sociological issues that embroil discussions of welfare, and about the cost efficiency of past or current policy in providing a social safety net.

26. Measures of present value translate dollars received or paid in the future to dollars received or paid today. Such an adjustment is necessary because most people prefer to receive money today rather than tomorrow and because a dollar today can be invested to yield more than a dollar next year. Mathematically, if we let r be the annual interest rate, the present value of x dollars received n years from today is $x/(1+r)^n$.

27. Generational accounting quantifies how much individuals will receive on net from government, taking into account both their contributions and what they receive (Kotlikoff 1992, Auerbach, Kotlikoff, and Leibfritz 1999).

28. In turn, children who would otherwise assist their parents may substitute taxes for such payments and save the same amount.

29. Because it is difficult to isolate empirically, we largely ignore the possibility that people invest less in their careers knowing that Social Security will provide for their retirement.

30. Applied to credibility, such statements may alternatively be interpreted as suggesting that some persons are willing to take the chance that government, private institutions, or their children will care for them should they live to retirement age.

31. For similar textbook statements, see Boadway and Wildasin 1984 and Blanchard and Fischer 1989. Analogous statements in scholarly articles can be found in Diamond 1977; Feldstein 1985, 1987; Atkinson 1987; Kotlikoff 1987.

32. One might maintain that the survival of Social Security is a fundamental issue and, therefore, that people will give it more attention than changes in benefits. That is, Social Security recipients may be less myopic than the evidence on modest changes in benefits implies.

33. Kotlikoff's study imputes benefits from Social Security on the basis of known characteristics rather than by asking individuals what benefits they expect to receive. Blinder et al. (1981) arrive at similar results when examining the relationship between increased benefits and savings.

34. This study surveyed 11,000 men and women aged 55 to 63 every two years from 1969 to 1979.

35. Indeed, other analyses indicate that Social Security may increase savings. Some claim that Social Security alerts people to retirement needs, making them save more; others postulate a "goal gradient effect" by which Social Security helps consumers approach their desired retirement income, inducing additional effort to meet the goal.

36. The Supplementary Security Income program provides a nationwide minimum income to the aged (usually to persons not eligible for Social Security), the blind, and the disabled.

37. AFDC was originally designed for one-parent families with children. Before 1990 some states also chose to support two-parent families where parents were unemployed. In October 1990 federal law was changed to mandate that all states with AFDC programs also offer an AFDC program for unemployed parents.

38. Moffitt, however, finds that stigma does not vary with the level of benefits.

39. A progressive tax makes the average tax increase with income. A proportional tax, which imposes the same tax rate on all persons, collects more dollars from a rich person than from a poor one and is thus also redistributive. For succinctness, however, we shall speak of a progressive tax.

40. A variant of taxation, the negative income tax, which makes payments to low-income persons, has been proposed as a welfare replacement. It could be adapted for the elderly by providing a grant that declines with income. Such a system, however, has many of the same potential problems of reduced work effort and lowered saving that we discussed earlier (see Ashenfelter and Plant 1990).

41. To understand the difference between nominal and effective taxes, consider how firms may react to increased taxes. Suppose firms are taxed at the rate of $1 per employee per hour. Let the market-clearing wage, where supply equals demand (say with the firm employing 10,000 persons), including taxes, be $6.50 per hour. Since the firm pays the tax, each worker receives $5.50 per hour. But the same equilibrium appears if workers are directly taxed, as workers are paid $6.50 but clear $5.50. Any pair of taxes summing to $1 (for exam-

ple, 75 cents paid by the worker and 25 cents by the employer) produces the same equilibrium. Thus, under certain conditions, taxes that appear to burden firms only increase the prices that consumers pay. This logic also implies that whether taxes for programs such as Social Security or any programs impacting all workers (for example, employer-mandated health insurance) are collected from employees, employers, or both is immaterial since take-home pay remains constant.

Admittedly, the world is often more complicated. For example, taxes on corporate profits can raise the price of a firm's goods, lower demand for these products, reduce dividends paid to shareholders, and reduce wages earned by workers; second-order effects can also appear, as changes in prices can affect demand for goods produced in other industries, changing associated prices, dividends, and wages. Nevertheless, the fundamental point that tax incidence is more complicated than a naive view might suggest holds.

42. Studies looking at a single year are criticized for ignoring lifetime incomes and tax burdens. For instance, a system taxing poor medical students heavily but rich doctors lightly is hardly regressive because the poor students become the rich doctors.

3. When Can Government Regulate?

1. To use the economist's language, an investment can reduce the marginal cost of compliance. Marginal cost measures the change in total cost resulting from a change in the quantity produced. The output can be interpreted as cleaning emissions, increasing worker safety, or meeting other regulatory requirements. A regulation that increases fixed costs but not marginal costs may be initially opposed but, once the fixed costs have been expended, little or nothing is to be gained from deregulation. By contrast, a regulatory requirement accomplishing the same goal but with high marginal costs may not be self-enforcing and may continue to stimulate opposition. Although, as we will discuss, such reasoning requires qualification, both regarding whether investments are reversible or irreversible and whether short-run or long-run views are adopted, this general distinction is valid. Note that economic actors may choose to finance a regulation-induced investment by borrowing, thus incurring costs for many years. But spreading costs created by regulation over many years in this manner will not reduce a regulation's credibility, since the borrower must repay the loan even if the regulation is abolished. As such, the marginal cost to those making the investment of meeting regulatory guidelines will be equivalent whether or not there is borrowing or a large capital outlay.

2. Command-and-control regulation specifies rewards and penalties for some specific behaviors; market-based solutions generate incentives to behave in a

manner that should produce the desired results. Thus, for example, command-and-control regulation may require polluters to meet certain emission guidelines; market-based regulation may set up a tax system or a tradable permit system that allows polluters to decide whether to reduce their emissions or pay the requisite price to pollute.

3. Sunstein (1990) emphasizes this point by noting that excessive regulation can lead to insufficient regulation. For example, federal law requires that once the Department of Labor has initiated a proceeding to regulate a toxic substance, it must impose rules controlling the substance even when the costs are enormous and the health benefits are small. Because regulation, once undertaken, must be draconian, the government avoids regulating many substances at all. Ironically, the consequence of a stringent statutory standard is weak protection of workers. Similarly, under the laws requiring the use of the best available technology in some environmental regulation, an offending plant or industry must install whatever technology is available to reduce the risk, even if the plant or industry must shut down. This requirement produces an "all-or-nothing" approach that leads the Environmental Protection Agency to forgo altogether the regulation of many substances.

4. The concern about cost recovery is, essentially, a variant of the *hold-up* problem (for seminal works, see Williamson 1975, 1979; Klein, Crawford, and Alchian 1978; for more recent analyses, see Graham and Pierce 1989; Milgrom and Roberts 1992; Rogerson 1992; De Fraja 1999; Gersbach and Glazer 1999). In the hold-up game, one side agrees to modify a contract either in the face of dire consequences or because it is too costly to make the other side comply with the agreement. The party that anticipates a hold-up may, therefore, refuse to enter into a contract in the first place. For example, consider a regulatory agency that promises a power company electricity prices that cover the total costs that it incurs in constructing a new plant. Suppose that, after the firm invests, the regulator reneges and announces that it will only allow rates that cover marginal costs of operating the plant and that the company will not be compensated for construction expenses. Having committed the capital, the firm may still find that it loses less by continuing to run it than by shutting it down. Consequently, unless a credible commitment is made, power companies may resist constructing new plants in the first place.

As we discuss in the next chapter on production, hold-up problems may also appear whenever government is the exclusive or the largest consumer of some output whose production entails high fixed costs. For instance, providers of military hardware may worry that they will construct a production facility with no commercial use and that the government will then only pay for the marginal costs of producing weapons.

5. Another option was to wash high-sulfur coal at the mine site. This too would

have raised marginal costs for utilities without requiring large, fixed cost, investments.

6. A firm is vertically integrated when it produces the inputs that it uses to produce its final products.

7. Crowding in may also be reinforced by the tendency of rational managers to invest only when others do so (Scharfstein and Stein 1990). An industry-wide regulation that directly induces a few firms to make a particular type of investment can cause a large increase in aggregate investment because of such herd behavior.

8. Of course, political factors may have shielded automobile manufacturers from heavy sanctions. Most obviously, the industry's concentration can originate political organization (Olson 1965). Yet the observation that the type of bargaining accords with that predicted by models incorporating credibility and associated economic constraints suggests that such factors are relevant.

9. Quayle, relying on the Motor Vehicle Manufacturers Association's assertion, voiced in opposition to legislative attempts in 1990 to increase the CAFE requirement to 40 miles per gallon (mpg) that 150,000 to 300,000 jobs would be lost (with a best guess of around 200,000), maintained that 300,000 jobs would disappear with the 45 mpg standard advocated by environmentalists in 1992.

10. Clearly, such willingness by firms to ask for waivers must be predicated on a belief that one is not opening a Pandora's box, where a whole gamut of policy is placed on the agenda and amended in an undesirable way. Policy will have more credibility if such a possibility exists.

11. A similar strategy is proposed for electric cars, where requirements that 2 percent of 1998 autos sold in California, New York, and Massachusetts be electric remain unmet. These states have considered a rule requiring all firms to offer electric cars once at least two viable electric car models are created, or that the mandate be enforced only two years after someone, somewhere, builds an acceptable vehicle (of course, acceptability is ambiguous and itself requires precise definition). Presumably, this could provide some firms (for example, battery manufacturers or upstart firms exclusively producing electric vehicles) with an incentive to develop such cars and perhaps also induce the major automobile companies to spend more on perfecting electric car technology.

12. Lead is well known to cause brain damage, as measured, for example, by lowered IQs. Although the effect of CFCs has been more controversial, they are generally considered to be the principal cause of the depletion of the stratospheric ozone layer protecting the earth from harmful ultraviolet rays. CFC use increased roughly fifteenfold from 1955 to 1988 before consumption began declining (see Porter and Brown 1996).

13. Sale of leaded gasoline in western Europe was restricted much later than in the United States. This difference suggests that explanations of U.S. events that fo-

cus on the appearance of statistical information demonstrating hazards of lead (e.g., Gray, Saligman, and Graham 1997, Weimer and Vining 1999), although they tell an important part of the story, are incomplete.

14. These data are taken from the World Resource Institute, http://www.igc.apc. org/wri/wr-98-99/ozone1.htm#CFC.

15. The tools available to politicians that we discuss here are relevant for the other types of policies that we examine, but are most central for regulation. Also, although the issues that we examine foreshadow some of our discussion in Chapter 5, they involve generic political features rather than differences between various political institutions.

16. Also, Moe and Caldwell (1994) suggest that the types of bureaucratic formalities that overcome credibility problems and establish durability lead to policy that is highly inefficient. That is, beyond a trade-off between political responsiveness and durability, there may be a trade-off between efficiency and commitment via delegation.

17. For example, Gabriel Hague, retired chairman of Manufacturers Hanover Trust and formerly President Eisenhower's chief economic advisor, proclaimed that "seldom has President Carter used his appointive power so well." Chase Manhattan Bank Chairman David Rockefeller concurred that "Paul is tough and determined" (Bennett 1979, p. A4) and could resist political pressures in shaping monetary policies. This belief was echoed by Salomon Brothers partner Henry Kaufman, who asserted that the Volcker appointment "ends the speculation on whether the White House is going to politicize monetary policy" (Pine and Berry 1979, p. A1).

18. Pertschuk, chairman of the Federal Trade Commission during the Carter administration, promoted bold initiatives at a previously moribund agency, angering elected officials (Pertschuk 1982). After the ascent of a Republican administration, he was quickly replaced with the conservative James Miller.

19. For a good, nontechnical discussion of reputation from the perspective of noncooperative game theory, see Kreps 1990.

20. Specifically, reputation may have limited effect because regulators gain nothing in their last period in office by building a reputation, and it is not rational for them to make such sacrifices. As a result, it is useless to make sacrifices in the next to last period, and so on. Ultimately, this logic of backward induction (making calculations by going from the last period to the first) implies that it may be irrational to invest in reputation in any period. The same logic essentially holds if regulators have high discount rates. Applied to our example, it follows that a regulator may not want to strictly enforce CAFE standards in the last period of his term. And he would not choose strict enforcement in the previous period because car companies would know that they would not have to conform in the final period. This logic can be extended to the initial period and leads to unraveling.

21. The example below differs from the previous discussion of unraveling by considering imperfect information about the regulator's preferences. This allows reputational considerations to affect behavior even when the number of periods is fixed.

22. Economists advocate use of economic incentives because they can (1) equate the marginal costs across regulatees, thereby lowering total costs for given compliance, and (2) give firms incentives to develop technologies and alternatives to meet the regulatory goals (Kahn 1998).

23. For the sake of parsimony, we concentrate here on creating markets and largely ignore efforts to change incentives.

24. Title IV of the Act created a market for sulfur oxides as part of a program to cut their production in half. Rights to produce sulfur oxides were distributed to coal-burning power plants that then had the option of keeping them or trading them to other current or new producers.

25. An unrelated problem that may reduce the safety benefits of antilock brakes is that drivers may not know how to operate them properly when they initially switch from conventional brakes. This effect will, presumably, disappear over time.

26. For example, forty-five American states instituted some form of no-fault divorce from 1969 to 1974, and the rate of divorce increased from 3.5 per 1,000 population in 1970 to 5.2 per 1,000 just ten years later.

4. Producing Goods and Services

1. The inability of the FAA to replace an aging, 1960s-style, air traffic control system has caused consternation and a presidential proposal to put the entire system in the hands of a government corporation (the agency spent $2 billion on a modernization program, which it then scrapped in 1994 when projected costs rose from $8 billion to $37 billion). The Model Cities program, initially intended to include only a few municipalities, was much expanded at its inception and exemplifies the difficulties of limiting eligibility (Arnold 1979).

2. Issues of multiple equilibria are unimportant for production, and are not discussed in this chapter.

3. We can distinguish such discussions from arguments about whether government should turn over some functions to the private sector, ranging from airports (Wilson-Smith 1995) to mail service (Ferrara 1990) to the guardianship of public lands (Lehman 1995). In such instances, government would either act exclusively as a regulator or play no role at all.

4. Regulation that bans or limits the use of goods that are not important inputs for government outputs has no production analogue—for example, government regulations that restrict the use of lead, CFCs, or any number of other pollutants.

5. Our earlier discussion of crowding out caused by redistribution is also relevant for understanding production. Though our analysis of redistribution focuses on how people respond to offers of money, goods, and services, and assumes that government can produce outputs such as housing or medical care at the desired levels, we now relax this assumption and investigate under what conditions the production goal is likely to be met.

6. We will, for the most part, assume that increased production satisfies the demand. In some circumstances, however, especially when congestion is heavy, added output only causes demand to increase and the market price may not decline. This result is most clearly shown with road construction, where more highways may merely increase traffic rather than reduce congestion (see Arnott and Small 1994). For example, consider two routes connecting two cities, with the first taking 15 minutes and the second requiring $10 + 10(F/C)$ minutes, where F is traffic flow and C is route capacity. If flow is 900 and capacity is 1,800 cars, travel time is 15 minutes on each route. Increasing capacity to 2,000 cars may merely increase flow to 1,000 cars, so that travel time remains 15 minutes; that is, increasing production leads to no decline in travel time (this is an example of the Pigou-Knight-Downs paradox).

   In what is known as the Downs-Thompson paradox, augmenting road capacity can even heighten congestion when travelers can switch modes of transportation (for example, from trains or buses to cars). Suppose that trains must cover some fixed share of their costs from fare revenues. If road capacity increases, some commuters may switch to cars from mass transit; in response, mass transit quality will be degraded by less frequent service, inducing still others to shift to the roads. For example, again denote flow and capacity as F and C, with subscripts r and t signifying roads and trains. Let road travel time be $10 + 10(F_r/C_r)$ minutes and train time be $20 - (F_t/300)$ minutes. Let the total number of travelers be 1,000. Because more train travelers induce more frequent service, travel time is 16.67 minutes when no roads exist and everybody uses trains, but rises to 20 minutes when road capacity is 1,000 and everybody uses the roads.

7. As we will discuss in depth shortly, private production will be especially discouraged if firms believe that government is committed to its own production over the long term. By contrast, when it is costly for firms to enter or to leave the industry, and when government's commitment is questionable, private producers may try to stick it out and to continue to supply the output. By contrast, private profitability may not be much reduced if the market the government serves is of little interest to the private sector. For example, if, as has been advocated in the United States, government adopts a "midnight basketball" program to keep poor youths from committing crimes or from abusing drugs and alcohol (Shogren 1994), prices at private athletic facilities will likely re-

main stable. In other words, public production that complements, rather than substitutes for, private output will cause less crowding out.

8. In total, 300,000 aircraft, 87,600 tanks, and 8.5 million tons of warships were built. An atomic bomb was developed, at a cost, using 1999 price levels, of about $75 billion (Milward 1977). In September 1942, tanks were produced at the rate of 4,000 a month (one every twelve minutes). Between 1940 and 1945 some 12,677 B-17 bombers were built. Munitions output in 1943 was 83 percent higher than in 1942, aircraft tonnage 140 percent higher, and production of merchant ships 100 percent higher (Goodwin 1994).

9. A similar story may be told about national park facilities. Politicians are accused of loving to establish new national parks but of losing interest in maintaining them (Ridenour 1994). Thus, for example, poorly maintained lodgings in the national parks may not crowd out better maintained facilities furnished by the private sector just outside park boundaries.

10. Critics may note that the substitution here may be imperfect because, to attract support, public broadcasting may have to adjust the programs that it presents and the way it shows them (for example, by including announcements that are tantamount to brief commercials). Nonetheless, the general lesson that crowding out working in reverse likely leads to reduced government support increasing private support still holds.

11. Economists label this increase in aggregate spending despite crowding out the "flypaper effect." Estimates of additional spending from a dollar of federal money range from 25 cents to one dollar. That is, most studies find that there is significant crowding out, but that local governments spend more than would be theoretically expected. Some argue that incomplete crowding results from the cognitive problem of understanding price effects, the difficulty of monitoring grants to localities, or the way issues are framed (for a discussion, see Hines and Thaler 1995). Nonetheless, most consider the flypaper effect to be an unresolved puzzle.

12. Contributors to this large literature include Andreoni (1989, 1990), Cornes and Sandler (1984, 1994), Kingma (1989), McClelland (1989), Roberts (1987), Sandler and Posnett (1991), and Steinberg (1986, 1987). Political scientists (e.g., Moe 1980, Wilson 1995) similarly speak of the role that purposive incentives play in contributions to political organizations.

13. Indeed, under such conditions, government action could crowd in production. For example, arts organizations, especially those supporting avant-garde art that is often viewed with suspicion, claim that government support is necessary to confirm the worthiness of (or, alternatively, partially discredit attacks on) the endeavor to potential donors (Hughes 1995). Public funding would then induce additional private support.

14. More concretely, consider a Cobb-Douglas production function, $q = \sqrt{(ab)}$,

where q is output, a is the variable input, and b is the capital input. The marginal product of input a is the derivative of q with respect to a, or $(\tfrac{1}{2})\sqrt{b/a}$. If aggregate contributions are e and contributions are allocated optimally, $a = b = e/2$. The marginal product of an additional contribution is then $\tfrac{1}{2}$. Given this production function, some potential contributors may decide to contribute nothing, regardless of the value of e. By contrast, if government provides e units of input b, the marginal product of a when $a = 0$ is high, higher than $\tfrac{1}{2}$, and, in equilibrium, private contributions can be positive. Put differently, although government provision of input b may crowd out its private provision, the greater impact of a contribution of input a may make its private provision more attractive, thereby resulting in increased private contributions.

15. Because the logic presented here resembles that already covered in our discussion of regulating firms in Chapter 3, we keep our analysis brief compared with our discussions of crowding out or of credibility problems that make limiting production difficult.

16. Some government projects will have few alternative uses not because of any conscious attempt to assure credibility but because of their inherent nature. For instance, an arms laboratory developing nuclear weaponry may have few other applications because taking over and converting such a facility for other production is unprofitable. By contrast, other activities may lend themselves to alternative uses. For example, the best site for a naval shipyard may be in a location that allows easy conversion to commercial production. A firm may, therefore, be willing to invest in a shipyard but not in ancillary facilities specialized to military production.

17. On the other hand, the purchase of nonunique goods reduces the support of firms for the governmental policy and thus may reduce policy credibility. Political factors may therefore make policy more credible when firms are induced to make investments that are profitable only when government continues the policy.

18. The effectiveness of such a strategy is partly predicated on how difficult it is for government to renege and allow additional firms into the market.

19. This is obviously an argument against second sourcing—where two or more firms build the same product—to improve the government's bargaining position (Farrell and Gallini 1988). This is not to say that second sourcing is undesirable but rather to suggest that getting firms and workers to make requisite investments will prove more difficult.

20. As will be discussed shortly, although abstract rationing has been used in other wealthy democracies and the United States has seen isolated cases of success, the most notable attempt in the United States did not work much better than specific rationing owing to flaws in the program design, which did little to discourage investment.

21. Awareness that treatment will be provided has encouraged practices such as "granny dumping," in which the sick and elderly are left at hospital doorsteps by their caregivers (Conrad 1992).
22. Our discussion here relies on Aaron and Schwartz (1984, 1990).
23. In fairness, in some instances Britain limits outlays for procedures requiring little capital or physician time. Most conspicuously, although most of the required drugs are plentiful, chemotherapy is used less than in the United States.
24. Only 14 percent of U.S. physicians made such complaints, compared with 20 percent in Germany and 50 percent in Canada.
25. To reiterate, in many situations abstract rationing *has* worked in the United States (for a list of such successes, see Glazer and Rothenberg 1999).
26. For instance, this problem is faced by New York state, where excess capacity due to a large number of campuses has made it difficult to limit enrollment at the State University of New York.
27. Santa Barbara, California, for example, has followed this strategy by restricting sewer capacity.
28. This suggests that mechanisms such as vouchers may be effective in producing education but not many other goods.

5. Economic Constraints and Political Institutions

1. To expand on a point described and illustrated previously, credible policy may *reduce* policy effectiveness if the harmful effects of offsetting behavior are strongly tied to beliefs that policy is credible. For example, as discussed in Chapter 1, because taxpayers will have less incentive to find alternative ways of earning or spending income that circumvent tax increases that will be rolled back shortly, increases that are expected to be short-lived may generate more revenue in a given period than those expected to endure. Or, in the spirit of Chapter 2's discussion of redistribution, minimum wage increases that employers expect to be repealed may reduce employment by less than permanent wage increases would because less substitution of capital for labor will be undertaken. Usually, however, we find that greater credibility increases the effectiveness of policy (see North and Weingast 1989, Greif, Milgrom, and Weingast 1994).
2. Since 1947–1948, party control has been divided in 1947–1948, 1955–1960, 1969–1976, 1980–1992, and 1995–2000, that is, in about thirty of the last fifty years.
3. Although some analyses claim that divided government produces bad policy, Mayhew's study is the best and the most comprehensive (for an overview and discussion, see Brady 1993). Experience with divided and unified American governments in the 1990s—for example, the seeming failure of two years of

unified government in 1993 and 1994, which led to Republican victory in Congress—also seems to validate Mayhew's perspective. Indeed, Mayhew finds no dramatic differences between unified and divided governments in the 1990s when he examines this period (see http://pantheon.yale.edu/~dmayhew/).

4. The principal exception to such descriptions appears in the Johnson administration, which implemented a large activist agenda in conjunction with a large Democratic majority in Congress.

5. As summarized by Moe and Caldwell (1994), this perspective states that the separation of powers yields an "organizational nightmare for American government. Winning groups and legislators would like to create agencies that are effective and accountable, but two forces inherent in politics itself—political uncertainty and fear of the state—prompt them to bury their agencies in bureaucracy and insulate them from ongoing control. The losers, meantime, usually must be accommodated through compromises over structure, and they demand structures fully intended to hobble agency performance. And then there is the president, who is the system's only champion of effective, responsible government—but whose efforts, in context, create still more bureaucracy and heighten the complexities and internal contradictions of the American administrative system. Not a pretty picture" (p. 176).

6. In the late 1940s the British Labor government nationalized production of coal, transportation, electricity, gas, iron, and steel. A later Conservative government privatized road haulage and denationalized iron and steel, and still later some Labor governments undid these changes and nationalized the aircraft and shipbuilding industries. The Conservative Thatcher government then reversed Labor policy, privatizing firms such as the British Gas Corporation, British Airways, British Steel, the British Transport Docks Board, and the National Freight Company.

7. On voter preferences for divided government, see Sigelman, Wahlbeck, and Buell 1997.

8. Although most of our discussion refers to the United States, it is relevant for other federal systems.

9. See the discussions in Rivlin (1992) and McKinnon and Nechyba (1997). On political innovation, see Walker (1969), Gray (1973), Polsby (1984), Berry and Berry (1990, 1992, 1994), Grady and Chi (1994), and Nice (1994).

10. Despite its importance, the latter criticism is beyond the scope of our analysis (for a discussion, see Revesz 1992).

11. In deriving the result that local regulation is efficient, Oates and Schwab (1988) suppose that each state sets limits on aggregate emissions, so that the addition of a polluting firm in a jurisdiction automatically requires lower emissions by each firm. Wellisch (1995) and Glazer (1999) show, however, that if a state sets emissions of each firm at a level that does not vary with the num-

ber of firms causing the pollution, then local regulation can be excessively stringent.

12. The arguments that we advance here have some clear similarities to those that claim that federalism is better at preserving property rights (e.g., Weingast 1995).

13. This discussion follows from work on option markets and principles for investment timing, which demonstrates that a firm (or a government) may gain by postponing a decision to adopt a profitable investment (Glazer 1985, Pindyck 1991, Dixit 1992).

14. Alternatively, if mobility arises from other factors not directly related to benefit levels, redistributive policy under federalism can be more successful, as individuals may worry that they will end up in a low-benefit locality.

15. These states were Alaska, Arizona, Arkansas, California, Colorado, Florida, Idaho, Maine, Massachusetts, Michigan, Mississippi, Missouri, Montana, Nebraska, North Dakota, Ohio, Oklahoma, Oregon, South Dakota, Utah, Washington, and Wyoming (Carey 1996). All such provisions were ruled unconstitutional by the U.S. Supreme Court in May 1995 in *U.S. Term Limits, Inc. v. Thornton.*

16. Texas agencies are subject to sunset every dozen years, and must gain approval from both legislative chambers and the governor.

17. Like term limits, campaign finance reform has often been found unconstitutional in the United States (see especially the 1976 Supreme Court case of *Buckley v. Valeo*).

18. Such implied criticisms differ from those typically levied against term limits or finance reform: legislative turnover is already common so the reforms are unnecessary; power will be shifted toward the bureaucracy, special interests, and congressional staffers, and away from senior legislators; or elected officials will be disproportionately wealthy.

19. Although this point has not been made about political reform, some authors recognize the importance of credibility. For example, Curry (1990, p. 62) notes that sunset review is used not only to determine if an agency should be abolished but also "to develop a broader base of political legitimacy."

20. Indeed, the improved credibility generated by institutional rules requiring policy scrutiny or encouraging turnover of public officials may provide one of the many explanations for the higher growth rates in democracies. Notably, credibility should generate investment (Leahy and Whited 1996), and investment should increase growth. Consistent with the theme that uncertainty reduces economic growth, studies have found that government instability (Alesina et al. 1992) and coups and assassinations (Barro 1991, 1996) are both associated with lower growth.

21. Indeed, political interference in other aspects of financial policy may have en-

hanced the Bundesbank's credibility concerning inflation. For instance, with German unification the government imposed a one-to-one East mark-West mark conversion ratio on the Bundesbank. This interference provided a clear demonstration by the government that, though it could interfere, it chooses not to disrupt the Bundesbank's anti-inflationary policies, that is, anti-inflationary policy is credible.

22. Findings that brief terms of office for the central banks in developed countries are associated with low currency depreciation are also consistent with this model (Cukierman 1992).

6. Final Thoughts

1. Even though we do not focus on explicitly political factors, credibility may also be useful for understanding such forces. For example, it may help us understand when policy might be enacted over, and successful despite, the opposition of special interests. Specifically, it is possible that a policy will be adopted or successfully implemented despite the opposition of special interests only if continued opposition is not credible. If continued opposition is credible (for example, the opposition of the elderly to any Social Security cuts), then the policy may never be adopted or it may be viewed as noncredible and fail after adoption. If continued opposition is not credible (for example, when the reduction of protective tariffs reduces or eliminates an industry and its workers), then policy may be more likely to be adopted and successful (and crowding in, given rational expectations, will come into play). Similarly, in investigating whether policies will be undermined by bureaucrats, we might ask whether the bureaucrats in question have the requisite credibility to exercise influence. For instance, bureaucrats opposed to a policy either because they disagree with its objectives or because they feel poorly compensated (either individually or through an agency budget) may be more successful in undermining policy (and more likely to threaten to do so) when their threats to withhold service are credible. Indeed, even a rational expectation that bureaucrats may sabotage policy can undermine it. Such threats, however, may be affected by the importance of an agency's programs. Perhaps counterintuitively, bureaucrats whose work is essential (for example, air traffic controllers, to cite a famous example of the 1980s) may find themselves in a disadvantageous bargaining position because they understand that politicians may move decisively to mitigate the effect of their actions. Consequently, at least to a point, it may be that bureaucrats will be more influential the less important their services.

References

Aaron, Henry J., and William B. Schwartz. 1984. *The Painful Prescription: Rationing Hospital Care.* Washington, D.C.: Brookings.

———— 1990. "Rationing Health Care: The Choice Before Us," *Science* 24: 418–422.

Abrams, Burton A., and Mark D. Schmitz. 1978. "The 'Crowding-Out' Effect of Government Transfers on Private Charitable Contributions," *Public Choice* 33: 29–41.

Ackerman, Bruce A., and William T. Hassler. 1981. *Clean Coal / Dirty Air.* New Haven: Yale University Press.

Alesina, Alberto. 1989. "Politics and Business Cycles in Industrial Democracies," *Economic Policy* 8: 55–98.

———— "Elections, Party Structure, and the Economy," in Jeffrey S. Banks and Eric A. Hanushek, eds., *Modern Political Economy: Old Topics, New Directions.* Cambridge: Cambridge University Press.

Alesina, Alberto, Sule Ozler, Nouriel Roubini, and Phillip Swagel. 1992. "Political Instability and Economic Growth." Working Paper No. 4173. Cambridge, Mass.: National Bureau of Economic Research.

Alesina, Alberto, and Howard Rosenthal. 1995. *Partisan Politics, Divided Government, and the Economy.* Cambridge: Cambridge University Press.

Alesina, Alberto, Nouriel Roubini, and Gerald D. Cohen. 1997. *Political Cycles and the Macroeconomy.* Cambridge: MIT Press.

Alexander, Herbert E. 1991. *Reform and Reality: The Financing of State and Local Campaigns.* New York: Twentieth Century Fund.

Alt, James E., and Robert C. Lowry. 1994. "Divided Government, Fiscal Institutions, and Budget Deficits: Evidence from the States," *American Political Science Review* 88: 811–828.

American Political Science Association. Committee on Political Parties. 1950. *Toward a More Responsible Two-Party System: A Report.* New York: Rinehart.

Anderson, Mikael Sikou. 1994. *Governance by Green Taxes: Making Pollution Prevention Pay.* Manchester: Manchester University Press.

Anderson, Torben M. 1994. *Price Rigidity: Causes and Macroeconomic Implications.* Oxford: Oxford University Press.

Andreoni, James. 1989. "Giving with Impure Altruism: Applications to Charity and Ricardian Equivalence," *Journal of Political Economy* 97: 1447–1458.

———— 1990. "Impure Altruism and Donations to Public Goods: A Theory of Warm-glow Giving," *Economic Journal* 100: 464–477.

"Antilock Brakes May Not Make the Difference That Many Expected." 1994. *Insurance Institute for Highway Safety Status Report* 29, p. 4 (January 29).

Arnold, R. Douglas. 1979. *Congress and the Bureaucracy: A Theory of Influence.* New Haven: Yale University Press.

Arnott, Richard, and Kenneth Small. 1994. "The Economics of Traffic Congestion," *American Scientist* 81: 446–455.

Ashenfelter, Orley, and Mark W. Plant. 1990. "Nonparametric Estimates of the Labor-Supply Effects of Negative Income Tax Programs," *Journal of Labor Economics* 8: S396-S415.

Atkinson, A. B. 1987. "Income Maintenance and Social Insurance," in Alan J. Auerbach and Martin Feldstein, eds., *Handbook of Public Economics,* vol. II. Amsterdam: North-Holland.

Auerbach, Alan J., Jagadeesh Gokhale, and Laurence J. Kotlikoff. 1994. "Generational Accounting: A Meaningful Way to Evaluate Fiscal Policy," *Journal of Economic Perspectives* 8: 73–94.

Auerbach, Alan J., Laurence J. Kotlikoff, and Willi Leibfritz, eds. 1999. *Generational Accounting around the World.* Chicago: University of Chicago Press, 1999

Babcock, Linda, John Engberg, and Amihai Glazer. 1997. "Wages and Employment in Public Sector Unions," *Economic Inquiry* 35: 532–543.

Bailey, Christopher J. 1998. *Congress and Air Pollution: Environmental Politics in the U.S.* Manchester: Manchester University Press

Baily, Mary Ann. 1993. "Policies for the 1990s: Rationing Health Care," in Richard J. Arnould et al., eds., *Competitive Approaches to Health Care Reform.* Washington, D.C.: Urban Institute.

Bardach, Eugene, and Robert A. Kagan. 1982. *Going by the Book: The Problem of Regulatory Unreasonableness.* Philadelphia: Temple University Press.

Barnes, Deborah E., and Lisa A. Bero. 1998. "Why Review Articles on the Health Effects of Passive Smoking Reach Different Conclusions," *Journal of the American Medical Association* 279: 1566–1570.

Barro, Robert J. 1974. "Are Government Bonds Net Wealth?" *Journal of Political Economy* 82: 1095–1117.

———— 1989. "The Ricardian Approach to Budget Deficits," *Journal of Economic Perspectives* 3: 37–54.

————— 1991. "Economic Growth in a Cross-section of Countries," *Quarterly Journal of Economics* 106: 407–444.

————— 1996. *Getting It Right: Markets and Choices in a Free Society.* Cambridge: MIT Press.

Barro, Robert J., and David Gordon. 1983. "Rules, Discretion, and Reputation in a Model of Monetary Policy," *Journal of Monetary Economics* 12: 101–121.

Barzel, Yoram. 1974. "A Theory of Rationing by Waiting," *Journal of Law and Economics* 53: 73–95.

Bawn, Kathleen. 1995. "Political Control versus Expertise: Congressional Choices about Administrative Procedures," *American Political Science Review* 89: 62–73.

Becker, Gary S., Michael Grossman, and Kevin M. Murphy. 1994. "An Empirical Analysis of Cigarette Consumption," *American Economic Review* 84: 396–418.

Benedick, Richard E. 1991. *Ozone Diplomacy: New Directions in Safeguarding the Planet.* Cambridge: Harvard University Press.

Bennett, Robert A. 1979. "Nominee Pledges to Fight Inflation and Restore Confidence in Dollar," *New York Times* 128, p. A1 (July 29).

Bergeijk, Peter A. G. van, Robert C. G. Haffner, and Pieter M. Waasdorp. 1993. "Measuring the Speed of the Invisible Hand: The Macroeconomic Costs of Price Rigidity," *Kyklos* 46: 529–544.

Bergman, B. J. 1996. "Car Talks—Motown Walks," *Sierra* 81: 36–37.

Bergstrom, Theodore, Lawrence Blume, and Hal Varian. 1986. "On the Private Provision of Public Goods," *Journal of Public Economics* 29: 25–49.

Bernheim, B. Douglas. 1986. "On the Voluntary and Involuntary Provision of Public Goods," *American Economic Review* 76: 789–793.

Bernheim, B. Douglas, and Laurence Levin. 1989. "Social Security and Personal Saving: An Analysis of Expectations," *American Economic Review* 79: 97–102.

Bernstein, Merton C., and Joan Brodshaug. 1988. *Social Security: The System that Works.* New York: Basic Books.

Berry, Frances S., and William D. Berry. 1990. "State Lottery Adoptions as Policy Innovations: An Event History Analysis," *American Political Science Review* 84: 395–405.

————— 1992. "Tax Innovation in the States: Capitalizing on Political Opportunity," *American Journal of Political Science* 36: 715–742.

————— 1994. "The Politics of Tax Increases in the States," *American Journal of Political Science* 38: 855–859.

Besley, Timothy, and Stephen Coate. 1992. "Understanding Welfare Stigma, Taxpayer Resentment and Statistical Discrimination," *Journal of Public Economics* 48: 165–183.

————— 1999. "Centralized versus Decentralized Provision of Local Public Goods: A Political Economy Analysis." Working Paper No. W7084. Cambridge, Mass.: National Bureau of Economic Research.

Bishop, John. 1982. "Discussion: Modeling the Decision to Apply for Welfare," in Irwin Garfinkel, ed., *Income-Tested Transfer Programs: The Case For and Against.* New York: Academic Press.

Blanchard, Olivier Jean, and Stanley Fischer. 1989. *Lectures on Macroeconomics.* Cambridge: MIT Press.

Blank, Rebecca. 1997a. *It Takes a Nation: A New Agenda for Fighting Poverty.* Princeton, N.J.: Princeton University Press

——— 1997b. "What Causes Public Assistance Caseloads to Grow?" Working Paper No. 6343. Cambridge, Mass.: National Bureau of Economic Research.

Blank, Rebecca, and Alan Blinder. 1986. "Macroeconomics, Income Distribution, and Poverty," in Sheldon Danziger and Daniel H. Weinberg, eds., *Fighting Poverty: What Works and What Doesn't.* Cambridge: Harvard University Press.

Blank, Rebecca M., and Patricia Ruggles. 1996. "When Do Women Use Aid to Families with Dependent Children and Food Stamps? The Dynamics of Eligibility versus Participation," *Journal of Human Resources* 31: 57–89.

Blendon, Robert J., et al. 1993. "Physician's Perspectives on Caring for Patients in the United States, Canada, and West Germany," *New England Journal of Medicine* 328: 1011–1016.

Blinder, Alan S. 1991. "Why Are Prices Sticky? Preliminary Results from an Interview Study," *American Economic Review Papers and Proceedings* 81: 89–100.

——— 1999. "Central Bank Credibility: Why Do We Care? How Do We Build It?" Working Paper No. 7161. Cambridge, Mass.: National Bureau of Economic Research.

Blinder, Alan S., Roger H. Gordon, and Donald E. Wise. 1981. "Rhetoric and Reality in Social Security Analysis—A Rejoinder," *National Tax Journal* 34: 473–478.

Blomquist, Glenn C. 1988. *The Regulation of Motor Vehicle and Traffic Safety.* Boston: Kluwer.

Boadway, Robin W., and David E. Wildasin. 1984. *Public Sector Economics.* Boston: Little, Brown.

Borjas, George G., and Valerie A. Ramey. 1994. "Time-series Evidence on the Sources of Trends in Wage Inequality," *American Economic Review* 84: 10–16.

Borland, Ron, et al. 1990. "Effects of Workplace Smoking Bans on Cigarette Consumption," *American Journal of Public Health* 80: 178–180.

Born, Richard. 1994. "Split-Ticket Voters, Divided Government, and Fiorina Policy-Balancing Model," *Legislative Studies Quarterly* 19: 95–115.

Boskin, Michael J., and John B. Shoven. 1988. "Poverty among the Elderly: Where Are the Holes in the Safety Net?" in Zvi Bodie, John Shoven, and David Wise, eds., *Pensions in the U.S. Economy.* Chicago: University of Chicago Press.

Brada, Josef C., and Saul Estrin. 1990. "Advances in the Theory and Practice of Indicative Planning," *Journal of Comparative Economics* 14: 523–530.

Brady, David W. 1993. "The Causes and Consequences of Divided Government: Toward a New Theory of American Politics?" *American Political Science Review* 87: 189–194.

Brady, David W., and Craig Volden. 1998. *Revolving Gridlock: Politics and Policy from Carter to Clinton.* Boulder, Colo.: Westview Press.

Brauner, Sarah, and Pamela Loprest. 1999. "Where Are They Now? What States' Studies of People Who Left Welfare Tell Us." Series A, No. A-32. Washington, D.C.: Urban Institute.

Brenner, Hans, and Andreas Mielck. 1992. "Smoking Prohibition in the Workplace and Smoking Cessation in the Federal Republic of Germany," *Preventive Medicine* 21: 252–261.

Breyer, Stephen. 1982. *Regulation and Its Reform.* Cambridge: Harvard University Press.

Brunelli, Richard. 1995. "Commercials to the Rescue," *Mediaweek* 5, p. 12 (June 19).

Bryant, John. 1983. "A Simple Rational Expectations Keynes-Type Model," *Quarterly Journal of Economics* 98: 525–528.

———— 1996. "Team Coordination Problems and Macroeconomic Models," in David Collander, ed., *Beyond Microfoundations: Post Walrasian Macroeconomics.* New York: Cambridge University Press.

Bryner, Gary C. 1995. *Blue Skies, Green Politics: The Clean Air Act of 1990 and Its Implementation,* 2d ed. Washington, D.C.: Congressional Quarterly Press.

Calvert, Randall, Mathew McCubbins, and Barry R. Weingast. 1989. "A Theory of Political Control and Agency Discretion," *American Journal of Political Science* 33: 588–611.

Cammisa, Anne Marie. 1998. *From Rhetoric to Reality? Welfare Policy in American Politics.* Boulder, Colo.: Westview Press.

Carey, John M. 1996. *Term Limits and Legislative Representation.* Cambridge: Cambridge University Press.

Carlton, Dennis W. 1986. "The Rigidity of Prices," *American Economic Review* 76: 637–658.

Carson, Dale A. 1994. "Designing Pollution Market Instruments: Cases of Uncertainty," *Contemporary Economic Policy* 12: 114–125.

Cechetti, Stephen G. 1986. "The Frequency of Price Adjustment: A Study of Newsstand Prices of Magazines," *Journal of Econometrics* 31: 235–274.

Centers for Disease Control and Prevention. 1994. "Preventing Tobacco Use among Young People: A Report of the Surgeon General" (Executive Summary). Washington, D.C.: U.S. Department of Health and Human Services.

Chaloupka, Frank J., Henry Saffer, and Michael Grossman. 1993. "Alcohol-Control Policies and Motor-Vehicle Fatalities," *Journal of Legal Studies* 22: 161–186.

Chaloupka, Frank J., and Kenneth E. Warner. 1999. "The Economics of Smoking." Working Paper 7047. Cambridge, Mass.: National Bureau of Economic Research.

Chappell, Henry W. Jr., Thomas M. Havrilesky, and Rob Roy McGregor. 1993. "Partisan Monetary Policies: Presidential Influence through the Power of Appointment," *Quarterly Journal of Economics* 108: 185–218.

Collins, William J. 1997. "Occupational Mobility and Governmental Intervention in the World War II Era." Unpublished manuscript, Department of Economics, Vanderbilt University.

Congressional Quarterly, Inc. 1983. *Social Security and Retirement: Private Goals, Public Policy.* Washington, D.C.: Congressional Quarterly Press.

———— 1997. *Federal Regulatory Directory,* 8th ed. Washington, D.C.: Congressional Quarterly Press.

Conlan, Timothy J. 1988. *New Federalism: Intergovernmental Reform from Nixon to Reagan.* Washington, D.C.: Brookings.

———— 1998. *From New Federalism to Devolution: Twenty-Five Years of Intergovernmental Reform.* Washington, D.C.: Brookings.

Conrad, Jane Reister. 1992. "Granny Dumping: The Hospital's Duty of Care to Patients Who Have Nowhere to Go," *Yale Law and Policy Review* 10: 463–487.

Cook, Gareth G. 1995. "The Case for (Some) Regulation, Part 2," *Washington Monthly* 27: 34–39.

Cornes, Richard, and Todd Sandler. 1984. "Easy Riders, Joint Production, and Public Goods," *Economic Journal* 94: 580–598.

———— 1994. "The Comparative Static Properties of the Impure Public Good Model," *Journal of Public Economics* 54: 403–421.

Council of State Governments. 1994. *The Book of the States, 1994–1995.* Lexington, Ky.: Council of State Governments.

———— 1998. *The Book of the States, 1998–1999.* Lexington, Ky.: Council of State Governments.

Cowen, Tyler, Amihai Glazer, and Katrina Zajc. 2000. "Credibility May Require Discretion, Not Rules," *Journal of Public Economics,* 76, no. 2: 295–306.

Cox, Gary W., and Samuel Kernell, eds., 1991. *The Politics of Divided Government.* Boulder, Colo.: Westview Press.

Craig, Peter. 1991. "Costs and Benefits: A Review of Research on Take-up of Income-related Benefits," *Journal of Social Policy* 20: 537–565.

Cukierman, Alex. 1992. *Central Bank Strategy, Credibility, and Independence: Theory and Evidence.* Cambridge: MIT Press.

Cukierman, Alex, Steven B. Webb, and Bilin Neyapti. 1992. "Measuring the Independence of Central Banks and Its Effects on Policy Outcomes," *World Bank Economic Review* 6: 353–398.

Curry, Landon. 1990. "Politics of Sunset Review in Texas," *Public Administration Review* 50: 58–63.

Danziger, Sheldon, and Peter Gottschalk. 1995. *America Unequal.* Cambridge: Harvard University Press.

Danziger, Sheldon, Robert Haveman, and Robert Plotnick. 1981. "How Income Transfers Affect Work, Savings, and the Income Distribution: A Critical Review," *Journal of Economic Literature* 19: 975–1028.

——— 1986. "Antipoverty Policy: Effects on the Poor and the Nonpoor," in Sheldon Danziger and Daniel H. Weinberg, eds., *Fighting Poverty: What Works and What Doesn't.* Cambridge: Harvard University Press.

Davis, Stacy C., ed. 1995. *Transportation Energy Data Book: Edition 14.* Oak Ridge, Tenn.: Oak Ridge National Laboratory.

Dawson, John E., and Peter J. E. Stan. 1995. *Public Expenditures in the United States: 1952–1993.* Santa Monica, Calif.: The Rand Corporation.

De Fraja, Gianni. 1999. "After You Sir: Hold-Up, Direct Externalities, and Sequential Investment," *Games and Economic Behavior* 26: 22–39.

Diamond, Peter A. 1977. "A Framework for Social Security Analysis," *Journal of Public Economics* 8: 275–298.

DiNardo, John, and Thomas Lemieux. 1992. "Alcohol, Marijuana, and American Youth: The Unintended Effects of Government Regulation." Working Paper No. 4212. Cambridge, Mass.: National Bureau of Economic Research.

Dixit, Avinash. 1992. "Investment and Hysteresis," *Journal of Economic Perspectives* 6: 107–132.

——— 1996. *The Making of Economic Policy.* Cambridge: MIT Press.

Donohue, John J. III. 1989. "Using Market Incentives to Promote Auto Occupant Safety," *Yale Law and Policy Review* 7: 449–485.

Dornbusch, Rudiger. 1976. "Expectations and Exchange Rate Dynamics," *Journal of Political Economy* 84: 1161–1174.

Dotsey, Michael. 1996. "Some Not-So-Unpleasant Monetarist Arithmetic," *Federal Reserve Bank of Richmond Economic Quarterly* 82: 73–91.

Dubin, Jeffrey A. 1992. "Market Barriers to Conservation: Are Implicit Discount Rates Too High?" Social Science Working Paper No. 802. Pasadena, Calif.: California Institute of Technology.

Duffy, Michael. 1993. "Now Comes the Porklock," *Time* 141, pp. 20–22 (April 26).

Economic Report of the President. 1997. Washington, D.C.: United States Government Printing Office.

Edwards, George C. III, Andrew Barrett, and Jeffrey Peake. 1997. "The Legislative Impact of Divided Government," *American Journal of Political Science* 41: 545–563.

Eichengreen, Barry. 1998. "European Monetary Unification: A Tour d'horizon," *Oxford Review of Economic Policy* 14: 24–40.

Eijffinger, Sylvester, Eric Schaling, and Marco Hoeberichts. 1998. "Central Bank Independence: A Sensitivity Analysis," *European Journal of Political Economy* 14: 73–88.

Ellis, Christopher J., and Mark A. Thoma. 1995. "The Implications for an Open Economy of Partisan Business Cycles: Theory and Evidence," *European Journal of Political Economy* 11: 635–651.

Elmendorf, Douglas W., and N. Gregory Mankiw. 1998. "Government Debt." Working Paper No. 6470. Cambridge, Mass.: National Bureau of Economic Research.

Epple, Dennis, and Thomas Romer. 1991. "Mobility and Redistribution," *Journal of Political Economy* 99: 828–858.

Epstein, David, and Sharyn O'Halloran. 1996. "Divided Government and the Design of Administrative Procedures: A Formal Model and Empirical Test," *Journal of Politics* 58: 373–397.

———— 1999. *Delegating Powers: A Transaction Cost Politics Approach to Policy Making under Separate Powers.* Ann Arbor, Mich.: University of Michigan

Erfle, Stephen, and Henry McMillan. 1990. "Media, Political Pressure, and the Firm—The Case of Petroleum Pricing in the Late 1970s," *Quarterly Journal of Economics* 105: 115–134.

Erfle, Stephen, John Pound, and Joseph Kalt. 1981. "The Use of Political Pressure as a Policy Tool during the 1979 Oil Supply Crisis." Discussion Paper E-80–09. Cambridge, Mass.: John F. Kennedy School of Government.

Erikson, Robert S., Gerald C. Wright, and John P. McIver. 1993. *Statehouse Democracy: Public Opinion and Policy in the American States.* Cambridge: Cambridge University Press.

Fair, Ray C. 1988. "Explaining Votes for President," *Political Behavior* 10: 168–179.

Farrell, Joseph, and Nancy T. Gallini. 1988. "Second-sourcing as a Commitment: Monopoly Incentives to Attract Competition," *Quarterly Journal of Economics* 103: 673–694.

Farrell, Joseph, and Matthew Rabin. 1996. "Cheap Talk," *Journal of Economic Perspectives.* 10: 103–118.

Feldstein, Martin S. 1974. "Social Security, Induced Retirement, and Aggregate Capital Accumulation," *Journal of Political Economy* 82: 905–926.

———— 1982. "Social Security and Private Savings: Reply," *Journal of Political Economy* 90: 630–642.

———— 1985. "The Optimal Level of Social Security Benefits," *Quarterly Journal of Economics* 100: 303–320.

———— 1987. "Should Social Security Benefits Be Means Tested?" *Journal of Political Economy* 95: 468–484.

———— 1994. "American Economic Policy in the 1980s: A Personal View," in Martin S. Feldstein, ed., *American Economic Policy in the 1980s.* Chicago: University of Chicago Press.

Feldstein, Paul J. 1993. *Health Care Economics.* Albany, N.Y.: Delmar Publishers.

Ferejohn, John A. 1974. *Pork Barrel Politics: Rivers and Harbors Legislation, 1947– 1968.* Stanford, Calif.: Stanford University Press.

Ferrara, Peter, ed., 1990. *Free the Mail: Ending the Postal Monopoly.* Washington, D.C.: Cato Institute.

Fiorina, Morris P. 1981. *Retrospective Voting in American National Elections.* New Haven: Yale University Press.

——— 1989. *Congress: Keystone of the Washington Establishment,* 2d ed. New Haven: Yale University Press.

——— 1994. "Split-Ticket Voters, Divided Government, and Fiorina's Policy-Balancing Model—Response," *Legislative Studies Quarterly* 19: 117–125.

——— 1996. *Divided Government,* 2d ed. Boston: Allyn and Bacon.

Forder, James. 1998. "The Case for an Independent European Central Bank: A Reassessment of Evidence and Sources." *European Journal of Political Economy* 14: 73–88.

Foster, Vivien, and Robert W. Hahn. 1995. "Designing More Efficient Markets: Lessons from Los Angeles Smog," *Journal of Law and Economics* 38: 19–48.

Freeman, Richard B. 1993. "How Much Has De-unionization Contributed to the Rise in Male Earnings Inequality?" in Sheldon Danziger and Peter Gottschalk, eds., *Uneven Tides: Rising Inequality in America.* New York: Russell Sage Foundation.

Freeman, Richard B., and Lawrence Katz. 1994. "Rising Wage Inequality: The United States vs. Other Advanced Countries," in Richard B. Freeman, ed., *Working under Different Rules.* New York: Russell Sage Foundation.

Fullerton, Don, and Diane Lim Rogers. 1993. *Who Bears the Lifetime Tax Burden?* Washington, D.C.: Brookings.

Gagnon, Joseph E., and Michael M. Knetter. 1995. "Markup Adjustment and Exchange Rate Fluctuations: Evidence from Panel Data on Automobile Exports," *Journal of International Money and Finance* 14: 289–310.

Gallagher, Maggie. 1996. *The Abolition of Marriage: How We Destroy Lasting Love.* Washington, D.C.: Regnery.

Galston, William A., and Geoffrey L. Tibbetts. 1994. "Reinventing Federalism: The Clinton / Gore Program for a New Partnership among the Federal, State, Local and Tribal Governments," *Publius* 24: 23–48.

Garfinkel, Michelle, and Amihai Glazer. 1994. "Does Electoral Uncertainty Cause Economic Fluctuations?" *American Economic Review* 84: 169–173.

——— 1996. "Politics with and without Policy," *Economics and Politics* 8: 251– 265.

Garfinkel, Michelle R., Amihai Glazer, and Jaewoo Lee. 1999. "Election Surprises and Exchange Rate Uncertainty." *Economics and Politics* 11: 255–274.

Gartner, Manfred. 1986. "Some Political Economy of Flexible Exchange Rates," *European Journal of Political Economy* 2: 153–168.

Gates, Max. 1991. "Small Shops Likely to Lose Smog Check Business," *Automotive News* 5424, p. 18 (December 16).

—— 1992. "VP Debate Raises Question of CAFE, Jobs," *Automotive News* 5469, pp. 1, 52 (October 19).

Gersbach, Hans, and Amihai Glazer. 1999. "Markets and Regulatory Hold-Up Problems," *Journal of Environmental Economics and Management* 37: 151–164.

Gilmour, John B., and Paul Rothstein. 1993. "Term Limitations in a Dynamic Model of Partisan Balance," *American Journal of Political Science* 38: 770–796.

Glazer, Amihai. 1985. "The Advantages of Being First," *American Economic Review* 75: 473–480.

—— 1989. "Politics and the Choice of Durability," *American Economic Review* 79: 1207–1213.

—— 1999. "Local Regulation May Be Excessively Stringent," *Regional Science and Urban Economics* 29: 553–558.

Glazer, Amihai, Daniel B. Klein, and Charles Lave. 1995. "Clean on Paper, Dirty on the Road: Problems with California's Smog Check," *Journal of Transport Economics and Policy* 29: 85–92.

Glazer, Amihai, and Henry McMillan. 1992. "Pricing by the Firm under Regulatory Threat," *Quarterly Journal of Economics* 107: 1089–1099.

Glazer, Amihai, and Lawrence S. Rothenberg. 1999. "Increased Capacity May Exacerbate Rationing Problems: With Applications to Medical Care," *Journal of Health Economics* 18: 671–680.

Goldin, Claudia, and Robert Margo. 1992. "The Great Compression: The Wage Structure in the United States at Mid-century," *Quarterly Journal of Economics* 107: 1–34.

Goodwin, Doris Kearns. 1994. *No Ordinary Time: Franklin and Eleanor Roosevelt—The Home Front in World War II.* New York: Simon & Schuster.

Gore, Albert. 1994. *Rethinking Program Design: Accompanying Report of the National Performance Review.* Washington, D.C.: U.S. Government Printing Office.

Grady, Dennis O., and Keon S. Chi. 1994. "Innovations in State Government," in *The Book of the States: 1994–1995.* Lexington, Ky.: Council of State Governments.

Graham, Daniel A., and Ellen R. Peirce. 1989. "Contract Modification: An Economic Analysis of the Hold-Up Game," *Law and Contemporary Problems* 52: 9–32.

Grasmick, Harold G., Robert J. Bursik, Jr., and Bruce Arneklev. 1993. "Reduction in Drunk Driving as a Response to Increased Threats of Shame, Embarrassment, and Legal Sanctions," *Criminology* 31: 41–67.

Gray, George M., Laury Saligman, and John D. Graham. 1997. "The Demise of

Lead in Gasoline," in John D. Graham and Jennifer Kassalow Hartwell, eds., *The Greening of Industry: A Risk Management Approach.* Cambridge: Harvard University Press.

Gray, Virginia. 1973. "Innovation in the States: A Diffusion Study," *American Political Science Review* 67: 1174–1185.

Greider, William. 1987. *Secrets of the Temple: How the Federal Reserve Runs the Country.* New York: Simon & Schuster.

Greif, Avner, Paul R. Milgrom, and Barry R. Weingast. 1994. "Coordination, Commitment, and Enforcement: The Case of the Merchant Guild," *Journal of Political Economy* 102: 745–776.

Grier, Kevin B. 1989. "On the Existence of a Political Monetary Cycle," *American Journal of Political Science* 33: 376–389.

——— 1991. "Congressional Influence on United States Monetary Policy—An Empirical Test," *Journal of Monetary Economics* 28: 201–220.

——— 1996. "Congressional Oversight Committee Influence on U.S. Monetary Policy Revisited," *Journal of Monetary Economics* 38: 571–579.

Hall, Robert E. 1991. *Booms and Recessions in a Noisy Economy.* New Haven: Yale University Press.

Haveman, Robert, and Jonathan Schwabish. 1999. "Macroeconomic Performance and the Poverty Rate: A Return to Normalcy?" Institute for Research on Poverty Discussion Paper No. 1187–99. Madison: University of Wisconsin.

Hayes, Michael T. 1992. *Incrementalism and Public Policy.* New York: Longman.

Heclo, Hugh. 1977. *A Government of Strangers: Executive Politics in Washington.* Washington, D.C.: Brookings.

Herrnstein, Richard J., and Charles Murray. 1994. *The Bell Curve: Intelligence and Class Structure in American Life.* New York: Free Press.

Hibbs, Douglas. 1977. "Political Parties and Macroeconomic Policy," *American Political Science Review* 71: 1467–1487.

——— 1992. "Partisan Theory after Fifteen Years," *European Journal of Political Economy* 8: 361–374.

Hibbs, Douglas A. Jr., and Christopher Dennis. 1988. "Income Distribution in the United States," *American Political Science Review* 82: 467–490.

Hilts, Philip J. 1995. "Black Teenagers Turning Away from Smoking, but Whites Puff On," *New York Times* 144, p. B7 (April 19).

Hines, James R. Jr., and Richard H. Thaler. 1995. "The Flypaper Effect," *Journal of Economic Perspectives* 9: 217–226.

Hird, John. 1994. *Superfund: The Political Economy of Environmental Risk.* Baltimore, Md.: Johns Hopkins University Press.

Horn, Murray J. 1995. *The Political Economy of Public Administration: Institutional Choice in the Public Sector.* Cambridge: Cambridge University Press.

Hu, The-wei, Hai-yen Sung, and Theodore E. Keeler. 1995a. "Reducing Cigarette Consumption in California: Tobacco Taxes vs. an Anti-smoking Media Campaign," *American Journal of Public Health* 85: 1218–1222.

—— 1995b. "The State Antismoking Campaign and the Industry Response: The Effects of Advertising on Cigarette Consumption in California," *American Economic Review* 85: 85–90.

Hughes, Robert. 1995. "Pulling the Fuse on Culture: The Conservatives' All-out Assault on Federal Funding Is Unenlightened, Uneconomic and Undemocratic," *Time* 146, pp. 60–68 (August 7).

Huntington, Samuel P. 1953. "The Marasmus of the ICC: The Commission, the Railroads, and the Public Interest," *Yale Law Journal* 61: 467–509.

Ito, Takatoshi. 1992. *The Japanese Economy.* Cambridge: MIT Press.

Jacobson, Gary C. 1990. *The Electoral Origins of Divided Government.* Boulder, Colo.: Westview Press.

Janofsky, Michael. 1994. "Oregon Takes First Step in Its March toward Extending Health Care to All," *New York Times* 143, p. 6 (February 19).

Joskow, Paul L., Richard Schmalensee, and Elizabeth M. Bailey. 1998. "The Market for Sulfur Dioxide Emissions," *American Economic Review* 88: 669–685.

Kahn, James A. 1986. "Gasoline Prices and the Used Automobile Market: A Rational Expectations Asset Price Approach," *Quarterly Journal of Economics* 101: 323–339.

Kahn, James R. 1998. *The Economic Approach to Environmental and Natural Resources,* 2d ed. Orlando, Fla.: Harcourt Brace & Company.

Karoly, Lynn A. 1993. "The Trend in Inequality among Families, Individuals, and Workers in the United States: A Twenty-five Year Perspective," in Sheldon Danziger and Peter Gottschalk, eds., *Uneven Tides: Rising Inequality in America.* New York: Russell Sage Foundation.

Kearney, Richard C. 1990. "Sunset: A Survey and Analysis of the State Experience," *Public Administration Review* 50: 49–57.

Keech, William R. 1995. *Economic Politics: The Costs of Democracy.* Cambridge: Cambridge University Press.

Keeler, Theodore E. 1994. "Highway Safety, Economic Behavior, and Driving Environment," *American Economic Review* 84: 684–693.

Kelly, Benjamin. 1992. "How the Auto Industry Sets Roadblocks to Safety," *Business and Society Review* 83: 50–53.

Kettl, Donald F. 1993. *Sharing Power: Public Governance and Private Markets.* Washington, D.C.: Brookings.

—— 1994. *Reinventing Government?: Appraising the National Performance Review.* Washington, D.C.: Brookings.

—— 1998. *Reinventing Government: A Fifth-Year Report Card.* Washington, D.C.: Center for Public Management, Brookings.

Kidd, Michael P. 1995. "The Impact of Legislation on Divorce: A Hazard Function Approach," *Applied Economics* 27: 125–130.

Kilborn, Peter T. 1999. "Oregon Falters on a New Path to Health Care," *New York Times* 148, p. 1 (January 3).

Kingma, Bruce Robert. 1989. "An Accurate Measurement of the Crowd-out Effect, Income Effect, and Price Effect for Charitable Contributions," *Journal of Political Economy* 97: 1197–1207.

Klebnikov, Paul. 1993. "Pollution Rights, Wronged," *Forbes* 152, p. 128 (November 22).

Klein, Benjamin, Robert G. Crawford, and Armen A. Alchian. 1978. "Vertical Integration, Appropriable Rents, and the Competitive Contracting Process," *Journal of Law and Economics* 21: 297–326.

Kotlikoff, Laurence J. 1979. "Testing the Theory of Social Security and Life Cycle Accumulation," *American Economic Review* 69: 396–410.

——— 1987. "Justifying Public Provision of Social Security," *Journal of Policy Analysis and Management* 6: 674–689.

——— 1992. *Generational Accounting: Knowing Who Pays, and When, for What We Spend.* New York: Free Press.

Kramer, Gerald H. 1983. "The Ecological Fallacy Revisited: Aggregate-versus Individual-level Findings on Economics and Elections, and Sociotropic Voting," *American Political Science Review* 77: 92–111.

Kramer, Michael. 1996. "Where Candidates Fear to Tread," *Time* 147, p. 38 (April 1).

Krause, George A. 1994. "Federal Reserve Policy Decision Making: Political and Bureaucratic Influences," *American Journal of Political Science* 38: 124–144.

Krause, George A., and Jim Granato. 1998. "Fooling Some of the People Some of the Time? A Test for Weak Rationality with Heterogeneous Information Levels," *Public Opinion Quarterly* 62: 135–151.

Kreps, David M. 1990. "Corporate Culture in Economic Theory," in James E. Alt and Kenneth A. Shepsle, eds., *Perspectives on Positive Political Economy.* Cambridge: Cambridge University Press.

Krugman, Paul R. 1994. *The Age of Diminished Expectations: U.S. Economic Policy in the 1990s.* Cambridge: MIT Press.

Kunioka, Todd, and Lawrence S. Rothenberg. 1993. "The Politics of Bureaucratic Competition: The Case of Natural Resource Policy," *Journal of Policy Analysis and Management* 12: 700–725.

Landy, Marc K., Marc J. Roberts, and Stephen R. Thomas. 1994. *The Environmental Protection Agency: Asking the Wrong Questions from Nixon to Clinton,* expanded ed. Oxford: Oxford University Press.

Lave, Lester B., and W. E. Weber. 1970. "A Benefit-Cost Analysis of Auto Safety Features," *Applied Economics* 2: 265–275.

Leahy, John V., and Toni M. Whited. 1996. "The Effects of Uncertainty on Investment: Some Stylized Trends," *Journal of Money, Credit and Banking* 28: 64–83.

Lehman, Scott. 1995. *Privatizing Public Lands.* Oxford: Oxford University Press.

Leimer, Dean L., and Selig D. Lesnoy. 1982. "Social Security and Private Saving: New Time-series Evidence," *Journal of Political Economy* 90: 606–629.

Lemieux, Thomas. 1993. "Unions and Wage Inequality in Canada and the United States," in David Card and Richard Freeman, eds., *Small Differences That Matter.* Chicago: University of Chicago Press.

Leonard, Jonathan S. 1985. "What Promises Are Worth: The Impact of Affirmative Action Goals," *Journal of Human Resources* 20: 3–20.

——— 1990. "The Impact of Affirmative Action Regulation and Equal Employment Law on Black Employment," *Journal of Economic Perspectives* 4: 47–63.

Levinson, Arik. 1997. "A Note on Environmental Federalism: Interpreting Some Contradictory Results," *Journal of Environmental Economics and Management* 33: 359–366.

Levy, Brian, and Pablo T. Spiller. 1996. "A Framework for Resolving the Regulatory Problem," in Brian Levy and Pablo T. Spiller, eds., *Regulations, Institutions, and Commitment: Comparative Studies of Telecommunications.* Cambridge: Cambridge University Press.

Levy, Frank, and Richard J. Murnane. 1992. "U.S. Earnings Levels and Earnings Inequality: A Review of Recent Trends and Proposed Explanations," *Journal of Economic Literature* 30: 1333–1381.

Lindsay, Cotton M., and Bernard Feigenbaum. 1984. "Rationing by Waiting Lists," *American Economic Review* 74: 404–417.

Lipford, John W., and William R. Dougan. 1995. "A Public Choice-theoretic Test of Ricardian Equivalence," *Public Finance Quarterly* 23: 467–483.

Litterman, Robert B., and Laurence Weiss. 1985. "Money, Real Interest Rates, and Output: A Reinterpretation of Postwar U.S. Data," *Econometrica* 53: 129–156.

Lowery, David, and Virginia Gray. 1995. "The Population Ecology of Gucci Gulch, or the Natural Regulation of Interest Group Numbers in the American States," *American Journal of Political Science* 39: 1–28.

Lowi, Theodore J. 1964. "American Business, Public Policy Case Studies and Political Theory," *World Politics* 16: 677–715.

——— 1972. "Four Systems of Policy, Politics, and Choice," *Public Administration Review* 33: 298–310.

——— 1979. *The End of Liberalism: The Second Republic of the United States,* 2d ed. New York: W. W. Norton.

Malabre, Alfred L. 1994. *Lost Prophets: An Insider's History of the Modern Economists.* Boston: Harvard Business School Press.

Mankiw, N. Gregory, Jeffrey A. Miron, and David N. Weil. 1987. "The Adjustment of Expectations to a Change in Regime: A Study of the Founding of the Federal Reserve," *American Economic Review* 77: 358–374.

Marmor, Theodore R., Jerry L. Mashaw, and Philip L. Harvey. 1990. *America's Misunderstood Welfare State.* New York: Basic Books.

Mashaw, Jerry L., and David L. Harfst. 1990. *The Struggle for Auto Safety.* Cambridge: Harvard University Press.

Matsusaka, John G., and Argia M. Sbordone. 1995. "Consumer Confidence and Economic Fluctuations," *Economic Inquiry* 33: 296–318.

Mayhew, David R. 1991. *Divided We Govern: Party Control, Lawmaking, and Investigations, 1946–1990.* New Haven: Yale University Press.

McCallum, Bennett T. 1999. "Recent Developments in Monetary Policy Analysis: The Roles of Theory and Evidence." Working Paper No. 7088. Cambridge, Mass.: National Bureau of Economic Research.

McClelland, Robert. 1989. "Voluntary Donations and Public Expenditures in a Federalist System, Comment and Extension," *American Economic Review* 79: 1291–1296.

McCubbins, Mathew, Roger G. Noll, and Barry R. Weingast. 1987. "Administrative Procedures as Instruments of Political Control," *Journal of Law, Economics, and Organization* 3: 243–277.

———— 1989. "Structure and Process, Politics and Policy: Administrative Arrangements and the Political Control of Agencies," *Virginia Law Review* 74: 431–482.

McDonald, Maurice. 1977. *Food, Stamps, and Income Maintenance.* New York: Academic Press.

McGarry, Kathleen. 1996. "Factors Determining Participation of the Elderly in Supplementary Security Income," *Journal of Human Resources* 31: 331–358.

McKay, David. 1994. "Divided and Governed? Recent Research on Divided Government in the United States," *British Journal of Political Science* 24: 517–534.

McKinnon, Ronald, and Thomas Nechyba. 1997. "Competition in Federal Systems: The Role of Political and Financial Constraints," in John A. Ferejohn and Barry R. Weingast, eds., *The New Federalism: Can the States Be Trusted?* Stanford, Calif.: Hoover.

McNeely, Dave. 1994. "Is the Sun Setting on the Texas Sunset Law?" *State Legislatures* 20: 17–20.

Melnick, R. Shep. 1994. *Between the Lines: Interpreting Welfare Rights.* Washington, D.C.: Brookings.

Milgrom, Paul, and John Roberts. 1992. *Economics, Organization and Management.* Englewood Cliffs, N.J.: Prentice-Hall.

Milward, Alan S. 1977. *War, Economy, and Society, 1939–1945.* Berkeley: University of California Press.

Moe, Terry M. 1980. *The Organization of Interests: Incentives and the Internal Dynamics of Political Interest Groups.* Chicago: University of Chicago Press.

———— 1984. "The New Economics of Organization," *American Journal of Political Science* 28: 739–777.

Moe, Terry M., and Michael Caldwell. 1994. "The Institutional Foundations of Democratic Government: A Comparison of Presidential and Parliamentary Systems," *Journal of Institutional and Theoretical Economics* 150: 171–195.

Moffitt, Robert. 1983. "An Economic Model of Welfare Stigma," *American Economic Review* 73: 1023–1025.

———— 1992. "Incentive Effects of the U.S. Welfare System," *Journal of Economic Literature* 30: 1–61.

Mueller, Dennis C. 1989. *Public Choice II.* Cambridge: Cambridge University Press.

Munnell, Alicia H. 1977. *The Future of Social Security.* Washington, D.C.: Brookings.

Murray, Charles A. 1984. *Losing Ground: American Social Policy, 1950–1980.* New York: Basic Books.

National Institute on Drug Abuse. 1998. *Nicotine Addiction: What Is Nicotine?* Washington, D.C.: Government Printing Office.

Neustadt, Richard E., and Ernest R. May. 1986. *Thinking in Time: The Uses of History for Decision-Makers.* New York: Free Press.

Nice, David C. 1994. *Policy Innovation in State Government.* Ames, Iowa: Iowa State University Press.

Nivola, Pietro S., and Robert W. Crandall. 1995. *The Extra Mile: Rethinking Energy Policy for Automotive Transportation.* Washington, D.C.: Brookings.

North, Douglas C., and Barry R. Weingast. 1989. "Constitutions and Commitment: The Evolution of Institutions Governing Public Choice in Seventeenth-Century England," *Journal of Economic History* 49: 803–832.

Oates, Wallace E., and Robert M. Schwab. 1988. "Economic Competition among Jurisdictions: Efficiency Enhancing or Distortion Inducing?" *Journal of Public Economics* 35: 333–353.

Okun, Arthur M. 1962. "Potential GNP: Its Measurement and Significance," pp. 98–103. Proceedings of the Business and Economic Statistics Section of the American Statistical Association, Washington, D.C.

———— 1975. *Equality and Efficiency, the Big Tradeoff.* Washington, D.C.: Brookings Institution.

Olmstead, Alan, and Paul Rhode. 1985. "Rationing without Government: The West Coast Gas Famine of 1920," *American Economic Review* 75: 1044–1056.

Olson, Mancur. 1965. *The Logic of Collective Action: Public Goods and the Theory of Goods.* Cambridge: Harvard University Press.

———— 1982. *The Rise and Decline of Nations: Economic Growth, Stagflation, and Social Rigidities.* New Haven: Yale University Press.

Ordeshook, Peter C. 1986. *Game Theory and Political Theory: An Introduction.* Cambridge: Cambridge University Press.

Orleans, C. Tracey, and John Slade, eds. 1993. *Nicotine Addiction: Principles and Management.* Oxford: Oxford University Press.

Orr, Larry L. 1975. *Income, Employment, and Urban Residential Location.* New York: Academic Press.

Osborne, David, and Ted Gaebler. 1992. *Reinventing Government: How the Entrepreneurial Spirit Is Transforming the Public Sector.* Reading, Mass.: Addison-Wesley.

Osterman, Paul. 1991. "Welfare Participation in a Full-employment Economy—The Impact of Neighborhood," *Social Problems* 38: 475–491.

Page, Benjamin I., and Robert Y. Shapiro. 1992. *The Rational Public: Fifty Years of Trends in Americans' Policy Preferences.* Chicago: University of Chicago Press.

Patton, Robert. 1993. "Japan Stimulus Package Goes High-tech as Trade Surplus Soars," *Electronics* 66, p. 4 (April 26).

Pechman, Joseph. 1985. *Who Paid the Taxes, 1966–85?* Washington, D.C.: Brookings.

Peltzman, Sam. 1975. "The Effects of Automobile Safety Regulation," *Journal of Political Economy* 83: 677–725.

Persson, Torsten. 1988. "Credibility of Macroeconomic Policy: An Introduction and a Broad Survey," *European Economic Review* 32: 519–532.

Persson, Torsten, and Guido Tabellini. 1990. *Macroeconomic Policy, Credibility, and Politics.* Chur: Harwood Academic Publishers.

Pertschuk, Michael. 1982. *Revolt against Regulation: The Rise and Pause of the Consumer Movement.* Berkeley: University of California Press.

Peterson, Paul E. 1981. *City Limits.* Chicago: University of Chicago Press.

——— 1995. *The Price of Federalism.* Washington, D.C.: Brookings.

Peterson, Steven, George Hoffer, and Edward Millner. 1995. "Are Drivers of Air-Bag-Equipped Cars More Aggressive? A Test of the Offsetting Behavior Hypothesis," *Journal of Law and Economics* 38: 251–264.

Pindyck, Robert S. 1991. "Irreversibility, Uncertainty, and Investment," *Journal of Economic Literature* 29: 1110–1148.

Pine, Art, and John M. Berry. 1979. "Fed Chairman, Carter Advisor Named," *Washington Post* 102, p. A4 (July 26).

Plotnick, Robert D., et al. 1998. "The Twentieth Century Record of Inequality and Poverty in the United States." Institute for Research on Poverty Discussion Paper No. 1166–98. Madison: University of Wisconsin.

Polsby, Nelson W. 1984. *Political Innovation in America: The Politics of Policy Initiation.* New Haven: Yale University Press.

Porter, Gareth, and Janet Welsh Brown. 1996. *Global Environmental Politics,* 2d ed. Boulder, Colo.: Westview Press.

Posnett, John, and Todd Sandler. 1989. "Demand for Charity Donations in Private

Non-profit Markets: The Case of the U.K.," *Journal of Public Economics* 40: 187–200.

Rank, Mark R., and Thomas A. Hirschl. 1988. "A Rural-Urban Comparison of Welfare Exits—The Importance of Population Density," *Rural Sociology* 53: 190–206.

Ranney, Austin. 1954. *The Doctrine of Responsible Party Government: Its Origin and Present State.* Urbana: University of Illinois Press.

Reagan, Michael D. 1987. *Regulation: The Politics of Policy.* Boston: Little, Brown.

Reed, Donald. 1996. "Air Bag Side Effects," *Automotive Engineering* 104: 101.

Reed, W. Robert, and D. Eric Schansberg. 1994. "An Analysis of the Impact on Congressional Term Limits," *Economic Inquiry* 32: 79–91.

Reimers, Cordelia, and Marjorie Honig. 1996. "Response to Social Security by Men and Women: Myopic and Far-sighted Behavior," *Journal of Human Resources* 31: 359–383.

Revesz, Richard L. 1992. "Rehabilitating Interstate Competition: Rethinking the 'Race-to-the-Bottom' Rationale for Federal Environmental Regulation," *New York University Law Review* 67: 1210–1254.

———— 1997. "Federalism and Environmental Regulation: A Normative Critique," in John A. Ferejohn and Barry R. Weingast, eds., *The New Federalism: Can the States Be Trusted?* Stanford, Calif.: Hoover.

Ridenour, James. 1994. *The National Parks Compromised: Pork Barrel Politics and America's Treasures.* Merrillville, Ind.: ICS Books.

Rivlin, Alice M. 1992. *Reviving the American Dream: The Economy, the States and the Federal Government.* Washington, D.C.: Brookings.

Roberts, Russell D. 1984. "A Positive Model of Private Charity and Public Transfers," *Journal of Political Economy* 92: 136–148.

———— 1987. "Financing Public Goods," *Journal of Political Economy* 95: 420–437.

Robinson, John P., and Tibbett L. Speer. 1995. "The Air We Breathe: Public Attitudes toward Smoking Are Complex, but the Facts for Business Are Clear," *American Demographics* 17: 24–29.

Rogerson, Richard. 1988. "Indivisible Labor, Lotteries and Equilibrium," *Journal of Monetary Economics* 21: 3–16.

Rogerson, William P. 1992. "Contractual Solutions to the Hold-Up Problem," *Review of Economic Studies* 59: 777–794.

———— 1994. "Economic Incentives and the Defense Procurement Process," *Journal of Economic Perspectives* 8: 65–90.

Rogoff, Kenneth. 1985. "The Optimal Degree of Commitment to an Intermediate Monetary Target," *Quarterly Journal of Economics* 110: 1169–1190.

Romer, Thomas, and Barry R. Weingast. 1991. "Political Foundations of the Thrift Debacle," in Alberto Alesina and Geoffrey Carliner, eds., *Politics and Economics in the Eighties.* Chicago: University of Chicago Press.

Roosevelt, Franklin D. 1941. "Address to the American Retail Federation," in Samuel I. Rosenman, ed., *The Public Papers and Addresses of Franklin D. Roosevelt, 1939.* New York: Random House.

Rosen, Harvey S. 1988. *Public Finance.* Homewood, Ill.: R. D. Irwin.

Rosenthal, Elisabeth, with Lawrence K. Altman. 1998. "China, Land of Heavy Smokers, Looks into Abyss of Fatal Illness," *New York Times* 148, p. A10 (November 20).

Rothenberg, Lawrence S. 1992. *Linking Citizens to Government: Interest Group Politics at Common Cause.* Cambridge: Cambridge University Press.

———— 1994. *Regulation, Organizations, and Politics: Motor Freight Policy at the Interstate Commerce Commission.* Ann Arbor: University of Michigan Press.

———— 2000. "If It's Broken, Don't Fix It: The Politics of Campaign Finance Reform." Unpublished manuscript, Department of Political Science, University of Rochester.

Sandler, Todd, and John Posnett. 1991. "The Private Provision of Public Goods: A Perspective on Neutrality," *Public Finance Quarterly* 19: 22–42.

Sargent, Thomas J., and Neil Wallace. 1981. "Some Unpleasant Monetarist Arithmetic," *Federal Reserve Bank of Minneapolis Quarterly Review* 5: 1–17.

Scharfstein, David S., and Jeremy C. Stein. 1990. "Herd Behavior and Investment," *American Economic Review* 80: 465–479.

Scherrer, Huel C., and David B. Kittelson. 1994. "I/M Effectiveness as Directly Measured by Ambient CO Data." SAE Technical Paper No. 940302. Warrendale, Pa.: Society of Automotive Engineers.

Schmedel, Scott R. 1993. "A Retroactive Tax Rise Could Leave Many Filers Owing Big Payments Next April," *Wall Street Journal* 221, p. A1 (May 26).

Schoenfeld, Elizabeth. 1996. "Drumbeats for Divorce Reform," *Policy Review* 77: 8–10.

Schultze, Charles. 1977. *The Public Use of Private Interest.* Washington, D.C.: Brookings.

Shapiro, Matthew D., and Joel Slemrod. 1995. "Consumer Response to the Timing of Income—Evidence from a Change in Tax Withholding," *American Economic Review* 85: 274–283.

Shenon, Philip. 1994. "Asia Having One Huge Nicotine Fit," *New York Times* 143, p. 1, sec. 4 (May 15).

Shogren, Elizabeth. 1994. "Midnight Basketball Is Winner on the Street," *Los Angeles Times* 113, p. A18 (August 19).

Shubik, Martin. 1982. *Game Theory in the Social Sciences: Concepts and Solutions.* Cambridge: MIT Press.

Sigelman, Lee, Paul J. Wahlbeck, and Emmett H. Buell, Jr. 1997. "Vote Choice and the Preference for Divided Government: Lessons of 1992," *American Journal of Political Science* 41: 879–894.

Skocpol, Theda. 1996. *Boomerang: Clinton's Health Security Effort and the Turn against Government in U.S. Politics.* New York: W. W. Norton.

Small, Kenneth, and Camilla Kazimi. 1995. "On the Costs of Air Pollution from Motor Vehicles," *Journal of Transport Economics and Policy* 29: 7–32.

Smith, James P., and Finis R. Welch. 1989. "Black Economic Progress after Myrdal," *Journal of Economic Literature* 27: 519–564.

Stein, Herbert. 1994. *Presidential Economics: The Making of Economic Policy from Roosevelt to Clinton,* 3rd ed. Washington, D.C.: American Enterprise Institute.

Steinberg, Richard. 1986. "Charitable Giving as a Mixed Public / Private Good: Implications for Tax Policy," *Public Finance Quarterly* 14: 415–431.

———— 1987. "Voluntary Donations and Public Expenditures in a Federalist System," *American Economic Review* 77: 24–36.

———— 1989. "The Theory of Crowding Out: Donations, Local Government Spending, and the 'New Federalism,'" in Richard Magat, ed., *Philanthropic Giving.* Oxford: Oxford University Press.

Stevens, Rosemary. 1989. *In Sickness and in Wealth: American Hospitals in the Twentieth Century.* New York: Basic Books.

Stewart, Richard B. 1977. "Pyramids of Sacrifice? Problems of Federalism in Mandating State Implementation of National Environmental Policy," *Yale Law Journal* 86: 1196–1272.

Stieber, Jack. 1972. *Public Employee Unionism: Structure, Growth, Policy.* Washington, D.C.: Brookings.

Stockman, David A. 1987. *The Triumph of Politics: The Inside Story of the Reagan White House.* New York: Avon.

Stokey, Edith, and Richard Zeckhauser. 1978. *A Primer for Policy Analysis.* New York: W. W. Norton.

Sung, Hai-yen, The-wei Hu, and Theodore E. Keeler. 1994. "Cigarette Taxation and Demand: An Empirical Model," *Contemporary Economic Policy* 12: 91–100.

Sunstein, Cass R. 1990. *After the Rights Revolution: Reconceiving the Regulatory State.* Cambridge: Harvard University Press.

Thorpe, Kenneth E., and Charles E. Phelps. 1991. "The Social Role of Not-for-Profit Organizations: Hospital Provision of Charity Care," *Economic Inquiry* 29: 472–484.

Tiebout, Charles. 1956. "A Pure Theory of Local Expenditures," *Journal of Political Economy* 64: 416–424.

Tufte, Edward R. 1978. *Political Control of the Economy.* Princeton, N.J.: Princeton University Press.

U.S. Bureau of the Census. 1993. *Statistical Abstract of the United States.* Washington, D.C.: Government Printing Office.

U.S. Congress. House Committee on Ways and Means. 1992. *Overview of Entitle-*

ment Programs: Background Material and Data (Green Book). Washington, D.C.: Government Printing Office.

———— 1998. *Overview of Entitlement Programs: Background Material and Data (Green Book).* Washington, D.C.: Government Printing Office.

U.S. Department of Health and Human Services. 1988a. *Surgeon General's Workshop on Drunk Driving: Background Papers.* Washington, D.C.: Government Printing Office.

———— 1988b. *The Health Consequences of Smoking—Nicotine Addiction: A Report of the Surgeon General.* Washington, D.C.: Government Printing Office.

———— 1994. "Cigarette Smoking among Adults—United States, 1993," *Morbidity and Mortality Weekly Report* 43, pp. 925–930 (December 23).

———— 1995. "Air-bag-associated Fatal Injuries to Infants and Children Riding in Front Passenger Seats—United States," *Morbidity and Mortality Weekly Report* 44, pp. 845–847 (November 17).

U.S. Department of Labor. 1960–1991. *Current Wage Developments.* Washington, D.C.: Government Printing Office.

———— 1991–1993. *Compensation and Working Conditions: CWC.* Washington, D.C.: Government Printing Office.

U.S. Environmental Protection Agency. 1993. *Respiratory Health Effects of Passive Smoking: Lung Cancer and Other Disorders.* Washington, D.C.: Environmental Protection Agency.

———— 2000. *National Air Pollutant Emission Trends, 1900–1998.* Washington, D.C.: Environmental Protection Agency.

Viscusi, W. Kip. 1985. "Cotton Dust Regulation: An OSHA Success Story?" *Journal of Policy Analysis and Management* 4: 325–343.

———— 1994. "Health and Safety Regulation," in Martin Feldstein, ed. *American Economic Policy in the 1980s.* Chicago: University of Chicago Press.

Viscusi, W. Kip, John M. Vernon, and Joseph E. Harrington. 1995. *Economics of Regulation and Antitrust,* 2d ed. Cambridge: MIT Press.

Vogel, David. 1995. *Trading Up: Consumer and Environmental Regulation in a Global Economy.* Cambridge: Harvard University Press.

Walker, Jack. 1969. "The Diffusion of Innovations among the American States," *American Political Science Review* 63: 880–899.

Wallace, Jeremy. 1994. "Perspective: Social Security—Youths Find UFO's More Credible Than Social Security System," *Orange County Register,* p. A3 (September 27).

Warr, Peter G. 1982. "Pareto Optimal Redistribution and Private Charity," *Journal of Public Economics* 19: 131–138.

Weale, Albert. 1992. *The New Politics of Pollution.* Manchester: Manchester University Press.

Weaver, R. Kent. 1988. *Automatic Government: The Politics of Indexation.* Washington, D.C.: Brookings.

Weaver, R. Kent, and Bert A. Rockman, eds. 1993. *Do Institutions Matter? Government Capabilities in the United States and Abroad.* Washington, D.C.: Brookings.

Weber, Axel. 1991. "EMS Credibility." *Economic Policy* 12: 57–102, (April).

Wechsler, Henry, et al. 1998. "Increased Levels of Cigarette Use among College Students: A Cause for National Concern," *Journal of the American Medical Association* 280: 1673–1678.

Weimer, David L. 1982. *The Strategic Petroleum Reserve: Planning, Implementation, and Analysis.* Westport, Conn.: Greenwood.

Weimer, David L., and Aidan R. Vining. 1999. *Policy Analysis: Concepts and Practice,* 3rd ed. Englewood Cliffs, N.J.: Prentice-Hall.

Weingast, Barry R. 1995. "The Economic Role of Political Institutions: Market-Preserving Federalism and Economic Development," *Journal of Law, Economics, and Organization* 11: 1–31.

Wellisch, Dietmar. 1995. "Locational Choices of Firms and Decentralized Environmental Policy with Various Instruments," *Journal of Urban Economics* 37: 290–310.

White, Joseph, and Aaron Wildavsky. 1989. *The Deficit and the Public Interest: The Search for Responsible Budgeting in the 1980s.* Berkeley: University of California Press.

White, Lawrence J. 1982. *The Regulation of Air Pollutant Emissions from Motor Vehicles.* Washington, D.C.: American Enterprise Institute.

Wilcox, David W. 1989. "Social Security Benefits, Consumption Expenditure, and the Life-Cycle Hypothesis," *Journal of Political Economy* 97: 288–304.

Williamson, Oliver E. 1975. *Markets and Hierarchies: Analysis and Antitrust Implications.* New York: Free Press.

———— 1979. "Transaction Cost Economics: The Governance of Contractual Relations," *Journal of Law and Economics* 22: 233–261.

Wilson, James Q., ed. 1980. *The Politics of Regulation.* New York: Basic Books.

———— 1995. *Political Organizations.* Princeton, N.J.: Princeton University Press.

Wilson-Smith, Anthony. 1995. "A Hard Landing: Political Furor over Privatization of Toronto's Pearson International Airport," *Maclean's* 108, pp. 14–16 (April 17).

Wittman, Donald. 1995. *The Myth of Democratic Failure: Why Political Institutions Are Efficient.* Chicago: University of Chicago Press.

Wood, B. Dan, and Richard W. Waterman. 1994. *Bureaucratic Dynamics: The Role of Bureaucracy in a Democracy.* Boulder, Colo.: Westview.

Woodward, Bob. 1994. *The Agenda: Inside the Clinton White House.* New York: Simon & Schuster.

Zhang, Y., et al. 1994. "Final Report: Tucson Intersection Study of Automobile Emissions." Department of Chemistry. Denver, Colo.: University of Denver.

Index

Abrams, Burton A., 105
Ackerman, Bruce A., 78
Advertising, 14
AFDC. *See* Aid to Families with Dependent Children. *See also* Welfare programs
Affirmative action, 160–161 n. 24
Aid to Families with Dependent Children (AFDC). *See also* Welfare programs
    effects on labor supply, 61–62
    partisan effects on, 51–52
    spending, 62
    take-up rates, 66
Air bags. *See* Automobiles, air bags
Air pollution, 88–89, 129. *See also* Automobiles, emissions; Chlorofluorocarbon; Lead
Alcohol, 92, 93
Alesina, Alberto, 2, 24, 25, 120
Alexander, Herbert E., 131
Alt, James E., 120
Anderson, Mikael Sikou, 88
Anti-lock brakes. *See* Automobiles, anti-lock brakes
Appointments, 83–87
Arizona, 12
Arneklev, Bruce, 93
Australia, 58, 159 n. 11
Automobiles. *See also* Gasoline
    air bags, 80–81, 92
    anti-lock brakes, 90, 92
    drunk driving, 93
    electric, 165 n. 11
    emissions, 76, 81–83, 93
    fuel efficiency, 46, 76, 81
    seat belts, 80, 90, 91–92

Babcock, Linda, 109
Bailey, Christopher J., 80
Bailey, Elizabeth M., 89
Baily, Mary Ann, 111
Balanced budget multiplier, 155 n. 25
Bardach, Eugene, 110
Barrett, Andrew, 120
Barro, Robert J., 64, 156 n. 39
Barzel, Yoram, 111
Bawn, Kathleen, 84
Belgium, 114
Benedick, Richard E., 83
Bergman, B. J., 81
Bernheim, B. Douglas, 65
Bernstein, Merton C., 56
Besley, Timothy, 67, 126
Bishop, John, 66
Blank, Rebecca, 51, 62, 66
Blinder, Alan S., 32, 51
Blomquist, Glenn C., 91
Borjas, George G., 51
Borland, Ron, 17
Born, Richard, 120
Boskin, Michael J., 63
Brady, David W., 120
Brauner, Sarah, 62
Brenner, Hans, 17
Breyer, Stephen, 73
Brodshaug, Joan, 56
Bryner, Gary C., 84

197

Budgetary policy, 21
Budget deficits, 42–47
Bundesbank, 135, 136
Bursik, Robert J., 93
Bush, George, 46

Caldwell, Michael, 124, 172 n. 5
California, 11, 12, 82
Calvert, Randall, 84
Campaign finance, 131
Canada, 62, 158 n. 4, 159 n. 11, 171 n. 24
Capacity. *See* Investment; Rationing
Capital. *See* Investment
Carson, Dale A., 89
Carter, Jimmy, 85, 121, 122, 155 n. 29
Catalytic converters, 80, 82–83
Cechetti, Stephen G., 28
Central bank, 32, 85, 135. *See also* Federal
    Reserve Bank
Chaloupka, Frank J., 93
Chappell, Henry W. Jr., 20
Chi, Keon S., 126
China, 9, 11
Chlorofluorocarbon (CFC), 82, 83
Cigarette smoking, 8–18, 90–91, 93
Citibank, 38–39
Clean Air Act, 80, 84, 89
Clinton, William J., 25, 35, 102, 122, 123,
    145
Coal, 78
Coate, Stephen, 67, 126
Cohen, Gerald D., 24
Command-and-control regulation, 77, 163
    n. 2
Commitment, 3, 58. *See also* Credibility
Competition
    across states, 125–128
    effect on regulation, 79–80
Complementarities. *See* Strategic
    complementarities
Congestion, 168 n. 6
Congress, 77, 78, 80, 81, 120–123, 133
Conlan, Timothy J., 125
Consolidated Omnibus Budget
    Reconciliation Act, 111
Cook, Gareth G., 81
Corporate Average Fuel Economy (CAFE)
    standards, 80, 81
Cotton dust, 77–78
Courts, 84, 111

Cox, Gary W., 120
Craig, Peter, 66
Crandall, Robert W., 101
Credibility, 139–140, 141. *See also* Political
    support
    of central banks, 32
    defined, 6
    by delegation, 84–86
    and divided government, 122–123
    effect of rational expectations, 7–8
    effect of sunset laws, 134–135
    effect of term limits, 134–135
    effects of crowding in, 7
    increases with discretion, 32, 135
    to induce investment, 72, 97
    jawboning, 38
    of policies, 17–18, 99, 126–128
    and property rights, 7
    of rationing, 110–112
    of regulatory policy, 72, 75–83, 88–89, 94
    relation to institutions, 119
    reputation, 85–87
    of transfer programs, 50–51, 52–58, 70,
        71
    used by politicians, 136–137
Crowding in and crowding out, 139–140,
    142. *See also* Social pressures
    automobile emissions, 18
    cigarette smoking, 18, 90
    defined, 6
    effect on credibility, 7
    of fiscal policy, 33–35
    of philanthropy, 102–106
    of poverty programs, 48–51, 60–62, 66–
        68
    in production, 97, 99, 100–102, 106–116
    of regulations, 73, 79, 89–92, 93
    relation to institutions, 119
    of Social Security, 64–65
Cukierman, Alex, 2
Curry, Landon, 133

Danziger, Sheldon, 52, 60
Davis, Stacy C., 82
Dawson, John E., 96
Deficit. See Budget deficits; Trade,
    international
Delegation, 83–87, 129
Democratic party. *See* Partisan effects
Denmark, 88, 114

Dennis, Christopher, 51
Dependency ratio, 159 n. 13
DiNardo, John, 92
Discretion, 32, 135
Divided government, 119–125, 134, 145
Divorce, 93–94
Dixit, Avinash, 3
Donohue, John J. III, 81
Downs-Thompson paradox, 168 n. 6
Duffy, Michael, 35

Education, 11, 106
Edwards III, George C., 120
Elderly, 62–66
Elections
    affected by macroeconomic conditions,
        22–24
    effect on monetary policy, 30–31
    effect on wage contracts, 29–31
Elmendorf, Douglas W., 46
Engberg, John, 109
Entitlements, 54
Environment, 126. *See also* Air pollution
Environmental Protection Agency, 82, 85,
    136
Epstein, David, 120
Equilibria, multiple, 139, 140, 142
    automobile emissions, 15–16, 82
    cigarette smoking, 15–16, 90–91
    defined, 6
    investment, 39–42, 83
    in macroeconomic policy, 35
    in regulation, 83, 90, 92–94
    relation to institutions, 119
    in welfare programs, 66–68
Erfle, Stephen, 37
Erikson, Robert S., 126
Exchange rate, foreign, 26–27, 154 n. 21
Exhortation, 21, 35–39, 140
Expectations, 36, 39–42, 97. *See also*
    Rational expectations
Externalities, 13

Fair, Ray C., 22
Federal Aviation Administration, 96
Federalism, 125–131, 145, 169 n. 11
Federal Reserve Bank, 25–27, 31, 85, 155 n.
    29
Federal Trade Commission, 85
Feigenbaum, Bernard, 111

Feldstein, Martin S., 45, 65
Feldstein, Paul J., 114
Ferejohn, John A., 1
Fiorina, Morris P., 20, 70, 120
Fiscal policy, 21, 33–35, 140
Flypaper effect, 169 n. 11
Food stamps, 62, 66, 67
Ford, Gerald, 156 n. 29
Forder, James, 135
Foster, Vivien, 89
France, 9, 155 n. 27, 159 n. 11
Free riding, 100, 106
Fullerton, Don, 69

Gaebler, Ted, 118
Gallagher, Maggie, 94
Galston, William A., 125
Gasoline, 82–83, 100–101, 102
Gates, Max, 17
Generational accounts, 63–64
Germany, 135, 136, 159 n. 11, 171 n. 24
Gilmour, John B., 133
Glazer, Amihai, 12, 38, 77, 109, 110
Gore, Albert, 118, 131
Gottschalk, Peter, 52
Government. *See* Divided government;
    Federalism
Government failure, 1, 139–146
    attributed to institutions, 124
    automobile emissions, 11–13, 80–82
    automobile fuel efficiency, 81
    autombile safety, 80–81, 91–92
    Clean Air Act, 80
    long-term monetary policy, 27–28
    redistribution by taxation, 69–70
    regulation of personal behavior, 73
    restricting production, 109–116
    supplementing philanthropy, 102–106
    supplementing private production, 100–
        102
Government success, 1, 120–122, 139–146
    automobile emissions, 81–82
    automobile fuel efficiency, 80
    limiting chlorofluorocarbon production,
        82
    limiting lead production, 82
    long-term economic growth, 46, 47
    redistributing income, 51, 60, 62, 65, 69,
        71
    reducing cigarette smoking, 9–11

short-term economic growth, 27–28, 34–35
war production, 101
Grady, Dennis O., 126
Granato, Jim, 45
Grasmick, Harold G., 93
Gray, Virginia, 126
Great Britain. *See* United Kingdom
Greenspan, Alan, 85
Grier, Kevin B., 20
Gross Domestic Product, 22
Grossman, Michael, 93
Growth, economic, 43–44
Gulf of Tonkin Resolution, 137

Hahn, Robert W., 89
Hall, Robert E., 41
Harfst, David L. 76
Harrington, Joseph E., 73
Harvey, Philip L., 54, 56
Hassler, William T., 78
Havrilesky, Thomas M., 20
Health. *See* Medical care
Heclo, Hugh, 84
Herrnstein, Richard J., 48, 59
Hibbs, Douglas A., Jr., 22, 51
Hird, John, 122
Hirschl, Thomas A., 67
Hoffer, George, 92
Hold-up, 108, 164 n. 4
Honig, Marjorie, 65
Hu, The-wei, 11
Huntington, Samuel P., 1

Ignorance, 143
Indiana, 61
Indicative planning, 42
Inefficiency, 114–115, 144
Inflation, 36–37
and credibility, 32, 85, 135
and elections, 22–24
rational expectations of, 27, 45
Institutions, political, 118–138, 144–145.
See also Divided government
Interest groups, 1
Interest rates
effect of budget deficits, 46
jawboning, 38–39
monetary policy, 26
prime, 38–39

seasonality of, 31
Investment, 39–41, 145
automobile emissions, 17
in capacity, 110
cigarette smoking, 17, 90
under divided government, 123
effects of credibility, 76–78, 116
effects on redistribution, 58
for government production, 97, 99, 107–109, 112–115, 116
under local policies, 128, 130
in medical facilities, 112–114
under regulation, 72, 79, 94
strategic complementarities, 40–42
under sunset laws, 135
under uncertainty, 129
Iran, 38–39
Ireland, 155 n. 27
Italy, 155, n. 27, 159 n. 11
Ito, Takatoshi, 42

Jacobson, Gary C., 120
Janofsky, Michael, 111
Japan, 9, 35, 42, 43–44, 159 n. 11
Jawboning. *See* Exhortation
Johnson, Lyndon B., 52, 137
Joskow, Paul L., 89

Kagan, Robert A., 110
Kahn, James A., 1986
Kalt, Joseph, 37
Kearney, Richard C., 133, 134
Keech, William R., 2
Keeler, Theodore E., 92
Kelly, Benjamin, 81
Kemp, Jack, 37
Kennedy, John, 37, 52, 121, 122
Kernell, Samuel, 120
Kettl, Donald F., 98, 118
Kidd, Michael P., 94
Kilborn, Peter T., 111
Kittelson, David B., 12
Klebnikov, Paul, 89
Klein, Daniel B., 12
Korea, 159 n. 11
Kotlikoff, Laurence J., 65
Kramer, Michael, 56
Krause, George A., 45
Krugman, Paul R., 46
Kunioka, Todd, 84

Labor supply, 60–62
Labor unions, 158, n. 4
Landy, Marc K., 85
Lave, Charles A., 12
Lave, Lester B., 91
Lead, 82
Legislation, 120–122
Leimer, Dean L., 65
Lemieux, Thomas, 92
Lesnoy, Selig D., 65
Levin, Laurence, 65
Levinson, Arik, 126
Levy, Brian, 109
Levy, Frank, 52
Lindsay, Cotton M., 111
Loprest, Pamela, 62
Lowery, David, 126
Lowi, Theodore J., 1, 5, 157 n. 1
Lowry, Robert C., 120

Macroeconomics, 20–47, 140, 143
    budgetary policy, 21
    budget deficit, 42–47
    effect on poverty, 51
    exhortation, 35–39
    fiscal policy, 21, 33–35, 140
    literature on policy constraints, 2
    monetary policy, 21, 25–33, 51, 140
    policies, defined, 5
    political cycles, 22–24, 39–42
Malabre, Alfred L., 37
Mankiw, N. Gregory, 31, 46
Marginal cost, 163 n. 1
    effects on restricting production, 109–
        110
    regulation, 77–78
Markets
    effect of structure on regulation, 78–83,
        130
    production, 98
    for regulation, 87–89, 93, 114, 163 n. 2
Marmor, Theodore R., 54, 56
Mashaw, Jerry L., 54, 56, 76
Matsusaka, John G., 41
May, Ernest R., 137
Mayhew, David R., 120–122, 123
McCallum, Bennett T., 32
McCubbins, Mathew, 84
McDonald, Maurice, 67
McGarry, Kathleen, 66, 67

McGregor, Rob Roy, 20
McIver, John P., 126
McKay, David, 120
McMillan, Henry, 37, 38
McNeely, Dave, 133
Medicaid, 111, 114
Medical care, 96, 111–114, 123, 163 n. 41
Medicare, 111, 114
Mielck, Andreas, 17
Military procurement, 107, 108–109
Millner, Edward, 92
Milward, Alan S., 101
Minnesota, 12
Miron, Jeffrey A., 31
Mississippi, 61
Mobility, 130–131
Model Cities, 96
Moe, Terry M., 124, 172 n. 5
Moffitt, Robert, 60, 61, 67
Monetary policy, 21, 25–33, 51, 140
Money supply, 26. *See also* Monetary policy
Moral stigma. *See* Social pressures
Mueller, Dennis C., 4
Multiple equilibria. *See* Equilibria, multiple
Munnell, Alicia H., 65
Murnane, Richard J., 52
Murray, Charles A., 48, 59
Myopia. *See* Rational expectations

Netherlands, 88, 159 n. 11
Neustadt, Richard E., 137
New Zealand, 32
Nivola, Pietro S., 101
Nixon, Richard, 122, 136
Noll, Roger G., 84

Oates, Wallace E., 126
O'Halloran, Sharyn, 120
Okun, Arthur M., 61, 151 n. 2
Olmstead, Alan, 37
Olson, Mancur, 1, 100
Options, 173 n. 13
Ordeshook, 4
Oregon, 111
Osborne, David, 118
Osterman, Paul, 66

Parks, national, 169 n. 9
Parliamentary governments, 58, 119–120,
    122, 124, 145

Partisan effects. *See also* Political cycles
  legislation, 120–121, 123
  redistribution, 51–52
Patton, Robert, 35
Peake, Jeffrey, 120
Peltzman, Sam, 91
Persson, Torsten, 2
Pertschuk, Michael, 85
Peterson, Steven, 92
Philanthropy, 102–106
Phillips curve, 156 n. 30
Pigou-Knight-Down paradox, 168 n. 6
Policy. *See also* Government failure;
    Government success
  reform, 2, 145–146
  reversal, 76–77, 79–81, 101, 105, 107–
    108, 124, 131, 144
Political cycles, 22–24, 39–42
Political institutions. *See* Institutions,
    political
Political support, 142–143. *See also* Special
    interests
  effect of term limits, 134
  for local policies, 128
  for philanthropy, 105
  for production, 109
  for redistribution, 53–54
Pork barrel, 1, 35
Portugal, 114
Posnett, John, 105
Pound, John, 37
Poverty, 49. *See also* Aid to Families with
    Dependent Children
  effect of tax-and-transfer programs, 49–
    50, 53–54
  rates, 49–50, 53, 60, 62
Pregnancy, 92
Presidents of the United States, 22–25. *See
    also* under individual names
Prices, 27–29, 100
Prisoners' dilemma, 156 n. 34
Private production, 99, 100–106
Production, 96–117, 141, 159 n. 11. *See* also
    Investment
  of chlorofluorocarbons, 82
  crowding in and crowding out, 97, 99,
    100–102, 106–116
  of lead, 82
  limiting, 97, 115

policies, defined, 5, 98–100
  political support for, 109
  reducing cigarette smoking, 9–11
  restricting, 109–116
  unemployment, 101
  in war, 101
Property rights, 7
Public policy. *See* Government failure;
    Government success; Policy

Quayle, James Danforth, 80

Race to the bottom, 126
Railroads, 76
Ramey, Valerie A., 51
Rank, Mark R., 67
Ranney, Austin, 120
Rational expectations, 37, 140
  automobile emissions, 16
  cigarette smoking, 16
  defined, 6
  effect on credibility, 7–8
  effects of budget deficits, 44–47
  of monetary policy, 27–33
  relation to institutions, 119
  reputation, 86–87
  response to appointments, 85
  Ricardian equivalence, 44–47, 64
  of Social Security benefits, 64–65
  of taxes, 46
  of transfer programs, 50–51, 58–59, 71
  wage contracts, 29–31
Rationing, 110–112, 114–115
Reagan, Ronald, 37, 51, 52, 85, 136
Redistribution, 5, 48–71, 98, 130, 140–141,
    168 n. 5. *See also* Aid to Families with
    Dependent Children; Poverty; Social
    Security; Welfare programs
  partisan effects, 51–52
  political support, 53–54
  by taxation, 69–70
Reed, W. Robert, 133
Reimers, Cordelia, 65
Regulation, 5, 72–95, 98. *See also*
    Automobiles, fuel efficiency; Cigarette
    smoking
  agencies, 74
  banking, 122
  effect of competition, 79–80

by local governments, 126, 130
multiple equilibria, 83, 90, 92–94
regulatory capture, 84
and social pressures, 92–94
and unemployment, 101
under vertical integration, 79, 81, 83
Republican party. *See* Partisan effects
Reputation, 86–87
Reuss, Henry, 38–39
Rhode, Paul, 37
Ricardian equivalence, 44–47, 64
Ridenour, James, 1
Roberts, Marc J., 85
Rockman, Bert A., 124
Rogers, Diane Lim, 69
Rogerson, Richard, 41
Rogerson, William, 108
Rogoff, Kenneth, 32
Romer, Thomas, 122
Roosevelt, Franklin D., 44, 136–137
Rosen, Harvey, 65
Rosenthal, Elisabeth, 11
Rosenthal, Howard, 2, 120
Rothenberg, Lawrence S., 84, 110, 133
Rothstein, Paul, 133
Roubini, Nouriel, 24
Ruckelshaus, William D., 85, 136
Ruggles, Patricia, 66

Sacrifice ratio, 36–37
Saffer, Henry, 93
Sandler, Todd, 105
Savings
affected by fiscal policy, 34
effect of budget deficits, 42–47
effect of Social Security, 64–65
Sbordone, Argia M., 41
Schansberg, D. Eric, 133
Scharfstein, David S., 41
Scherrer, Huel C., 12
Schmalensee, Richard, 89
Schmedel, Scott R., 46
Schmitz, Mark D., 105
Schoenfeld, Elizabeth, 94
Schwab, Robert M., 126
Scrubbers, 78
Seat belts. *See* Automobiles, seat belts
Shapiro, Matthew D., 46
Shenon, Philip, 11

Shoven, John B., 63
Shubik, Martin, 4
Skocpol, Theda, 123
Slemrod, Joel, 46
Smog check. *See* Automobiles, emissions
Smoking. *See* Cigarette smoking
Social pressures
automobile emissions, 15
cigarette smoking, 14, 90
and regulation, 92–94
welfare programs, 66–68
Social Security, 53, 54–58, 62–66, 136–137,
157 n. 40
Special interests, 10, 12, 13, 84
Spending. *See also* Budget deficits; Fiscal
policy
environmental, by state, 126–127
by government programs, 96
on medical care, 113–114
Spiller, Pablo T., 109
Stan, Peter J. E., 96
States, individual U.S. ,131–134, 136. *See*
also Federalism
Stein, Jeremy C., 41
Stewart, Richard B., 125
Stieber, Jack, 109
Stockman, David A., 37
Stokey, Edith, 4
Strategic complementarities, 17, 40–42
Strategic Petroleum Reserve, 100–101, 102
Sung, Hai-yen, 11
Sunset laws, 131–134
Sunstein, Cass R., 164 n. 3
Superfund, 122
Surgeon General of the United States, 14
Sweden, 58, 114, 159 n. 11

Tabellini, Guido, 2
Taxes. *See also* Budget deficits; Fiscal policy
on cigarettes, 11
incidence, 68
negative income tax, 162 n. 40
rational expectations of, 46
for redistribution, 68–71
Social Security, 56, 63–65
on welfare benefits, 54
Term limits, 131, 133–134, 135
Texas, 133
Thomas, Stephen R., 85

Tibbetts, Geoffrey L., 125
Trade, international, 45, 51
Transfer programs. *See* Poverty;
    Redistribution; Social Security;
    Welfare programs
Truman, Harry S., 121
Tufte, Edward R., 20
Turkey, 114

Unemployment, 22–24, 101
Unified government. *See* Divided
    government
United Kingdom, 9, 66, 105, 112, 114, 122,
    159 n. 11

Vernon, John M., 73
Vertical integration, 79, 81, 83
Vining, Aidan R., 4
Viscusi, W. Kip, 9, 73, 77, 85
Vogel, David, 125
Volcker, Paul A., 37, 38, 85
Volden, Craig, 120

Wages, 29–31
Waiting lines. *See* Rationing
Wallace, Jeremy, 56

Washington, George, 42
Waterman, Richard W., 85
Weaver, R. Kent, 57, 124
Weber, Axel, 136
Weber, W. E., 91
Weil, David N., 31
Weimer, David L., 4, 100
Weingast, Barry R. 84, 122
Welfare programs, 48–49, 51–54, 57, 59–62
    credibility, 50–51, 52–58, 70, 71
    effect on labor supply, 60–62
    reform in 1996, 54, 62
    tax on benefits, 54
White, Joseph, 37
White, Lawrence J., 81
Wilcox, David W., 65
Wildavsky, Aaron, 37
Wilson, James Q., 73
Wisconsin, 62
Wood, B. Dan, 85
Woodward, Bob, 25
World War II, 101
Wright, Gerald C., 126

Zeckhauser, Richard, 4
Zhang, Y., 12